Religion, Culture, History

A Philosophical Study of Religion

Steven Brutus

Daimonion Press ◆ Portland, Oregon

Religion, Culture, History:
A Philosophical Study of Religion

ISBN: 1479109681
ISBN-13: 978-1479109685

Contents / Religion, Culture, History

Preface

1/overview

The United Nations estimates that the total human population on earth is just over seven billion.*

Among all peoples living around the globe, more than two billion are Christians, at least a billion and a half are Muslims, and nearly a billion are Hindus. There are perhaps 500 million Buddhists in the world. There are perhaps 400 million adherents of Chinese traditional religion, including both Confucianism and Taoism. There are 100 million followers of Shinto.

Some of these figures are overlapping. For example, the current *Houghton Mifflin Almanac* describes the religion of Japan, whose total population is 128 million, as follows: 112 million Shintoist, 93 million Buddhist. The United States Department of State *Report on International Religious Freedom*, 2009, describes the same population as follows: 107 million Shinto, 89 million Buddhist.

These abstract categories, such as 'Buddhist,' collect together a very large variety of divisions and sects. For example, the US State Department *Report* recognizes 154 forms of Buddhism in Japan.

There are perhaps 400 million primal, indigenous, animist, shamanist, spiritist, or other traditionists, including adherents to several African diasporic religions; this includes perhaps 20 million Yoruba religionists and followers of the Kardecian religion, including Santeria, BaKongo, Palo Monte and Amanda traditions. There are 27 million Sikhs and 20 million Juche (the government-authorized ideology of North Korea). It is estimated that there are 14 million Jews in the world. There are seven million followers of Baha'i, four million Jains, four million followers of the Cao Dai religion (a creation of modern Vietnam, sometimes regarded as a form of Buddhism), and two million followers of Tenrikyo (followers of Miki Nakayama, also called Oyasama; a creation of modern Japan, sometimes considered a modern form of Shinto). Zarathustrians or Zoroastrians are thought to number approximately two and a half million. Followers of Wicca, Druidism, Asatru, Pagan and other revivalist traditions number perhaps a million or fewer.

Over a billion people in the world call themselves secularists, atheists, agnostics, non-believing or non-religious or non-practicing, which is roughly one seventh of the world's population. By sheer numbers, this group would be the third largest 'religion' in the world.

These figures suggest that religion looms large in human affairs – this is confirmed almost daily in newspaper headlines – a survey of human history discovers a similar import in times past.

---

*See notes, beginning on page 175.

This essay provides some background for a study of religion in culture and through history.

The goal is to see religion clearly – also to see broadly – not to limit research to a single religious idea or a few, but to bring in as much as possible – limited only by reason and empirical science.

2/the current moment

"For the first time in history," Hannah Arendt wrote in 1957, "all peoples on Earth have a common present... Every country has become the neighbor of every other country, and every man feels the shock of events which take place at the other end of the globe." Arendt feared that this "new unity of the world" would become a "permanent theatre of war" unless it was accompanied by "renunciation, not of one's own tradition and national past, but of the binding authority and universal validity which tradition and the past have always claimed" (*Men in Dark Times*).

Arendt's generation lived through the carnage of the First World War, the Russian Revolution, the political chaos of the Weimar years, the Great Depression, the rise of the Nazi movement in Germany and the Nazi invasion of Poland, the Warsaw uprising, the Allied invasion, the horrors of Auschwitz, liberation by the Allies at the close of WWII, the creation of the United Nations, Stalinism, the Soviet invasion of Eastern Europe, the Cold War, America's tangled history in Vietnam, President Nixon's opening to the People's Republic of China, the Solidarity movement, Glasnost and the end of the Cold War, and the first stages of globalized capitalism.

Reflecting on this complex history, Arendt and many thinkers of her generation predicted the gradual disappearance of religion – a diminishing importance for religion in world affairs – especially in light of advances in science, the evident trend towards secularization in world society and the emergence of a working framework for world government. This was their hope, and they feared what might happen if religion continued to inspire war. A half-century later, some of their hope is realized – also some of what they feared. There is a decline in religiosity, evident both by the number of people who call themselves secular, and by sheer demographics: about 2 billion people live in secular societies, and 1.7 billion live in traditional religious societies. Yet demographics also support an opposite trend: secular societies' population growth is half that of traditional societies. The economic circumstances of traditional societies tend to increase birth rate and decrease gender equality, making religion more rather than less important. Thus secularization advances, but we are also living through a period of religious revival. Religion is becoming more important, rather than less, both in world affairs and in domestic politics, nearly everywhere in the world. Theism and atheism appear to be closely entangled. The current moment in history shows both trends: religious fundamentalism, notably of a violent and intolerant strain, and strident atheism, taking religion to task for reigniting ancient hatreds, and for the horrors of world history.

The British writer and scholar Karen Armstrong, the author of twelve books on comparative religion – such as 2009's *The Case for God* – argues that religious fundamentalism is a reaction to secular modernity, just as the "new atheism" is a reaction to religious fundamentalism. Armstrong argues that these strains of thought, and factions in the culture wars, are alike "fiercely reductive" – refusing to acknowledge any legitimacy to their counterparts; both are "essentially political discourses" – offering opposite dictates regarding national or ethnic or social identity – both advocating very different politics; and both develop "an exaggerated view of their enemy as the epitome of evil" – when in fact these are two sides of the same historical moment.

Islam takes much of the popular energy surrounding the idea of fundamentalism, yet Islam was the last of three Abrahamic faiths (Judaism, Christianity, Islam) to develop a fundamentalist strain. Note that the *hijab* (a Muslim woman's headscarf or veil, from the Arabic word 'to cover') was largely unknown in Muslim countries in the 1950s. Yet beginning in the 1970s, and coincident with the rise of fundamentalist Islam, the hijab became nearly universal in Muslim countries; a recent report by the *New York Times* states that 90% of Egyptian women live behind the veil (January 28, 2007). The history in Egypt has since been replayed throughout the Muslim world. Egyptian President Gamal Abdel Nasser (1918–1970) pursued a rapid program of modernization and secularization after WWII. He saw Muslim clerics and religious organizations as an obstacle to his ambitious program of bringing Egypt into the twentieth century. He jailed thousands of members of the "Muslim brotherhood" without trial. In prison they became radicalized and laid the foundation for the Islamist movement that plays such a large role in world affairs today. One among these prisoners was Sayyid Qutb (1906–66), a novelist and literary critic who had taken a degree in education at Colorado State College. Qutb wrote his influential text *Milestones* (1964) during his ten-year stay in a Cairo prison – the text was smuggled out in pieces – completed shortly before he was hanged (1966). This is a sample of the view that emerges in Qutb's work:

"There are two parties in all the world: the Party of Allah and the Party of Satan – the Party of Allah, which stands under the banner of Allah and bears his insignia, and the Party of Satan, which includes every community, group, race and individual that does not stand under the banner of Allah."

Jewish fundamentalism has its origin in reaction to Antisemitism and to events such as the Kishinev pogrom that took place in Russia in 1903. State-approved and state-ignored massacres against Jews in Russia and Eastern Europe around the turn of the century became a rallying point for protest and for religious conservatives who wished to reestablish a theocratic state in Palestine. The result was a messianic form of Judaism that Albert Einstein denounced as little more than a religious form of fascism (*New York Times*, December 4, 1948).

Christian fundamentalism has an important beginning with Pope Pius X's declaration in 1907 that modernism is a satanic heresy. Pius excommunicated a large number of modern authors and banned their books, including René Descartes, Michel de Montaigne, John Locke, Jonathan Swift, Voltaire, Denis Diderot, Thomas Paine and, of course, Charles Darwin. Hitler was never excommunicated; but Kant was.

All forms of fundamentalism portray themselves as restoring an earlier, ideal past – returning to a tradition that recent, 'modern' ideas have put in jeopardy – yet as historians of religion explain, fundamentalism is a late development in religious life. Religions, just like the cultures of which they are a part, traverse cycles of change, beginning in dynamism, self-confidence and experimentation, and later hardening into orthodoxy. Fundamentalism distorts the tradition that it is trying to defend; it emerges from a cornered, embattled position and responds to change with defensiveness and a demand for absolute loyalty. The upshot is polarization and the tendency to demonize one's opponent. Thus even in modern times we return to the demon-haunted world of distant antiquity.

3/the role of education

For most of human history, young people, often only boys, spent the school day in rhythmic chanting, memorizing a sacred text in a singsong cadence. Education was learning by singing the sacred texts of one's tribe.

The five Confucian classics – which include *The Book of Rites* and *The Book of Changes* – originating in the Shang dynasty – formed the main substance of education in China for nearly 5000 years.

The *Vedas* (*veda*, knowledge) dating from perhaps 2000 BCE, formed the curriculum in ancient India.

The *Torah* formed the curriculum in ancient Israel – *Torah* meaning 'teaching' or 'instruction,' also 'scribe,' as in the person who copies the teaching down. According to tradition, Moses is the author of the *Torah*. Recent scholarship asserts that the earliest parts of the *Torah* date from ~1000 BCE, a period in which the first 'Hebrew Schools' (*beth hamidrash*, school of learning) were founded; the student was expected to memorize large sections of the *Torah* and also show some personal initiative in understanding and practicing the teaching by age 13.

Jesus is said to have entered such a school at age 12 and shown extraordinary skill in posing difficult questions. Christian education, beginning with the Apostles, has been centered in reading, reciting, memorizing, singing, telling the story, understanding and living the 'good message,' Greek *Euangelion*, English *Gospel*, of the Resurrection.

It is said that Muhammad liked to wander the caves in the mountains encircling Mecca, especially around Mt. Hira, to find some quiet, to meditate and reflect. According to tradition, it was in the foothills of Mt. Hira that Muhammad first heard the message sent by Allah, the Merciful, whose angel Gabriel (*Jibril*) appeared amidst the rocks and bade Muhammad speak the words that stand at the beginning of the *Qur'an*: "Recite (*iqra*) in the name of the Lord who first made men from clots of blood." The record of his teaching, the *Qur'an* (recitation) is thought to have been completed by 632. The first *madrasah*, or school, was founded in Morocco in the ninth century. Muslim education in many parts of the world today carries on the tradition of educating young people by training them by rhythmic chanting of sacred texts.

If we take in the history of China and India and add the traditions beginning with Judaism, Christianity and Islam, we have before us a picture of the education of nearly all mankind, centered on the transmission of religious culture from generation to generation.

Two thinkers – one from the East, one from the West – have played an enormous role in upsetting this scheme of education. Siddhartha, who pronounced himself Awake (*buddha*) (563–483 BCE) and Socrates, considered a founder of philosophical reasoning (469–399 BCE), sought to detach wisdom from its basis in fixed truths and offer it instead as a moral and spiritual project for individuals. Neither offers a dogma – these thinkers do not call upon us to trust them or repeat any teaching – instead they ask us to inquire for ourselves and teach ourselves.

Meeting-places of the ancient world such as Naucritis, Melitus and Gandhara were among the first multilingual, multiethnic, multireligious communities. Peoples with wildly different lifeways settled down together, started to talk, and tried to articulate their ideas and differences. Education in these places had *many* sacred texts instead of just one – teaching became *many* -sided and people began to learn *many* traditions – education became a discussion, rather than the passing down of a tradition. This is very like the situation of the Western liberal arts curriculum today, which begins again in the Renaissance with Greek, Hebrew and Latin texts, finding Chinese, Sanskrit and Egyptian texts over a long course of history, and ultimately holds together ideas, images and stories from every part of the world and every history. This is the history that makes possible the very words that appear on this page.

Perhaps one note is worth inserting before beginning the main inquiry that this text records. This is the striking fact that so much of education through history has been religious education by means of rote memorization. At present and even in ancient times, these same practices have been condemned as unworthy of being called 'education.' The inquisitive freedom taught by Buddha and Socrates has a kind of mirror opposite in the uncritical loyalty taught by Hitler and Stalin. "Surrender to the Führer," Soviet "re-education" programs and what Mao called "Thought Reform" in the years of the Cultural Revolution are new instances of very old techniques of establishing intellectual obedience. The philosopher Michael Oakeshott argued that these techniques, based on the power of fear and conformity, should rather be called *indoctrination*. "It is the softening of the mind by force, by alarm, by the hypnotism of the endless repetition of what was scarcely worth saying even once" (*Religion, Politics and the Moral Life*, 1993).

Christiaan Hurgronje (1857–1936), a famous Orientalist and student of Islam, made a similar observation in 1916:

"This book, the *Koran*, once a world reforming power, now serves little purpose but to be chanted over and over again without ever giving thought to the meaning of the words…The result is a numbing practice in which a valuable portion of the education of Muslim youths is wasted."

Hurgronje was a progressive and advocated independence of thought through universal access to a properly scientific education, and via critical inquiry, breaking with the claim of superiority of any people or tradition. He counted on the link between education in technologically advanced civilizations and a broad resultant decline in traditional religious affiliation.

"Every global opinion poll shows religion declining among the youngest generation," writes Jeremy Rifkin, the American economist and writer, also citing evidence for the increase in spirituality. "Spirituality refers to the very individual quest to find meaning in the broader scheme of things," as Rifkin describes it.* His work *The Empathic Civilization* (2009) hints at a broader phenomenon than the opposition between believers and critics, reaching to a universal category of understanding or mode of sense, as argued earlier by Max Müller (*Introduction to the Science of Religion*, 1873), William James (*The Varieties of Religious Experience: A Study in Human Nature*, 1902) and, more recently, by Donald Brown (*Human Universals*, 1991). The present study pursues a line of thought like these, arguing from a conception of education as inquiry, rather than the passing down of a tradition.

4/point of view

This subject is dangerous. Many voices in society try to scare us off having too close a look at it.

My approach is philosophy. My approach is to speak to the philosopher in myself and in everyone. In my conception, philosophy is something that takes place in every person. Every person may also refuse philosophy.

Everyone can think – everyone has this power. Everyone can also fail to think – everyone has this weakness.

Both possibilities apply to every single human being.

As I understand it, the study of religion is also the study of politics, and takes place in a contested space of ideas. Karl Jaspers, an influential thinker for much of the twentieth century, taught that philosophy must lose both its humility before theology and its arrogance towards the everyday life of man. It must live in the world of opinion, including the apogee of competing claims that we call 'religion' (*An Inquiry into the Possibility of Religion without Myth*, 1954). Jaspers referred back to Kant, who taught that philosophy must not cower before religion, but instead "carry the torch in front of her gracious lady rather than the train of her dress behind" – philosophy must lead because thinking must lead – or else we lead unexamined lives (*To Eternal Peace*, 1795). As I understand it, this practice of philosophy lays out evidence and the arguments in which evidence weighs for a conclusion. It works through arguments. It is not important in all cases that we reach a conclusion, but it is important in all cases that we work through arguments. Philosophy is the *elenchus* – the Socratic method of oppositional discussion and critical cross-examination – this is how philosophy enters a contested space of ideas. The good of it is, that some things become less possible, whenever we become thoughtful. This is the other side of Hannah Arendt's teaching about the "banality of evil" – the idea that evil does not come from evil intentions, but simply from mindless conformity.

I count on the love of learning, the passion for truth, the free range of inquiry across all subjects, and the duty of self-criticism, to keep the goal in sight and not lose track of the project of comparative religion. The distinction between *comparative* religion and every other kind of inquiry into religious subjects is the difference between preaching, on the one hand, and searching, on the other.

If you do not love learning, have no passion for truth, do not permit yourself every freedom to follow argument wherever it may lead, and cannot criticize yourself and what you hold dear, do not read this book.

(1) the word 'religion'

The English word 'religion' has a Latin root: *religare*, to tie or bind. It is related to the English word *rely*, to be dependent on, to place confidence in, to trust. Both derive ultimately from the Indo-European root *leig-*, to place together, to bind. Related terms include the English words *rally, league, liaison, ligament, ally,* and *oblige.*

Common synonyms in English for the word 'religion' (with varying senses) include faith, belief system, (religious) belief, (religious) denomination, (religious) persuasion, worship, devotion, creed, sect and church.

The following are common definitions for the word 'religion' –

Reverence for a supernatural power regarded as creator of the universe
Belief in a supernatural power or deity that controls human destiny
Spiritual practice or discipline making one or more transcendent claims
Personal or institutionalized system stating the terms and rules of worship
The life or condition of a person in a worshipping order
A body of people adhering to a set of worshipping beliefs or practices
A set of beliefs and practices based on the teachings of a spiritual leader

Sometimes the word is used in secular contexts to indicate passionate conviction.

A cause, principle, or activity pursued with zeal or conscientious devotion

The following words from other languages are often translated with the word 'religion' into English. Their meanings – likewise their roots – appear to get at the subject from various angles.

Chaio or *Jiao* (Mandarin) – religion; way, path; school; often used in the phrase *san-chiao*, 'the three ways,' i.e. the three religions of China, Confucianism, Taoism, and Buddhism (the beginnings of Chinese religion date from ~3000 BCE). The root meaning of *chaio* is 'teach, guide, incite.'

Dharma (Sanskrit) – religion; righteousness, duty; often used in the phrase *santana dharma*, the 'Eternal Religion,' i.e. the Hindu religion, the religion formulated by the *risis* (the revealers, or seers of truth) who authored the *Vedas*, the ancient Hindu scriptures (the oldest dating from ~2000 BCE). The root meaning of *dharma* is 'to hold firmly, to stand.'*

Dat (Hebrew) – religion; law, observance; ceremony; used to indicate religious practices of any kind whatsoever, e.g. as practiced by the Hebrews or by people in distant lands (plural *datot*). The history of the Hebrews (from Hebrew *ivar*, 'to cross over,' in reference to the patriarch Abraham, said to have crossed over the river Euphrates migrating west) dates from ~2000 BCE. The root meaning of *dat* is 'decree, law, commandment.'

The root meaning of the term *Islam* is 'submission' – the term from which the word *Buddhism* is derived means 'wakefulness' – the term from which the word *Shinto* is derived means 'spirit' – the Greek root of the term *Christ* means 'anointed.'

From this brief survey the inquirer quickly comes to the result that religious life arises in many tribes, appears in many forms and has many root ideas.

The American pragmatist philosopher William James, in his classic work *The Varieties of Religious Experience* (1902), confronting the problem of defining the word 'religion,' offers the parallel case of 'government' and quickly draws some conclusions. 'Government,' he says, is a word like this, and a person might tell us that the most important thing about government is authority, or obedience, or police, or an army, or an assembly, or a system of laws – or any number of things. James thinks that a person who really knows something about government is not going to trouble much with defining it. He even says that any abstract conception of it might be more misleading than helpful. Government may be all these things, one of which is more important at one moment and others at another. Let us say that government is this very complex thing; but surely *religion* is no less so.

"Let us not fall immediately into a one-sided view of our subject, but let us rather admit freely at the outset that we may very likely find no one essence, but many characters which may alternatively be equally important, in religion."

James notes that the theorizing mind "tends to the oversimplification of its materials." "This is the root of that absolutism and one-sided dogmatism" that we see all too often both in philosophy and in religion. Religion is therefore a "collective name" and not any single fact, principle, essence, object, act or idea. But James cannot maintain this openness or the near infinity it suggests – instead he decides to investigate *one* kind of feeling, act and experience, an experience "which we discover in solitude," and in which we "apprehend ourselves in relation to the divine" – the divine, in whatever way a human being may consider it. And at the end of a long study and a review of hundreds of cases, he says that the special province of *religious* feeling, act and experience is marked by several characters: the belief in an encompassing spiritual universe; the sense that our work is to get in harmony with this higher world; a new zest and sense of the gift of life; and a complex feeling of safety, peace and outreach of love.

James is convinced that people have a sense for the sacred in the same sense that people have a grasp of logic and a moral sense and a feeling for beauty. However, his humility and sense of humor forbid him to say too much about it – he says that it is an "underbelief" to ignore the sense for holiness, but equally an "overbelief" to conclude anything sure about it. Our "transmarginal" consciousness quickly carries over the brink. James is a kind of hardboiled humanist. He owns up to having feelings, but he tries to keep his head, even if he has them. He asks for the reader's indulgence for his tendency to begin to say strange things – "the same indulgence which in a converse case I should accord to you." He also asks for, and offers, criticism of every idea in the wide arena of religion. The way to offer respect to a believer is to treat him as a serious thinker who is responsible for what he believes, says and does – in particular, let us see what he does. Oddly, James is not interested in "institutional" religion – religion in the form of official doctrine and churches. He thinks that the sense for the sacred is a human universal, whereas religions themselves appear to be cultural artifacts. He regards the manifestations of religion to be largely absurd, yet also holds the sense for the sacred to be the most important among all human powers.

James' sober view of religious phenomena is a useful companion for this inquiry – he himself tests his sobriety against many famous definitions of 'religion' – and since his time many more have become famous – here are several that try to capture the special province of religious life:

Confucius: religion is showing reverence towards the sacred.

Pericles: religion is devotion to the city.

Aristotle: religion is to honor the gods.

Spinoza: religion may be summed up as respect for priests.

Voltaire: religion is best understood by those who have lost all power of reasoning.

Ambrose Bierce: religion is the daughter of Hope and Fear, explaining to Ignorance the nature of the Unknowable.

Paul Radin: religion is a feeling and an act; the feeling takes form in a belief in spirits who exist outside of human experience but control it; and the act is a humbling, worshipping, reverencing, but also a pleading, bargaining and blaming; in sum religion is a means for retaining life-values.

Paul Tillich: religion is the ground of our being; the name of this inexhaustible depth and ground of our being is God; this depth is what the word 'God' means; and if this word has not much meaning for you, translate it, and speak of the depth of your being, the source of your being, your ultimate concern, the thing you take seriously without any reservation.

Clifford Geertz: religion is a confrontation with the problems of meaninglessness, suffering and injustice; a strategy for trying to reduce these problems; and an approach to dealing with the fact that despite all effort, they continue.

Abraham Joshua Heschel: religion is the awareness of God's interest in human beings; its task is to concur with this interest; God is in need of man to carry out His ends, and religion is a way of serving these ends. Religion is more than inwardness. It lives in deeds, not only in thoughts.

Jared Diamond: religion is supernatural beliefs serving to justify central authority, the transfer of wealth and the maintenance of social rules.

Daniel Dennett: 'religion' equates to 'social system,' whose participants avow belief in supernatural agency whose approval is sought.

Karen Armstrong: religion is a practical discipline, whose insights are derived from spiritual exercises and a dedicated lifestyle, whose task is to help us live creatively with our mortality, and which teaches us to discover new capacities of mind and heart. It is not simply what people believe; it is a program of action; it is not what people think but what they do. Religion requires the disciplined cultivation of a special mode of consciousness; religion takes place in an *ecstasis*, a stepping-outside the norm. As religion 'steps outside' it comes to three perennial conclusions: material reality is symbolic of an unseen dimension of existence; the attempt to grasp this dimension pushes human intelligence to the limits of language and understanding; and the thing we sense 'outside' is not alien but intimate, it is ourselves, and it inspires in us an unselfishness and desire to serve.

The above definitions and conceptions of religion fall (roughly) into two categories – advocates and opponents. The American author Upton Sinclair began thinking about this twofold reality during the First World War and summed up his conclusions in 1917:

"It is the fate of many abstract words to be used in two senses, one good and the other bad...So it is with the word 'religion'...Religion signifies the most fundamental of the soul's impulses, the impassioned love of life, the feeling of its preciousness, the desire to foster and further it. In that sense every thinking man must be religious; in that sense religion is a perpetually self-renewing force, the very nature of our being...Yet religion is also institutions having fixed dogmas and revelations, creeds and rituals, with an administering caste claiming supernatural sanction. Religion in this sense becomes the natural ally of every form of oppression and exploitation."

Perhaps there is a third option – neither for nor against, but *searching* – this is the point of view attempted here – a kind of appreciative inquiry, and critical inquiry, and equilibrium of both.*

(2) the subject 'religion'

It is controversial that the subject of 'religion' even exists. Congregants often deny that what they practice and believe has any comparison among other peoples. For example, the Canadian scholar of religion and Presbyterian minister, Wilfred Cantwell Smith (1917-1995), argued that the concept of 'religion' is a merely European construct, of recent origin, which has no general validity (*The Meaning and End of Religion*, 1962):

"...while there is a staggering amount of data, phenomena, of human experiences and expressions that might be characterized in one culture or another, by one criterion or another, as religion – there is no data for religion. Religion is solely the creation of the scholar's study. It is created for the scholar's analytic purposes by his imaginative acts of comparison and generalization. Religion has no existence apart from the academy."

To the extent that people following a tradition regard themselves as believing what God has revealed to them, they are not free in conscience to entertain contrary beliefs. They refer to their own belief, not as *religion* but as *truth*. Smith states this idea as follows: "One's own 'religion' may be piety and faith, obedience, worship, and a vision of God. But an alien 'religion' is merely a system of beliefs or rituals, an abstract and impersonal pattern of observables."

Experience of the world presents the problem that the claims of unlike religious traditions flatly *contradict* each other; and two claims that contradict each other cannot both be held as truths. This fact puts the believer in the position of tempering his own beliefs or rejecting those of others. Smith, for example, held that Christianity is truth, whereas Confucianism, Islam and Buddhism were accounted as various kinds of belief.

The traditional solution to the problem of religious controversy works by introducing the notion of *false religion* (idolatry, blasphemy, sacrilege, heresy, superstition, deviation). This idea allows the believer to acknowledge the existence of beliefs other than his own, without jeopardizing his faith.

Thus we have 'truth' and various kinds of belief; or we have 'true' religion and various kinds of false religion; or, more simply and with less presumption, we *accept* the notion of religion. Acceptance makes room for many sorts of approach – a large space between zeal and lenience.

Granting that the subject of 'religion' exists, it is radically contentious, and is widely held to be *the* most controversial among questions of belief. The difficulty is that argument is impossible when opponents do not share any common ground. There is an issue between the opponents, but in the extreme case the positions are so opposite that opponents have no basis to communicate. They may triumph over one another or wholly reverse their positions, but cannot face, listen and speak to their opponent.

If speakers manage to get beyond the war of words and begin to carry on a real conversation about religion, it is still unlikely that they will make any progress, because the subject is too hard. The Greek sophist Protagoras (490-420 BCE) was famous in his own time for having written:

"Concerning the gods I am unable to discover whether they exist or not, or what they are like in form; for there are many obstacles to knowing, especially the difficulty of the subject and the brief span of human life."

Supporting the idea of religion, as well as the conviction that we may still have something to learn about it, it is useful to note that sacred writings from many ancient traditions – such as the *Vedas* and the *Torah* and the *I Ching* – often use words meaning 'religion' to refer both to their own form of worship and that of other communities – words such as *chiao, dharma,* and *dat* – which implies an awareness of others' beliefs. Awareness, of course, does not imply agreement. But it is unnecessary to frame the subject as a debate between opposing parties.

Contention is a kind of *first* reaction to the discovery that other people believe things that we do not believe. In a cosmopolitan community, strangers come into contact with one another, and traditions intersect, e.g. in the Ionian cities of the ancient sixth-century or in ancient third-century Alexandria in Egypt – or in Portland, Oregon today. The essential condition in the holder of a traditional faith is that he does not know that he is a traditionalist – becoming aware of the existence of other traditions comes as a shock – eventually however this shock wears off. This makes it possible to develop other responses besides those of rejection or conversion. It becomes possible to acknowledge the diversity of religious beliefs without thereby concluding that there is anything 'wrong' with any of them.

The Athenians, for example, solved this problem by assuming that the deities they worshipped were given other names in foreign lands.

This 'solution' would not satisfy someone who believed that his god was the one and only true God. Nor would it satisfy someone who believed that all talk of gods is patent nonsense. But a person with a philosophical turn of mind, someone who was able to look broadly at religious phenomena, someone who noticed differences of custom and belief among different peoples, might see something in this strategy.

One way of expressing this change in attitude is to say that even in the extreme case, where the inquirer still regards unlike religious traditions as rival truth-claims – thus reducing all religious phenomena to matters of belief – he still might study other peoples' traditions, taking note of them and learning about them. Faith does not exclude curiosity or, even, respect.

(3) the term 'history'

The English word 'history' comes from the Greek root *historia* meaning research, inquiry, empirical investigation, many-sided curiosity, disinterested observation, collecting and recording traditions and geographical and ethnological data. Herodotus, often called 'the father of history' (also 'the father of lies'), writing in the fifth century BCE, often uses the words "customs" and "conventions," and describes in great detail the odd practices of alien peoples ("barbarians"), but he also recounts the conflict between the Greeks and Persians from its beginnings, thus writing its *history* in the familiar sense of a chronological record of events, a narrative or story. Herodotus traveled widely over the entire civilized world of his time – the Near East, Asia Minor, Egypt, Italy and Greece – and makes a special effort to record and study religious ideas. He is struck by the conflict of manners between peoples, e.g. noting that some people bury their dead, some burn their dead, some expose their dead to the elements and some eat their dead; and he adopts a standpoint that attempts to respect all these practices, often observing that any custom that is ancient and that has withstood the test of time is worth consideration and study.

Thucydides (460-400 BCE) is sometimes called the first *true* historian because he separated physical science or research from the mere chronology of events and because he specifically denied that Herodotus wrote history – calling it "mythology" instead – he insists that he records eyewitness accounts, checks his sources, applies critical tests, and corrects for errors that arise from imperfect memory and the partiality of witnesses. He was famous in his own time for writing these words:

"The absence of mythology in my history will I fear detract somewhat from its interest for people who like a good story; but I shall be content if it is judged useful by inquirers who desire an exact knowledge of the past as an aid to the interpretation of the future, for in the course of human things the future must resemble the past or perhaps even exactly repeat it."

Thucydides says that his purpose as an historian is to record from a dispassionate point of view the unfolding of the enormous event which divided his world into two hostile armies – The Peloponnesian War – saying that he began to compose his work "at the moment that the war broke out." He says that he is attempting to transfer his scientific attitude from the study of timeless nature to the political struggle of his own age, a scene complicated by conflicting passions and party-causes. For certain he is the father of western *political* history – a branch of learning that is largely a record of man's destructive activities or, as Gibbon calls it, "little more than the register of the crimes, follies and misfortunes of mankind." Historians today recognize at least two broader kinds of history: economic history (an account of man's constructive activities) and social history (an account of daily life in past ages;

7

an account of family and household life; of the relation of different classes to one another; and a record of the conditions of labor and leisure). Most writers today define *social history* as a study of the *culture* of an age as it arose out of general conditions of life, as it takes form in all kinds of human activities and productions, and as it changes through time.

The comparative study of religions is a part of social history that digs into the problem of religious custom, conceived as having a purely natural origin in human experience and exactly like philosophy and science and art as an element of culture.

(4) the term 'culture'

The ancient world did not possess a concept of 'culture.' Where the sense of the term refers to the intellect ('a cultured person' or 'high culture'), the Greeks used words like *mathesis* and *paideia* that have to do with education and its result. The Romans used words like *artes liberales* and *humanitas.* Where the sense of the term has to do with the life of a people ('cultural change' or 'French culture'), the Greeks used words like *ethos* and *nomos* (customs and laws) and the Romans used words like *mores* and *rites* (morals and rites).

The term 'culture' derives from the Indo-European root *kwele,* to dwell, to till the soil, to farm, the basis of words like 'agriculture' and 'cultivate' and 'bacterial culture.' The term has to do with taking germ, taking hold and residing, nurturing, and growing, and thus by extension to what is grown, to what thrives and dies. Some common definitions of the term 'culture' in reference to the life of a people are –

The totality of socially transmitted practices, arts, beliefs, institutions and products of human work and thought; the world of shared meaning.

Practices considered as the expression of a particular period, class, community, or population: *alternative culture; Victorian culture; the culture of poverty.*

Practices considered in reference to a particular category, such as a subject or mode of expression: *religious culture in the Middle Ages; oral culture.*

Practices that characterize the functioning of a group or organization: *corporate culture.*

The strategy of using the word 'culture' to refer to the life of a people in these broad senses is a creation of the eighteenth century – of the European Enlightenment – and owes its origin to writers beginning with Voltaire and Diderot and Gibbon – the first volume of *The Decline and Fall of the Roman Empire* was published in 1776. The modern comparative study of cultures dates from nearly a hundred years later. Some important milestones in the development of the general theory of culture and of the 'science of religion' include the works of Max Müller (*Comparative Mythology*, 1856; *Introduction to the Science of Religion*, 1873), Edward Tylor (*Primitive Culture*, 1871) and Emile Durkheim (*Elementary Forms of the Religious Life*, 1912). These writers and a great many others beginning with their epoch – e.g. Marx, Nietzsche, Weber – Sir James Frazer, William James, Franz Boas, Ernst Renan, Ruth Benedict, Margaret Mead – Robertson Smith, Paul Radin, Robert Marett, Marcel Mauss, Jane Harrison, F.B. Jevons – all these writers share the premise that it is possible to abstract from an account of specific social practices to broader categories and thus to *kinds* and *stages* of society, to *types* and *structures* of culture, and to *forms* and *ideas* of religion.

This is an application of the scientific method – empirical investigation and mathematical reasoning – as if we were studying biology or chemistry or physics, instead of society and culture and religion.

(5) religion/culture/history

History is relevant to religion not to explain it but to describe what it has been – to show what it has done – to uncover the religious sense in its raw form and suggest pathways for its development.

"No retrospective will take us to the true beginning" – as George Eliot warns – but as she also says we must look to history to see "how the mysterious mixture behaves under the varying experiments of time" – beginning as far back as we can reach, and taking into view everything we can discover. For religion, this sets us back to the Middle Paleolithic, the origin of our species 200,000 years ago, or perhaps even to our prehuman ancestors, and takes in innumerable good and evil things. On first review there is too much to look at and no easy way to pursue the search.

Petroglyphs discovered in Northern Australia are thought to be at least 60,000 years old. Prehistoric statuettes from the Upper Paleolithic period – called "Venus figurines" – have been dated to ~40,000 BCE. Cave paintings from Paleolithic times, beginning as early as ~40,000 BCE and falling into disuse with the beginnings of agriculture somewhere between 10,000 and 8,000 BCE, have been found in Africa, India, South America and Southeast Asia. To take an important example, there are nearly three hundred fifty decorated caves in the region stretching between Southern France and Northern Spain. The paintings appearing in caves such as Altamira and Lascaux date from ~35,000 BCE to ~9,000 BCE. It is widely held that all these ancient artworks have a religious significance and that they played a role in different kinds of rituals.

Ancient religiosity throws considerable light on the problem of understanding *contemporary* religious life. It discloses the religious instinct in its humblest form. It also suggests some first stages in a timeline for religiosity, from worship of the Great Mother, to hunting magic, shamanism, agricultural religion and prayers for the fecundity of the soil, to ancestor worship, protector gods, forest, mountain and ocean gods, temple gods, to the Sky Father and the first inklings of monotheism.

Religion is ancient – this may be the most important thing about it – its great age even suggests itself as a kind of guide. It connects shamanism and fertility rites with what people are up to today in mosques, churches and temples. The big truth here is that we need a context to make sense of important experiences – we need a context to make sense of suffering and injustice and inexplicable happenings – we need a context to make sense of the whole sweep of our lives and our connection to ancestors and future generations. Religion offers itself as this context. Religion is the answer to the puzzle of life on earth and bears the burden of all things that cannot be comprehended except by supernatural power. This big truth suggests that matters of doctrine are trivial – e.g. whether to pray standing up, kneeling, or prostrate; whether to worship Allah, Tian (天), or Zeus; or whether is it important to believe anything, or act, or to obey certain rules. In practice these differences seem huge or even the essential piece. Thus the inquiry confronts enormous variety and must range around for a place to stand and sort out all these differences.

Pick up the argument from William James: he wants to instruct us about religion by talking about the many ways of talking about government, noting that government is usually misgovernment.

There are many ways of talking about religion, but not all of them make any sense. James argues that a person has a duty to develop his or her moral sense, and sense of logic, and sense of beauty; he also argues that the same duty applies to the religious sense. He argues that these powers are all inborn in us but are also inchoate or unformed, subject to accident, and may thrive or fail. Human powers need some nourishing to develop. James also argues that if we keep working at developing our religious sense, we will find the religious 'big truth' or 'context' in ourselves. James of course is a 'hardboiled humanist' – a pragmatist – more to the point, he is a philosopher, and he arrives at an *individual* solution. James spent many years at war with himself – battling his depression. He refused to go out into the world until he had solved the problem of belief. Ultimately he arrived at belief in himself – what he called "fatal courage" and "partnership with fate" and "using your death" – better known by his formula "the will to believe."

James' is an unusual case. Few people carve out a faith completely on their own. *Most* of us come to religion by being part of a culture. The present text approaches religion as part of social history, not as James does with a focus on highly personalized ideas regarding "the realm of spirits."

Culture is relevant to religion as its outward form, its special rites, special words, special symbol – for example, the cross. But not simply the cross: instead the Ankh, the Talisman, the Basque cross, the Canterbury cross, the Celtic cross, the Coptic cross, the Sun cross, the Greek cross, the cross of Lorraine, the Tau cross, the Jerusalem cross, the Saltire, the Maltese cross – and many others. Culture is the language in which we think and pray – also the language in which we think and doubt; but not simply the language: instead the speech of a place and time; the local dialect, accent, slang; – the point being that culture is *local* and binds a people to a here and now.

Culture is local, but it is also *shared*. It has a communitarian sort of being. Margaret Mead: "Culture is the learned behavior of a *society* or *social subgroup*"; Talcott Parsons: "Culture is the system of norms and values that regulate *social* action symbolically"; Clifford Geertz: "Culture is the ensemble of stories we tell about ourselves."

Because it is *shared* meaning, the driving issue in culture is how far this *sharing* extends. The big issue in culture is who gets to be part of it – thus also the division between 'tacit' knowledge and 'objective' knowledge – knowledge gained via membership in a group, and knowledge advanced with universal claims – us vs. them, local vs. global, contingent vs. necessary.

If a religion were only intended for a small group of people and never claimed any force outside that group – a tribal custom intended for the tribe – then no one need know about it, no one could benefit from it nor insult it. The *sharing* in a case like this does not extend very far. 'Us' is very small and 'them' is quite large. There are cases like this, but they play no role in history.

Sharing in that part of social history that we are calling *religious custom* is dynamic – ever-changing – including new members and excluding old ones; becoming more popular and losing ground – and plays itself out in polarities such as clergy and lay people, mainstream vs. alternative, native vs. immigrant, dominant culture vs. marginalized culture, empire vs. colony. Culture is a principle of difference. It speaks to what is unique about a people in contradistinction to other peoples' lifeways. Thus it is possible to envision a planetary culture – a culture to unite all persons in a common system of values and stories – either as liberation or tyranny. Some related ideas here include "cultural imperialism," (also cultural invasion, cultural conquest, cultural domination) – what happens when one society imposes its culture onto another society; also "hybridity," a term coined by the British social thinker Homi Bhabha to indicate the idea of reversing the process of cultural imperialism – i.e., a kind of cultural revenge; and "multiculturalism," a concept that tries to capture the sense that the diversity of cultures is a fundamental condition of human existence – thus an attempt to normalize cultural diversity and try to develop a cosmopolitan vision that respects it and grows up in it.

Overall the thought-complex 'religion/culture/history' tries to get at the subject of religion by asking three related kinds of questions: What is the *grounding form* of religion, which we see at the beginning of its history? What is the *transcendental form* of religion, which we see at the end of all controversy? And what is the characteristic perversion, the *distorted form*, which plays a part in every religious history? The groundform, the dysform and transform of religion – the raw state and basic idea; the highest common principle and common ideal; and the characteristic distortion and corruption of this idea. What is the religious instinct in its germ-form or seed-form? And what is the precipitate, essence, epitome, archetype, and completion – the great truth in which religious traditions converge – the common element rising above cultural variation – the highest common factor in all religious tradition? And what is the essential lie, falsehood, contradiction running through all its contingent exemplars – the disessence – which shows itself in history?

There is an astonishing variety of opinion regarding religion, culture and history. Religion, culture and history are also matters of fierce dispute that excite the advocate to defend his truth and denounce the infidel.

Conclusions in the discussion of religion, culture and history are hard to come by and rarely go unchallenged. Surely we must take note of this in our discussion.

The disputes are ancient. Believers from 'time immemorial' have claimed a purchase on truth.

Atheism likewise is as old as theism and is recorded in the most ancient texts of Europe, India and China – as documented extensively below in chapter 10 of this work. Many writers in the great traditions ascribe religious belief to fear, laziness and gullibility. They argue, that there is no ground-form, and there is no highest common factor, in religious controversy. They argue that religion is largely hokum intended to keep people down.

History guided by dispassionate neutrality can be found in such writers as Megasthenes, writing in the third century BCE; Ssu-Ma Ch'in, writing in the first century BCE; Plutarch, writing in the first century; Proclus, writing in the fourth; Sankara, writing in the eighth; Al-Biruni, in the eleventh; Rashid Al-Din, in the thirteenth; and Ibn Khaldun, writing in the fourteenth century.

Ibn Khaldun (1332-1406) makes a pioneering contribution to scientific history in his work known as the *Muqaddimah* or "Prolegomena," perhaps the first historical work to develop a comprehensive account of human affairs including political, economic, environmental, psychological and social factors governing the chain of events; he is particularly interested in what he calls "group-feelings" (*asibiyah*) as the origin to social and religious movements; he shows how group dynamics give rise to new political forces and ultimately to new civilizations.*

The Enlightenment or 'Age of Reason' takes a *critical* and *skeptical* attitude towards religion. Gibbon states the summit of learned skepticism about religion at the beginning of the second chapter of the *Decline and Fall*: "The various modes of worship, which prevailed in the Roman world, were all considered by the people, as equally true; by the philosopher, as equally false; and by the magistrate, as equally useful." Skepticism or inquiry is an attempt to understand the world purely on the strength of the unassisted human mind, without the help of revelation or tradition. Voltaire is the father of *expressly* skeptical history and is the first European thinker to describe "the spirit of the times" – such as Ibn Khaldun describes – instead of the sequence of events:

"My aim has not been to collect a vast quantity of facts, which are always self-contradictory, but to select the most important and best documented facts in order to guide the reader so that he may judge for himself concerning the extinction, revival, and progress of the human spirit, and enable him to recognize peoples by their customs."

Voltaire's *Essay on Manners* (1753) attempts to apply the model of Newtonian science to historical knowledge in order to reduce the mass of facts to simpler patterns and laws – using the word 'culture' for this enterprise implies an effort of detachment and an attempt to direct the same skepticism we hold toward others' traditions to our own – this is an enormous first step beyond its predecessors among the Arab historians and Church historians and the ancients including even Thucydides and Herodotus. Gotthold Lessing thought that Voltaire had to be counted among the greatest innovators in all of history because of this work – he says that Voltaire was "the first to take free steps in empty space" – in conceiving the idea that the purpose of writing history is to reveal the gradual progress of mankind – tracing all the steps through which humanity must pass in religion, art, science, philosophy – before it can arrive at knowledge and consciousness of itself.

There appear to be four important conditions for this advance, which are: intellectual curiosity, cosmopolitanism (and the opportunity to encounter other peoples and their varying doctrines), skepticism (that allows the inquirer some breathing space and critical distance from his own ingrained prejudices), and religious toleration – i.e. *political freedom to pursue this study* – for it seems certain that the 'natural history of religion' or 'science of religion' or 'comparative study of religions' would never have arisen as a subject if it had remained forbidden by religious law.

In our investigation of the term 'history' above, we noted Gibbon's view that political history is largely a record of man's destructive activities. But as we look at the thought-complex 'religion/culture/history,' we see that politics also creates the space in which thinkers get a chance to think. Politics is not a study of eternal truths but of changing opinions. It is precisely the *difference* of opinions – their variety – that makes 'opinions' possible. Otherwise there would only be truths. This is a rule for our study also. There is *comparative* religion only if there are religions, and history teaches us that there are religions only where politics has made their variety possible.

(6) terms of reference

Voltaire uses the word "culture" in the effort to look behind facts for the underlying mental principle that determines them. This is a change in focus: the words 'custom' and 'convention' emphasize the rituals of a society, its practices or outward doings, whereas the word 'culture' typically refers to *ideas*. After Voltaire, researchers pursue both lines of approach: looking at practices and looking at ideas.

Durkheim described religion as social glue; Marx described religion as social opium; Royce described religion as social insight; Freud described religion as social neurosis. Their conclusions are quite different but they use similar tools, ideas and methods. Chief among the terms of reference for the critical study of religion are the terms *magic*, *ritual*, *symbol*, *belief*, and *ideology*.

magic

According to the first generation of anthropological researchers, beginning with the Brothers Grimm, E.B. Tylor and Sir James Frazer, magic is the earliest form of human thought. Mankind thought originally only in magical terms; magic is the foundation of the universe of primitive man and is the first stage in the evolution of the human mind.

These thinkers were looking at data from ancient European and Semitic sources, but also drew conclusions from field studies conducted among aboriginal tribes in Australia such as the Arunta, Island peoples in the South Pacific such as the Tanna, and studies conducted in Mexico, India, China, Kenya and Assyria; in North America among the Cherokee, the Winnebago, the Ojibwa, the Huron, the Algonquin, the Iroquois; also from various settlements in Malaysia; first looking at Greek and Latin sources; later to folklore from Italy, Ireland and Finland. This broad experience helps explain the international character of anthropological terminology, including words such as *mana* ('power,' from Melanesia), *taboo* ('forbidden,' from Polynesia), *totem* ('watcher,' from Native America), *baraka* ('blessing,' from North Africa), *tumah* ('unclean,' from ancient Judea), *juju* ('supernatural power,' from West Africa) and *fetish* ('supernatural object,' from the Portuguese).

Magic is a kind of thinking – not a logical kind of thinking, not scientific or causal – but via a principle of association. In the background are several important ideas: the idea of human freedom and active agency in the struggle for existence; the idea that life is full of risk and that outcomes are subject to luck; the idea that human beings peer out into the world with an intense emotional interest; and the basic idea of animism, i.e. that all things are filled with life or spirit or soul.

These separate principles – first: freedom and human self-determination (sometimes called 'native optimism'); second: the idea of risk, fortune or luck (sometimes called 'the aleatory factor'); and third, the emotional element (e.g. desire, anger, hate, love, jealousy, fear, exhilaration, exaltation, awe, wonder; what Radin calls "an imperious affective need" – what Malinowski calls "the motivating thrill"); and the animistic thesis (in brief, the hypothesis of the spiritual universe) – are the raw materials. Magic bridges the connection between human intentions and desired outcomes, on the one hand, and actual events and outcomes of good or ill fortune, on the other. The magical element – the fantastic, make-believe, spirit-filled intervention – taking such forms as sorcery, witchcraft, spells, exorcism, ghosts, demons, goblins, sprites, omens, hexes, talismans, incantations, curses, the trickster and the shaman – completes the transition from wish to reality.

Anthropological literature distinguishes between various kinds of magic. A first is rudimentary magic, which appears to be a kind of substitute action and a form of catharsis (it counts on the principle of emotional causation; e.g. overcome by emotion, the actor resorts to make-believe to relieve tension, as when he throws into the fire a portrait of his enemy). Another is sympathetic magic, which appears to be an attempt at direct action (it counts on the principle of like producing like; e.g. the frustrated lover brings a hair or piece of clothing belonging to the would-be beloved to the sorcerer; the wizard then casts an attracting spell). Another is contagious magic, which appears to hypothesize a (supernatural) chain of contagion (it counts on the principle of the relative identification of things that are in contact; e.g. by accident a Hindu physically touches a Dalit – a member of the Untouchable caste – and has now caught a magical contagion; he or she must pass it on to someone else who is not a Hindu – e.g. a Moslem, a Jain, a Carvaka or atheist).

Anthropologists studying these phenomena are attempting to draw conclusions from associationist psychology about the nature of magical thinking. They take the spirit-world to be the mental world – mental processes, including primitive and childish kinds of thought processes, help to throw light on elementary forms of religious life. Further ideas about religion come into play from developments in psychology – from psychoanalysis and Gestalt psychology and the psychology of crowds – thus the idea that *mere thinking can change what happens in the world* is investigated over time and magical thinking is illuminated by talking about fantasy and dreams, mental disorders, cognitive deficits, powers of suggestion and indoctrination, and behavioral economics.

Perhaps the key idea underlying magical thinking is that of the spiritual universe itself. The Maori term *mana* is used to indicate the stuff from which magic is formed – also the stuff making up souls and the divine – a sacred impersonal force existing throughout the universe. Some like terms from other languages include *ka* (Egyptian), *ichor* (Greek), *numen* (Latin), *wakan* (Dakota), *manitiou* (Algonquin), *orenda* (Iroquois), *chi* (Mandarin), *kami* (Japanese), and *brahman* (Sanskrit).

Mana can be in a thing, an action, or in a human being. It can be stored up, as by a discipline of renunciation or trial (for which there is the Sanskrit term, *tapas*); it can be expended, as in a Potlatch ceremony in which the host offers his prize possession to a visitor; it can be wasted or traded, made a gift or withheld. Action can fulfill it or alternatively action may lack *mana* and fail to attain its object. A Maori shaman interviewed in 1921 by John Beattie explained that *mana* is exactly the same thing in human beings as it is in gods, save only that gods live forever.

The first generations of anthropologists who made these researches – notably in Fraser's *The Golden Bough* (1890) – held that mind passed through an evolution from magical fantasy, through religious devotion, to scientific experimentalism – from magic to religion to science. Succeeding generations in anthropology and kindred philosophers and social thinkers, having lived through world wars, pandemic outbreaks, natural disasters, social crises, economic swings, assassinations; – the Holocaust, the Iron Curtain, the Cultural Revolution; – no longer held this faith. They gave up claiming that history shows steady progress. This essay revisits this question in chapter 10 below. Arguably, political history shows advances, defeats, and compromises – *differences* of opinion persist; magic, for good or ill, also lives on; religion too.

ritual

"The first task of life is to live. Men begin with acts, not with thoughts. Every moment brings necessities which must be answered at once. Need is the impelling force. The method is trial and failure, rude experiment and selection ... There is a concurrence towards that which proves to be most expedient. This produces habits in the individual and customs in the group. This is how *folkways* arise. The young learn them by tradition, imitation and authority; they are uniform, universal in the group, imperative, and invariable. As time goes on, folkways or patterns of culture become more arbitrary, positive and imperative. If it is asked why they act in a certain way in certain cases, primitive people always answer that it is so because their ancestors have always done so. The ancestors would be angry if the living presume to change ancient folkways" (W.G. Sumner, *Folkways*, 1906).

This passage from Sumner's famous work *Folkways* lays out the case for the primacy of practice rather than ideas in shaping the life of a people. Sumner recounts a conversation he had with the chief of the Miranhas, a tribe in the Amazon – the chief is confused to hear that Europeans have such a negative view about cannibalism – the chief says "It is all a matter of habit. When I have killed an enemy, it is better to eat him than to let him go to waste. Big game is rare ... The bad thing is not being eaten, but death." Sumner coined the term "ethnocentrism" to capture the idea that each group thinks its own folkways are best. "Each group nourishes its own pride and its vanity, boasts itself superior, exalts its own divinities, and looks with contempt on outsiders."

Folkways show themselves in habits and customs – patterns of behavior built up from repeated trials both in individual experience and in the development of a culture – habits become character and customs become morals. Thus in investigating action, actual practice and *doing*, important terms of reference emerge both to describe the learning process and the development of society. These include the term 'habit' itself (Greek *hexis*, Latin *habitus*) – also the noun 'habit' meaning a garment worn by monks and nuns; and terms from various languages that discern social custom.

Aristotle focuses on the idea of habit as the main thing in the formation of character. Legislators try to make good citizens by helping people form good habits. Moral virtue is the result of practice and the steady development of habits of character – *not* the result of deliberation, weighing alternatives, or intellectual assent. Untutored nature is replaced by ingrained habit, which becomes second nature. Confucius has similar ideas – he would be confused by the modern idea that children should learn 'critical thinking' – he held that learning happens in stages and that rote learning is important at the beginning, to get a grasp of what great thinkers have said in former ages; when we have a good grasp of what our ancestors have said, we can begin to think critically and evaluate ideas from times past. Recent writers such as Michel de Certeau (*The Practice of Everyday Life*, 1980) and Pierre Bourdieu (*Practical Reason: A Theory of Action*, 1998) pursue this line of thought one step further. These writers try to examine the ways in which people re-appropriate cultural materials to make them 'their own.' Bourdieu uses the Latin term 'habitus' to indicate a pre-reflexive, lasting and acquired scheme of perception, thought and action that has a kind of autonomic character. He thinks that it is possible to re-assimilate mere habit, which has become second nature, to create something more authentic – a kind of third nature.

The Indo-European root *ri-*, 'to go, to flow,' is the basis of the Sanskrit term *riti*, 'a going, a way, a usage or custom,' itself the root of the Latin term *ritus*, 'a custom,' rendered into English as 'rite' and 'ritual' and signifying related ideas such as ceremony, observance, prescribed behavior.

As Sumner notes in *Folkways*, people gradually build up habits, whereas societies gradually create rites. One of the interesting things about social customs, rites, mores or norms is the selection as to *which* parts of human experience are called out for special attention and treatment so that by repetitive training the society gradually creates a pattern of culture that every new member of the society is made to learn.

The first answer to this problem appears to be: *wherever human behavior is closest to animal behavior*, society intervenes in the form of customs and rites to underscore the difference between animal life and human being. Briefly: this is why religion is so preoccupied with directing people's sexual lives.

18

The most universal and basic form of social ritual is the rite of initiation in which a child undergoes a trial and emerges as an adult. Thus the relationship between animal and human is closest in the sex cycle, which is why sexuality comes in as the first aspect of human experience to be remade and given a new significance by social teaching. It becomes "socially crystallized, re-organized and reinterpreted" (Paul Radin, *Primitive Religion*, 1957). Puberty ceases being a mere physiological change and arrival at sexual maturity; it becomes ritually dramatized as the idea of *transition* itself. Puberty becomes a life change taking form as a structured action – a ritual ceremony – so that a rite of passage is signaled by *doing*, rather than *thinking* giving rise to action. The ceremony is performed and implanted in our memory. Then we begin to think back on it, take it up and work our way through it. Thus the holiday exists before the story we tell about it; the image exists before its explanation; the command exists before the reason why. The sacred import is an action before it is a doctrine. "Savage religion is not so much thought out as danced out" (R.R. Marett, *The Threshold of Religion*, 1914).

Joseph Campbell states that the function of ritual is to "conduct people across the difficult thresholds of transformation that demand a change in the patterns of life" – rites of passage such as birth, naming, puberty, marriage, becoming a parent, death and burial – all these moments are certified by magic, given moral weight and sanctified by religion *in order to bar the way back*. The life pattern must change. So the initiate is reborn in the new stage on life's way (*The Hero with a Thousand Faces*, 1949).

Rites of passage, initiation rites, purification rites, rites of intensification – such as communal celebrations by the whole group at points in the annual cycle, e.g. the new year, or planting time, or times of political upheaval, such as appointing a new king – also sacrificial rites, secret rites, exorcisms, totemic rites, oath-taking and times for prayers and hymns – these and like occasions represent passing the threshold and a call to rebirth. Because this kind of action is *ritual* action, it is not simply empty repetition but is invested with spiritual power and therefore has moral force. Some pieces of the puzzle connecting ideas about action, practice, ritual and morality are invested in the Mandarin term *li*, the Sanskrit term *karma*, and the Greek term *praxis*, all of which might be translated as 'moral action' or 'religious action.'

Li: "The term *li* is usually translated as 'ritual.' However, neither this term nor words such as 'manners,' 'customs,' 'practices,' or 'prescribed actions' conveys an adequate idea of what *li* stood for in ancient China. This is because none of them denotes anything more than behavior growing out of and regulated by tradition. The ideas for which *li* stands seem to have had their origin in a religious attitude towards life and in ethical principles developing out of that attitude. *Li* means the performance with true piety of ritual through which the will of heaven (*tian ming*) is interpreted and made to prevail on earth. On the moral side, it means the sense of propriety, which, through training and developing into habit, makes possible right relationships both in personal life and in society" (*Commentary on the I Ching*, Richard Wilhelm).

Karma: "The term *karma*, literally meaning action, denotes both action in general and the fruit-producing subtle impressions that remain with the doer even after an action is outwardly performed. Thus the law of *karma* is the law of cause and effect in the moral world. *Karma* is the total effect of a person's action and conduct that is visited in the first instance on the actor himself but equally in outward terms in the world of practical effects. *Karma* projects the moral ideal surmounting mere ritualism – mere adherence to custom – and straining for the more transcendent concepts of moral understanding and moral freedom" (*Commentary on Shankara's Atmabodha*, Swami Nikhilananda).

Praxis: Heidegger notes that the Greek term *praxis* can mean moral action in one of its restricted uses; *praxis* can also be practical use; it can be the action, the ability to do or act, or the outcome – our problems are our *pragmata*; also just having something to do with a subject, knowing about it or having some business with it; also working on things, changing things, looking at things, examining things; in the widest sense, *praxis* is "all human doing, pursuing, and enduring, including *poesis*, i.e. all poetry, art and making." *Pragma* is the deed, the act, the thing done; but also the thing that was necessary, that had to be done, the right thing, the thing prescribed by custom (*What is a Thing?*, Martin Heidegger).

Religion was initially about magic and practical action; about what people did and not what they thought; books and even ideas played virtually no role in the earliest stages of religious life; there were no doctrines or explanations. In religion we honor the gods through ritual and sacrifice. With the change from prehistory into history, all religions developed an intellectual tradition and a preoccupation with doctrinal correctness; also new quietist strains of silence and unknowing; and also doubt. Theism and atheism are opposite reactions to the loss of a common world of rites.

One of the strengths of agreement in cultural rituals – society made from ritual forms – is its vagueness. Agreement in cultural forms does not imply agreement in principles, values or beliefs. The American legal scholar Cass Sunstein talks about Constitutional law *as a form of ritual* and cultural practice in terms of what he calls "incompletely theorized agreements." We the People of the United States uphold our First Amendment, that "Congress shall make no law respecting an establishment of religion, or prohibiting the free exercise thereof..." But to one man this protects religion from government, and to another it protects government from religion. As Kwame Appiah writes: "There is no agreed-upon answer – and there doesn't need to be. We can live together without agreeing what the values are that make it good to live together; we can agree what to do, without agreeing why it is right" (*Cosmopolitanism: Ethics in a World of Strangers*, Kwame A. Appiah).

The ritual, ceremonial, traditionally structured pattern of action is somehow the bearer of magic —"it is a unique form of symbolic action which creates a state that can be described broadly as one of emergence" (Godfrey Lienhardt, *Divinity and Experience: The Religion of the Dinka*) – this makes possible the ritual transformation of experience beyond a threshold to the next stage.

symbol

The word 'symbol' in its original meaning has to do with a coin or shield or weapon cut down the middle, one half being given to each of two close friends, who then passed it down through generations within their families. This was a way of keeping the bond of friendship alive long after its originators had passed away, and a kind of obligation, when one family presented the token to the other, to treat strangers as if they were close friends. Thus a 'symbol' is a way of keeping something in memory and a way of treating the unknown as if it were known.

A symbol is something that stands for something else. Thus it is familiar to all of us (for example) that the image of a fish may stand for the Christian community. The symbol in this case is a way of keeping the idea of the Christian community alive. Strangers instantly take on a familiar aspect if they are Christians welcomed into a Christian community.

A symbol is a kind of unit of cultural life: it is a principle of association between one idea (fish) and another (Christ). One can imagine a culture being built up gradually by such principles of association, somewhat like a language. Every word in the dictionary is explained by other words in the dictionary. Every symbol in the culture is explained by other symbols in the culture. Both processes are circular. If the circle is large enough, one has a genuine culture or a genuine language – rather than a *part* of culture or cultural practice, or a *part* of language or linguistic practice.

Durkheim studies the Arunta, an Australian aboriginal people, in his work *The Elementary Forms of Religious Life*. The Arunta practice totemism, a system in which a clan (a kin group) takes the name of, claims descent from, and attributes sacred properties to a plant or animal. Durkheim explains that the plant or animal is not the source of the totemism but a stand-in for the true source, which is society itself. He argues that *religion* – which takes the form of the totem ancestor, God, or other supernatural force – *is the symbolization of society*. By means of religious symbols, the group (in effect) worships itself. Society harnesses the enormous power inherent in people's perception of the sacred in order to animate a sense of communal oneness and moral authority. Thus the primary functions of religion (he claims) are the creation, reinforcement, and maintenance of social solidarity and control. He also argues that totems, taboos and simple vocabularies of symbols of small tribes villages become gradually *institutionalized* over time – in later stages they serve to justify central authority and group cohesion – and ultimately they are transformed into the larger structures we call 'religions.'

Several recent philosophers have seized on the idea that countless possible worlds may be created out of nothing by the use of *symbols*. They emphasize that the brute-fact element of experience does not dictate the way in which human beings negotiate their way through the world. As they express it, the world we live in is largely "underdetermined" by facts. Instead, these thinkers stress that there are *many* 'worlds' – as many as we can make out of symbols, as many as there are cultures – where no *one* culture stands above all others as an eternal sanity. They emphasize the creative power of the understanding – not the description of brute fact – and the variety and formative power of symbols.

C.G. Jung connected this idea with that of magic and ritual: the concept of the symbol corresponds to the *"magically powerful name* which gets a grip on the object" – more than this, the symbol (as Jung quotes Sabina Spielrein) "seems to owe its origin to the striving of a complex towards transformation" that shows itself in all art and creative work (*Symbols of Transformation*, 1912).

Another such thinker is Ernst Cassirer, whose *Philosophy of Symbolic Forms* (1923) undertakes a cross-cultural study of the development of myth, religion, language, art, and science. The American philosopher Nelson Goodman's book *Ways of Worldmaking* (1978) takes a similar approach through an analytic study of types and functions of symbols and symbol systems. Goodman asks: "What are worlds made of? And what role do symbols play in the making? And how is worldmaking related to knowing? These questions must be faced, even if full and final answers are far off." He says that the difference is not that fiction is fabricated and fact is found. Facts, he says, are "syncategorematic." They comprise many combinations and decisions. Experience comes in versions (rather than emerging for us as brute facts). Sometimes facts even vanish because of relationships between versions (and power wielded by people who uphold them). Goodman argues that it is better to talk about *versions* than *worlds* because with the former term it is obvious that perspective plays a role. There have to be *many* versions for there even to be *one*. Thus oftentimes selling a world makes more sense than arguing for it – worlds built up by human efforts need human actors to wield them. Goodman even proposes a new definition for the symbol: it should be a "category or scheme or organization, calling attention to a way of setting our nets to capture what may be significant" in experience – something we have missed up to now. Goodman also says that mere awareness that there are versions "paints no pictures." We still have to make them real and "a broad mind is no substitute for hard work." Ultimately, symbols are dangerous; they easily hoodwink us; real understanding is also an ability to *resist* them.

Much of religious life is expressed by means of symbols and in obviously symbolic language. But religious life is not merely symbolic, since in modern epochs it asks for assent. Belief implies more than mere association: association is succeeded by judgment, judgment is concluded with asserted truth, and conclusions are enacted in commitment – made real and effective in the world.

Luther hated ritual and even thought it was blasphemous (a "specter of the devil," "a reproach and mockery of true holiness," *Smalcald Articles*, 1537). He was equally dismissive of symbols, which he saw as a kind of ostentation. What counts is truth. Yet truth, magical at first, then ritualized, becomes symbolic, which means that it risks becoming *merely* symbolic. Symbolic thinking depends on achieving an affinity (*sympatheia*) with an unseen dimension of existence, entering a trance (*ekstasis*) and a self-forgetting (*kenosis*), "to assimilate oneself to the holy symbols" (Plutarch, fragment 168). A stone symbolizes the eternity of holiness, the moon its power of renewal, the sky its transcendence. That is to say: symbolic thinking requires effort; it requires a sharply directed focus in attention; it requires a highly unusual way of listening to sounds or of looking at images. Karen Armstrong puts this point in the first pages of her study *The Case For God*: "Religion is hard work. Its insights are not self-evident and have to be cultivated in the same way as an appreciation of art, music, or poetry ... like art, the truths of religion require the disciplined cultivation of a different mode of consciousness ... at such times, we feel that we inhabit our humanity more fully than usual and we experience an enhancement of being."

Symbolic truth, requiring this great effort, tends to get narrowed down to factual truth, requiring little or no effort at all. As another believer asks in 1888 (Mrs. Humphrey Ward, in her novel *Robert Elsmere*), "If the Gospels are not true in fact, as history, I cannot see how they are true at all, or of any value." The Greek scholar Walter Burkert has made this transition a special focus of his work (e.g. in *Greek Religion*, 1977) and has shown persuasively that just as fundamentalism is a reaction to secularism, so theology is a response in religious life to the innovation of philosophy. "Previously religion had been defined by forms of behavior and by institutions; [with the rise of philosophy] it becomes a matter of theories and thoughts." It is pointless to look for a doctrine behind a rite, but after the rise of philosophy, religiosity becomes equated with doctrinal assent. Religion was magical, symbolic *action*; religion becomes very unexceptional, literalist *belief*.

The belief, e.g. in the resurrection, counts as a *belief*, i.e. something that might be put into a declarative sentence, i.e. a statement that is true or false. Thus a kind of inspirational prompt and a way of bringing out the inner man – evoking wonder, enlivening the spirit, awakening the sense of awe – undergoes a kind of mutation and gets taken as a report of facts.

Now if a statement in religious expression is a statement like any other, then it is subject to normal sorts of criticism. The example statement cannot be self-contradictory. It cannot contradict obvious truths, well-known facts or derived claims in the system.

For this reason, believers have often held that religious expression is unlike any other kind of speech. Thus it need not obey normal rules of discourse. John Baillie's influential work *Our Knowledge of God* (1939) begins with the statement "We reject logical argument of any kind as the first chapter of our theology or as representing the process by which God comes to be known." Baillie is arguing for a kind of *Christian* knowledge, but it is easy to find equivalent statements in writers from every sort of religious tradition.

St. Thomas argued that on some questions it is wrong to apply strict logic or to try to be objective (*De Veritate*). Kierkegaard held that in some matters truth cannot be objective, but must be subjective (*Concluding Unscientific Postscript*). Tertullian ventured even further along this line by holding that some truths should be believed *because* they are illogical (*De Carne Christi*).

Part of the difficulty of such views is that it introduces a split among the believer's opinions – as it were, a split in his mind – applying normal thinking to one class of beliefs and an abnormal review process to a second, privileged set of beliefs. Religious conviction, so understood, comes at the cost of mental illness or, less drastically, involves a kind of theatrical state of mind, like the person who follows a story and gets caught up in the action by a willing suspension of disbelief.

Another approach to belief in religious contexts goes to the question of how they arise, how we become conscious of them, and how to regard them once they rise into conscious awareness.

If belief is a special sort of mental happening or *event*, it is something of which the believer might always be aware. Such an idea seems incompatible with the fact that some beliefs are evidently unconscious. Likewise it seems wrongheaded to connect every sort of belief with a datable event.

If belief is a *disposition*, then it is equivalent to a series of conditional statements describing what the believer would be likely to do in given circumstances. Believing a proposition, on such a view, would be like knowing how to ride a bike. (Note that we learn how to ride a bike gradually, even if there is an 'aha!' moment when we finally get the hang of it.) Believing a proposition on this model would be something that shows up when the subject arose. Yet it seems quite unremarkable to believe something without its arising as a question (I don't have to be thinking about mathematics to believe that '2 + 2 = 4').*

J.L. Austin argued that belief is less like an event or a disposition and more like a *performance*. That is, the statement 'I believe' invites my hearers to accept what I am uttering. Thus belief may be reluctant, noncommittal or enthusiastic, but whatever my emotion (or even if I have none), my belief proposes a kind of guarantee. A belief is not private. It shows itself and exists in society.

Austin also noted that there are degrees of belief. These might range from suspecting that P, or holding an opinion that P, or being almost sure that P, or being absolutely certain that P.*

Spinoza was the first philosopher to recognize a kind of 'primitive credulity' most responsible for human belief. Walter Bagehot, Alexander Bain, and William James developed the theory: the idea is that human beings tend to believe anything that is suggested to them. Bagehot said: "My theory is, that in the first instance the child believes everything." Belief in this sense is a natural endowment and not the express result of human effort. The important idea here is that the main thing to explain about belief is not belief itself but its absence. "The child learns by believing the adult; doubt comes afterwards" (Wittgenstein, *Philosophical Investigations*). Thus the question is not really about belief but about doubt. How do we learn to doubt? – How do we begin to think carefully? – Normally this is *not* the case, but instead we think instinctively, reactively, automatically, churning through habits of thought.

Experience suggests that the main cause of learning to doubt is the discovery of being wrong. To make a mistake and have it come to light is a gift: then you try to think more carefully and pay close attention to facts. In logic, this is 'disproof.' In the philosophy of science, this is called 'falsification.'

A difficulty here is that religious beliefs are typically not testable – not falsifiable – but have a kind of 'sacred' status that exempts them from unflinching critical review. A religious belief may be held without supporting evidence, or even in the face of contrary evidence, e.g. as an article of faith. Holding such a belief may be part of what it means to belong to a certain community. The idea that all belief should be subjected to empirical test is itself a cultural belief in the same sense – not e.g. of Christian culture but of modern scientific culture. Yet religious culture exempts itself from critical review, whereas scientific culture subjects itself to its own process of questioning.

The idea that a mode of expression can be meaningful, though exempt from logic and from empirical test, is much more familiar than it seems. Poetry is a good example. Alan Watts used to say that poetry is the art of saying what cannot be said. "Every poet knows that he is trying to describe the indescribable. Every poet knows that nothing is describable. Whether you take some sort of ineffable mystical experience at one extreme, or an ordinary rusty nail at the other, nothing is really describable" (*Buddhism: The Religion of No Religion*). The cliché is that we are all astonished by a change from a well-known and universally acknowledged routine norm – from an obviousness we have grown accustomed to – by the appearance of some kind of extraordinary and singular thing, which becomes the stuff of poetry. But, in truth, the poet is not astonished by a change from the obvious. The poet sees that *nothing* is obvious. Nothing is usual or normal.

A *poetic* interpretation of religious belief may free itself from logic and empirical test yet still discover meaning in a stone, a cloud, a day or a night, and especially in an individual human being.

Science generally is said to be 'empirico-deductive' (a term coined by Darwin). Thus in some cases we make faulty deductions and in some cases we get our facts wrong. Science confronts these two very different kinds of mistakes. Religion may free itself from both these problems and thus become a kind of poetry. Yet the fanatic is seldom satisfied with the poetry of his faith. He calls it 'truth' – he exempts it from any standard – he forbids us examining it – and he commands us to believe.*

Belief in context

Belief has a characterization at a biological level, at a psychological level, and at a social level, read from the satisfaction of basic drives, the expression of dynamic conflicts, or from the history of social interactions. That there is such a thing as belief also suggests that the agent attaches a *subjective* meaning to his or her behavior. The critical approach to belief should take all these and several other ideas into account.

The *biological* perspective addresses belief as a characteristic arising in the evolutionary process. This position holds that belief arises by the same process as every other biological adaptation. Beliefs are means by which biological units attempt to cope with their environment. Thus beliefs tend to survive if they lend some advantage to those who hold them. The species continues by its capacity for replicating, just as beliefs survive by their capacity for replicating. Richard Dawkins introduced the term "memes" on the model of biological 'genes' to get at problems like the "fitness" of belief and the "struggle for existence" among beliefs and the "evolution" of beliefs.

An example of belief that may be rooted in our biology is the idea that such things as food and drink and love are valuable.

The *psychological* perspective suggests that attention widens and narrows with affective states arising with instinctual compulsion. The condition of having unmet (instinctual) needs is experienced as *stress*. Stress is a state of tension caused by the intersection of internal and external stimuli within the body. Roughly: unmet needs result in adjustive demands experienced as stress. Empirical investigation appears to confirm the general claim that stress and concentration vary inversely – thus under the impact of stress the context for belief shifts from the external world to the troubled 'internal' environment – e.g. various beliefs are adopted on weak or no evidence whatever under the impact of guilt or anxiety or fear.

Some beliefs may be considered as means by which psychological units attempt to cope with their 'internal' environment. Instead of adopting beliefs based on objective review of evidence, agents adopt beliefs under psychological stress. This process is termed 'psychological defense.'

Examples of defense mechanisms include *scapegoating* (an innocent individual or group is singled out in blame for some undesired condition), *projection* (attribution to others of our own unwanted traits), *introjection* (in place of our own experiences, values and beliefs, we internalize the experiences, values, and beliefs of others), *denial* (we protect a favored self-concept by refusing to acknowledge some unpleasant circumstance), and *stereotyping* (we ignore individual differences and categorize people or things according to a rigid preconception). Psychological depth opens the problems of self-deception, hypocrisy, fragmentation of the self, and brings doubt to unshakable beliefs.

The *social* perspective teaches that belief arises in the circumstance and for the cause of communal life. Yet the community is finite. The result is that social life constrains belief within the circumstance of a specific time and place. Thus beliefs may be considered as means by which social units attempt to cope with their community. Beliefs appear as social practices.

Examples of ways in which social reality impacts beliefs are captured in such terms as parochialism, provincialism, and xenophobia. *Parochialism* is the idea that certain beliefs have primary application to local conditions and narrow interests. *Provincialism* refers to the idea that certain beliefs are assessed exclusively in relation to group loyalty (thus the bias for the community is the prejudice against its competitors). *Xenophobia* refers to the fear of strangers, which dictates a rejection of any belief seen to be unfamiliar or alien.

The believer's dismissal of rival religious traditions, and belief that other communities worship 'idols' and 'false gods,' may be said to be a *parochial* view shared by many religious traditions. It is typical of Americans, for example, to speak their own language and no other, to be ignorant of other people and places, and to care little about them – and to claim that the United States of America is the greatest nation that has ever been – which is surely an extreme form of *provincialism*. The French philosopher Simone de Beauvoir describes *xenophobia* as follows:

"In small-town eyes all persons not belonging to the village are strangers and suspect; to the native of a country, all who inhabit other countries are 'foreigners'; Jews are 'different' for the anti-Semite, Blacks are 'inferior' for the American racists, Aborigines are 'natives' for the colonists, working people are the 'lower class' to the privileged" (*The Second Sex*, 1949).

The above strategies – biological, psychological, and social – hold in common the basic idea that human action is meaningful. Each characterizes human agency at a differential level *below* that of the individual, explaining what we believe via our society, our brain or our physical body. Yet belief also has personal or idiosyncratic or subjective significance. When we ask someone why they believe something, normally they don't answer – 'because I am a biological or psychological or social unit.'

In some cases what a person believes links him or her to a wider community – belief in this sense has a cultural significance. In other cases, belief is strictly personal – in Greek *idiotes*, 'private' – e.g. a schizophrenic's belief that he hears voices. The skeptical approach to belief is the same, whatever the content. Instincts, emotions, personal preferences and ideas, as well as social arrangements, *have no truth value*. Likewise the complex frame of mind that Plutarch refers to as *symbolic thinking* cannot be assessed in terms of factual truth and error. Symbolism is not intended to assert truth, but to evoke a sense of awe.

After the rise of philosophy, symbolism falls before literalism, and ritual gets dislodged by belief. Belief in turn invites criticism, and criticism demands evidence. John Locke defends this principle by defining *the love of truth* as "the not entertaining of any proposition with greater assurance than the proofs it is built upon will warrant" (*An Essay Concerning Human Understanding*, 1689).

ideology

Basic concepts, practices, symbols and beliefs, taken all together, comprise the "form of life" (Wittgenstein, *Philosophical Investigations*). The form of life, web of belief, life practice, or worldview, always has a kind of ultimate reference in the historical community in which it is carried out – also called the pattern of culture. This last and ultimate context, superparadigm or supercontext, the pattern of culture, is what people mean when they use the word *ideology*.

Marx coined the term *ideology*, initially to refer to a statement that subtly promotes a bias while offering itself up as a perfectly neutral fact. Later he extended the term to get at the governing structure or framework for society as a whole and its inherent championing of one value over another, one class over another, and one life over another. Marx focused on the role religion plays as a painkiller for the frustration, deprivation and subjugation experienced by oppressed peoples. Religion motivates an otherworldly focus that diverts oppressed peoples from seeking radical change in *this* world. He noted that ideology is promulgated – mainly at an unconscious level – to make it seem that only a fool or a madman could reject such-and-such obvious truths, e.g. that blacks are inferior to whites or that women are inferior to men. When the man behind the curtain is exposed and people see that they are being manipulated, it becomes possible to lay out the ideology to display it and examine it. It finally appears as what it is: opinions, beliefs, hypotheses – not settled facts or obvious truths.

It is useful to think about ideology in three different ways: as descriptive, positive, and pejorative, as the Cambridge philosopher, Raymond Geuss, has argued in many works (*The Idea of a Critical Theory*, 1981; *History and Illusion in Politics*, 2001; *Politics and the Imagination*, 2010).

In the first and descriptive sense, the term 'ideology' has an anthropological background, and refers to a sociocultural system and the ways in which it changes over time. This is the system of symbols, concepts, attitudes, beliefs, and practices – the motives and values and products – the artforms, social structures, and dominant ways of thinking within a society. Every people has a widely shared, systematically interconnected field of cultural beliefs, underlying and driving action.

In the second and positive sense, 'ideology' represents a system of culture *that is intended to fulfill given purposes*. Ideology in this second and positive sense has an utopian content. It represents a requirement yet to be fulfilled. For example, the high-minded language of the American *Declaration of Independence* forms an important part of the American ideology.

Thus in the first case, ideology is an underlying principle, and in the second case, ideology is an utopian goal, but in both cases *the ideology is something the agents themselves within the society do not see*. People don't normally develop a consciousness about their sociocultural system and its development from remote ancient origins to prospective and utopian ideals. Ideology is a form of consciousness, a constellation of beliefs, attitudes, dispositions and practices that the agents themselves typically do not acknowledge. Part of what it means to be a member of a society is to have some measure of unconsciousness about the content and consequences of belonging to that society. Ideology in this sense is sometimes called 'false consciousness.' It is a form of delusion.

The term 'ideology' with this meaning was introduced at the beginning of the modern period by the philosopher and statesman Francis Bacon. Bacon held that human beings, gathering together into social organizations, give concrete form to guiding prejudices which are inseparable from their association. These are the *idola tribus*, the "idols of the tribe," which include all the words, practices, and organizing principles of the group (*Novum Organum*, 1620). Ideology in this sense is the summation of the life of a people. The defining problem for criticism is to establish sufficient objectivity such that analysis and evaluation do not simply mimic the reigning prejudices of a time and place, but instead apply principles that transcend local custom.

In any circumstance in which believers are made to 'believe' without any consciousness that they 'believe,' without reflection or examination, they realize a 'false consciousness' (a mind-state resulting from ideological control)

– this does not imply that they are in error – only that they believe without knowing that they believe and are still unconscious about themselves. But it seems difficult, or perhaps impossible, to sort out which among the contents of a culture are false, and which are true. If we confront one form of life or ideology with a rival form – if we judge a form of consciousness from the perspective of a form of consciousness external to it – then we engage the deep problems of cultural imperialism and ethnocentrism. The so-called *external critique of ideology* has the disadvantage of confronting people with judgments they have a motive to reject. Provincialism and xenophobia are normal phenomena in social life. Thus external critique is successful only if it is practiced as a form of democracy (political judgment has to make its case in the light of day). People from different backgrounds share many basic conceptions. This means that they can engage in a conversation and perhaps even reach consensus gradually by talking things out.

Ideology-critique has varied *internal* forms, in which the agents themselves within the society are accepted as final judges of right ideas, belief and practice. The strategy here is to engage the forms of criticism that agents in the society already use in daily life (to apply cultural ideas to the cultures that created them). Traditionally, there are three such forms of internal critique.

The reigning ideology within a given society refers to so-called 'descriptive beliefs' that assert the existence of objects or conditions. A first and straightforward form of critique along this line is to ask whether these beliefs are supported by evidence. "No society would survive for any length of time without basing a large part of its daily activities on beliefs derived from evidence" (Kwasi Wiredu, *How Not to Compare African Traditional Thought with Western Thought*, 1980). The same reliance on evidence can be applied by members of the society to question cultural beliefs that have attained an ideological status. Protagoras' questioning of the Olympian religion, and Copernicus' questioning of the geocentric hypothesis, are examples of epistemic ideology-critique.

A form of consciousness may be accounted false if it involves the consequence of supporting, stabilizing or legitimizing social institutions that involve unjust domination. This implies the strategy of emphasizing agents' desires for liberation and of rejecting beliefs that frustrate agents' capacities for fulfillment. Lincoln's questioning of the institution of slavery, and Susan B. Anthony's struggles for universal franchise, represent examples of functional social critique. They held that existing 'normal' social conditions should be abandoned, because they were unjust.

A form of consciousness may also be accounted false in view of the way in which it acquired or the way in which it is held. The idea here is that agents get stuck in a false consciousness if they hold beliefs on the ground of acceptances they could *never* acknowledge. Thus if a belief is causally related to the social standpoint of those who hold it, then there is a sufficient reason for doubting it. An example might be the common view among the wealthy that homeless people are lazy. A more difficult problem arises when agents hold beliefs whose grounds they explicitly deny. Suppose a young girl is constantly told that her desire to be a doctor is absurd because 'women can't be doctors.' Eventually she internalizes the judgment and abandons her plans for a medical career. She will judge herself, and judge other women, according to this adopted standard. Yet she could not *both* uphold this position and also acknowledge how she came to believe it. Her view of herself enshrines a false consciousness – an 'ideology' – mainly because of the way in which she formed it.

Researchers who study culture often focus on such problems of ideology-critique because they have to reckon with ways in which thinking is affected by *non-logical* factors that warp belief and action. The idea is that mere fictions assume the status of exalted truths. For example, the beliefs in demonic possession, or the prohibition against interfaith marriage, or prohibitions against miscegenation, have no status as facts, yet all of them have been taken as immovable truths.

*

The above brief survey of religious terms shows a kind of declension from magic to ideology in which religiosity has gradually less significance as a sense for grandeur and gradually more weight as intellectual obedience. Ancient religion is more practice than belief; modern religion is less awe and more theology. The term 'ideology,' which stands at the end of this declension, also indicates a *received* consciousness, or *normative* form of thought, which tends to replace careful analysis, and judging cases by their merits, with a loyalty test by the standard of fervor and ideological purity.

The American historian Gabriel Kolko writes that "from the turn of the twentieth century until this day, the American public mind has been the object of an ideological onslaught that is as unrelenting as it is diverse: ranging from the school to the press to mass culture in its multitudinous dimensions" (*The Limits of Power*, 1972). Kolko works through some of the steps by which the American ideology has been built up over a period of decades. In recent use, the term 'ideology' has lost some of its pejorative force and become accepted as merely descriptive – likely because the structures that people refer to with this term have become so familiar – social norms and political ideologies that are part of daily life. But this process runs much deeper in the case of religion; typically in religious life we are looking at constructions that have developed over centuries, or even millennia.

Because culture is built up from so many sorts of contingencies, and because cultural beliefs are affected by so many non-logical factors, Kolko concludes that every thoughtful person needs to be wary of "unshakable conviction" – especially so with deep convictions and beliefs laden with emotional power – because we want to be able to examine *everything*.

A critical thinker is part of her own culture, and can act in solidarity with people in culture, but her spirit of criticism keeps trying to find a foothold outside culture. In constructing an understanding of the thought-complex *religion/culture/history*, this is the most difficult problem we have to face.*

(7) approaches to the problem

The problem is *religion* in *culture* and through *history* – an attempt at the application of scientific method to the problem of religion – an attempt at bringing thoughtfulness and philosophic calm to the world of belief – requiring some experience of diverse beliefs, some skepticism, and some tolerance. Some orienting terms in the study are: magic, ritual, symbol, belief, and ideology. Some tools are: logic; empiricism; and ideology-critique, i.e. doubt regarding overarching assumptions.

Psychological theories include Max Müller's idea that human beings possess a sense for the sacred, similar to vision and the sense of touch; Tylor coined the term "animism" to refer to primitive man's attribution of life even to inanimate things; Marett held that religion originates in the feeling of awe; Wundt held that religion arises from fear; Freud developed a theory based on the idea that religion originates in the world of infantile sexuality, childhood dependency and helplessness: the child's guilt, reverence and general ambivalence toward parental figures is writ large in the idea of God.

Social theories include Xenophanes' sociological criticism and skepticism about religious ideas, including his notion that if cattle, horses and lions had hands and could draw or sculpt, then horses would make gods like horses; each would shape bodies of gods in their own likeness and think of them in relation to their own world of affairs. Aristotle held a similar view and noted "all people say that that the gods have a king because they themselves had kings formerly or now; for men create gods after their own image, not only with regard to form but with regard to their whole manner of life" (*Politics*, 1, 2, 7). Robertson Smith, J.F. McLennan and F.B. Jevons derived religion from ancient man's complicated feelings and realities of dependency on animals and on the guilt they felt about slaughtering animals for survival, which on the Smith theory underlies totemism and the ancient practice of tracing family and tribal lineage back to a spirit animal. Scholars such as Francis Cornford, Jane Harrison and Wilhelm Trotter derived religion from what they called "the herd instinct" and "herd-suggestion" and related anthropological theories of social or collective consciousness. Other writers such as Nicolai Bukharin claim that religion arises by gradual steps from ancestor-worship.

Cultural theories about religion focus on ideas about ethnocentrism (Herodotus), group-feelings (Ibn Khaldun), universalism (Rashid al Din), cultural growth and decay (Spengler, Toynbee), conflict among paradigms (Samuel Huntington, Benjamin Barber) – economic theories focus on hedonism (Hume), monopolies (Adam Smith), teleology (Hegel, Marx), rational choice (Rodney Stark), and a revisionist account of consumption (E.F. Schumacher) – Max Weber's *The Protestant Ethic and the Spirit of Capitalism* (1930) founds the sociology of religion and much work is being done presently in the biology of religion.

There are myriad approaches to the problem – many teachers offer ideas for the inquiry – I have immersed myself in many such ideas and as I write I am still studying new ones.

Generations of scholars have approached the problem of religion in culture and through history with many of the same orienting terms, and many of the same tools, in many rival forms – psychological, social, cultural; via the economics of religion and the biology of religion; with many believers' narratives and many atheistic accounts – and plainly I cannot claim any unheard-of depth in what I say here or pretend to a solution. How do I propose to approach the highly contested space of ideas that is *religion/culture/history*?

My approach is philosophy. I am speaking to the philosopher in myself and in everyone; I am trying to call up my strength for thinking; I am trying to hold back my weakness for not thinking. I have said that philosophy is limited only by reason and empirical science. Philosophy is inquiry – critical inquiry, appreciative inquiry, free inquiry – a means of educating oneself by inquiring. I have said that philosophy is devotion to learning, to objectivity, to self-criticism. Philosophy is a part of culture, but tries to find a foothold outside culture; philosophy is skepticism, and tries to aim this distrust at itself. Philosophy is not defensive, philosophy is not partisan, philosophy has no cause, philosophy lives in doubt. Philosophy is comparison and the consideration of arguments.

I am not taking philosophy as the advancing of a thesis, except as part of the *elenchus*, i.e. except as a part of the Socratic method of oppositional discussion and critical cross-examination. That is: I am constructing an understanding of the thought-complex *religion/culture/history* by working though arguments; and if I am able to draw any conclusion at the end of my reasoning, then I will advance a thesis that must itself be confronted, examined and led through the oppositional inquiry.

Philosophy is the *elenchus* – the method of critical examination – philosophy works through arguments. But what new position is reached by working through arguments? What is the gain in arguing?

According to its original conception by Socrates, the *elenchus* always has a negative result. The process begins with a thesis and proceeds to its refutation. Better hypotheses are found by identifying and eliminating those that lead to contradictions. We ask better questions and propose better answers. Truth is whatever survives the process of critical scrutiny up to a certain point. Knowledge advances by clearing away misunderstandings.

Two millennia following Socrates, Voltaire proposed a new conception of the *elenchus*. Argument over the ages traces a gradual course of development – these are the steps through which humanity must pass before it can arrive at knowledge and consciousness of itself – every generation forms a new stage of existence that recommences the project of knowledge at a higher level.

Thus the *elenchus*, initially a method of inquiry based on asking and answering questions, is revised into a thesis about history – a vision of human progress – the idea that generations conserve and transcend the experience of their ancestors – gradually attaining scientific understanding and perhaps even some wisdom.

A half-century after Voltaire, Hegel investigated this thesis – the idea of human progress – and proposed a still newer conception of the *elenchus*. He taught that philosophy is "its time comprehended in thought," which implies that philosophy comprehends every thought preceding its time – philosophy seeks out arguments from every kind of history and study that lead to the developments of its time. "In philosophy the latest birth of time is the result of all the systems that have preceded it" (*Logic, Encyclopedia of the Philosophical Sciences*, Part 1, sec 1, § 13). Hegel envisioned that behind all the above arguments about religion from psychology, sociology and every other study, there is a certain something, named Mankind, who is thinking these thoughts serially – the World Spirit embodied in Mankind, as distinct from individual men and women – Hegel envisions that Mankind's thinking is advancing by gradual stages to a higher knowledge that incorporates the learning of past ages.

Two centuries after Hegel, it is possible to see several steps beyond this conception – to see what is right and wrong with it – and thus reconceive philosophy once more, as well as its defining method of scrutiny. Hegel has captured something essential when he says that it is just as important to *assert* a thesis as it is to criticize it. Philosophy asks questions, but it also proposes answers. It is just as much imagination as reasoning. He also caught hold of the essence of philosophy in describing philosophy as a kind of dialogue in which new thinking emerges from old. What philosophy worth the name takes *no account whatever* of previous thinking? The growth of knowledge depends on proposing ideas and testing them, which makes history a platform from which we can jump to new ideas. Yet Hegel also envisioned that world history is *one* history, leading to the perfection of spirit that is his own philosophy. And from our perspective – in our *postmodern condition*, as Lyotard defines it, which is a kind of "incredulity towards metanarratives" – we no longer believe in one story that defines us all (*The Postmodern Condition*, 1979). We live in a world of many stories. There are many rituals, many systems of belief, many ideologies – many religions. They cannot be arranged in a single progressive line. Qualitative differences have no inherent order.

Thus I am *not* making the assumption that the World Spirit, embodied in Mankind, is advancing by gradual stages from magic to religion to science; or that every previous philosophy is superseded by the thinking I am recording in these words. I am making the opposite assumption. That is, I am arguing that all these many views are contemporaries – Sinuhe, Aristotle, Max Müller, Confucius, Al-Biruni, Marcel Mauss, Kabir, Margaret Mead, Enrique Dussel,

Kwasi Wiredu, Slavoj Zizek, Iris Murdoch, Chief Joseph – every source from every place in the world – every thinker who has weighed in on the question – every believer's account and every skeptic's reasoning, from ancient materialists to Christopher Hitchens. I am taking all these accounts as contemporaries, unmoored from their cultures, histories and the audiences they found – all the contents of the past, offered up to the individual – exactly what a present, living philosophizing has to confront and lead through the oppositional discussion and inquiry.

I am *not* asserting that all these accounts are equivalent or on a level or equally right or wrong. I *am* asserting that they all have to face scrutiny and that they cannot be arranged in any single order. I am looking to *consider them all* and normalize their variety. I am looking to *make them face each other* and communicate with each other. I am looking for an enlarged perspective and for a truth-content that survives this larger course of scrutiny. I am looking for something that is universally communicative – that speaks to *everyone*, whatever his or her perspective – that reaches bedrock in human experience.

Thus I am imagining philosophy as enlightened humanity in conversation with itself – to pursue philosophy is to try to become this enlightenment and to carry on this conversation. And thus I am looking to take from every offering what is useful for thinking.

Thinking is oriented towards the ongoing process of coming to be; it makes preliminary summaries for the purpose of taking the next step in time; it refuses monotony and welcomes learning. This is the approach to philosophy I am applying in this study.

The problem is *religion* in *culture* and through *history*. My approach is philosophy, which is a kind of approach to approaches, or perspective on perspectives, and which, in my conception, normalizes their variety. I am constructing an understanding of the thought-complex *religion/culture/history*, beginning with religions, cultures and histories themselves; also studying what medicine, natural science, social science and theology have to teach about these subjects; collecting this learning together by working though arguments; taking this on as *my* problem and trying to become the conversation it implies. In the end my goal is simply to bring some clarity to this difficult subject, to take some next steps in thinking, and carry the conversation forward.

Eastern traditions

Only Sumer and Egypt have an older written tradition than China, whose tradition stretches back 5000 years.

There are a number of themes that run throughout the Chinese tradition from its beginnings through contemporary Chinese thought. These include a few simple ideas and some basic methods. Chinese thinking may also be said to be largely concerned with one basic problem.

Central ideas in the Chinese tradition include the land, farming, and the cycles of natural change; the idea that *reversal* is inherent in all change, or that development always progresses to an extreme and is afterwards followed by progress towards an opposite extreme. Because the land is everything, so is the ancestor who first established himself and his descendants on the land. Chinese reflection is always concerned with *ethics*: it is 'humanistic' in that it is concerned with man's position in nature and 'conservative' in that it is concerned with man's position in the family system. Natural cycles and the movement of reversal teach the 'golden mean' or middle way, e.g., of caution in times of prosperity and hopefulness in times of misfortune. Because events and patterns of events are expected to occur despite human endeavor, this basic idea is sometimes characterized as 'fatalism.'

Regarding problems of method, there is no 'problem of knowledge' in Chinese philosophy, and epistemology was never seriously developed in any of the main Chinese schools. Subject and object are not separated but unified in a conception of cyclical nature. Chinese thinkers do not typically state *arguments*: they do not state premises and argue from them to conclusions. Likewise philosophy in China does not attempt to add to the sum of positive knowledge. Philosophy itself is not something to be known, but something to be experienced, and the purpose of philosophy is the elevation of the human mind. Philosophy attempts to satisfy the inherent human craving for what lies beyond the present actual world. In works of Chinese thinkers, one gets an impression of brevity, apparent disconnectedness of short sayings, even inconsistency. The use of language is not precise or scientific but artistic and suggestive. There is the express conviction that the essential thing cannot actually be said but only intimated or suggested. The ideal of Chinese art is *simplicity*. A whole world arises in a few words or a few strokes of a brush.

The main problem of Chinese thinking is the relation of 'this-worldliness' to 'other-worldliness.' The father of Chinese history, Ssu-Ma Ch'ien, writing in the first century BCE, and the most distinguished contemporary writer on Chinese intellectual history, Fung-Yu Lan, put the problem in roughly similar terms: What is the highest form of human achievement? And is it necessary to abandon society or even negate life in order to achieve it?

The ideal is one of "sageliness within and kingliness without" and thus a reconciliation between the claims of personal being and social life. This is called the "golden mean," the "Way," the "Way of Wen and Wu," or the "Way of the Superior Man." The problem is the relation between personal salvation and social responsibility. The tension between these extremes in represented in the conflict between Confucianism and Taoism; and the characteristic resolution of this tension is represented in the transformation of Indian Buddhism into specifically Chinese Buddhism.

¬ Philosophy and religion

'Philosophy' in this context means systematic, critical reflection, whose object is *being* itself.

'Religion' in this context means a superstructure of dogmas, rituals, and institutions, built around a core philosophy or conception of being.

Philosophy in the West is secular. It is an attempt to comprehend being purely on the strength of the unassisted human mind. Western philosophy develops in opposition to religion – it is tied up with skepticism and loss of faith and with replacing mythological thinking with scientific thinking. Many thinkers have speculated that philosophy took this course in the West because Western religions tend towards exclusivity. If a certain religion is the 'true' religion, then all other religions are 'false' religions. By this thinking, a particular expression of the ultimate, e.g., Judaism, Christianity, or Islam, tends to deny validity to its rivals, which then sink to the level of 'idolatry' or 'superstition.' Western writers have often characterized Chinese religions as 'superstitions.'

Philosophy in China is not expressly secular, but instead religion and philosophy are closely connected. People have become accustomed to saying that there are three great religions in China: Confucianism, Taoism, and Buddhism. Some Western scholars, especially Christian writers, have denied that these strains of thought actually count as 'religions,' but instead are merely 'philosophies.' This is an odd notion for the Buddhist, for example – odd and insulting. The Buddhist population of the world is at present roughly 500 million people.

More accurately: Confucianism is a philosophy and a religion; Taoism is a philosophy and a religion; and Buddhism is a philosophy and a religion; and each of these is a philosophy and a religion in different senses.

There is a core Confucian philosophy *and* a set of Confucian rites and religious practices – just as there is a core Christian philosophy and a set of Catholic doctrines and rituals. The Confucian philosophy, for example, develops a number of ideas about education and government; yet Confucianism also involves taboos and commandments, prayers and beliefs regarding the supernatural.

In the case of Taoism, Taoist 'philosophy' is directly opposed to Taoist 'religion.' Taoism as a philosophy teaches harmony with nature, whereas Taoism as a religion is an attempt to control nature – in particular to control death and achieve immortality. Taoism as a philosophy (*tao chia*) originates in the teachings of Yang Chu (fourth century BCE) whereas Taoism as a religion (*tao chiao*) dates from the later Han dynasty (the modern first through third century).

In the case of Buddhism, there is a core Buddhist teaching, though a variety of philosophical positions; and Buddhist religion has broken up into many different sects. Buddhism in China includes at least four main schools: Huayan and Ch'an, the Lotus school and the Pure Land school.

Nonetheless all Chinese philosophies and religions are *inclusivistic*: It is possible and even normal in China for the same person to practice rites from all three main traditions – for example, to mark the passage from childhood to adulthood in the Taoist rite, to set up a household and marry in the Confucian rite, and to bury one's dead and mourn in the Buddhist rite. There is a saying that there are three religions in China because there are three ages of life. Young people gravitate towards Taoism because it has no rules; adults uphold Confucianism because they want respect; and old people migrate towards Buddhism because they are afraid of death.

¬ The Book of Changes

The Shang dynasty is datable to the middle and the latter part of the second millennium BCE. Chinese civilization in this period attained mastery of bronze casting, possessed a writing system, and lived under a stratified and exacting military and political system. Material well-being was abundant and decorative art was already highly sophisticated. Religion in this period centered around weather, the land, and ancestor worship. For the student of philosophy and religion, the most striking developments of this period concern the *I Ching*, or Book of Changes. Parts of this book are among the most ancient writings known to man – only a few texts such as the *Song of the Harper* and the *Epic of Gilgamesh* are older.

The Book of Changes has within it all the main themes of Chinese thought: the land, the cycles of natural change, the idea of reversal, filial piety and ancestor worship, and the cautious and hopeful ethics of moderation. The Book of Changes also demonstrates the inclusiveness of Chinese traditions, because it includes contributions from thinkers of many historical periods and schools: by tradition both Confucius and Lao Tzu wrote parts of the text.

In order to grasp the significance of the Book of Changes for Chinese civilization, one has to reach back even further in history, from the Bronze Age to Neolithic times. Archeologists have theorized that the ancient Chinese of the third millennium BCE practiced a form of divination by heating tortoise shells over open fires and reading the cracks that then appeared as premonitions of events yet to unfold. Shell patterns became catalogued and were part of the traditions passed on from shaman to apprentice. According to tradition, eight basic patterns, known as "trigrams," were devised by Fu Hsi (~2900 BCE), China's legendary first ruler. Divination by chance fall arrangements of yarrow or milfoil plants developed from the earlier use of animal shells. King Wen, a Honan regent of the twelfth century BCE, reconceived and combined the eight basic patterns, to form sixty-four elemental "hexagrams." King Wen's son, known as the Duke of Chou, and King Wen's successor, King Wu, are credited with writing down the first reflections on these hexagrams, which over ages were developed by many hands into what are called *The Images* and *The Judgments*. Tradition holds that Confucius and Lao Tzu and Mencius and figures even of the later Han dynasty (modern second century) contributed further commentaries on these poems; new parts of the book were added in what we call medieval times and even in the early modern period.

The philosophy of the Book of Changes and the kind of changes it describes by the vocabulary of its hexagrams and commentaries is known to history as the Yin-Yang school. Divination was practiced by occultists or fang shih, their art being that of geomancy or feng shui ("wind and water"). These ancients held that man was a product of the universe and that his task is to live in harmony with it – harmony with wind and water. Currents of cosmic breath or energy (*qi*) flow in every geographic region and direction and influence human fortune: human action is effectual when it flows *with* and ineffectual when it rushes *against* the currents of wind and water. Yet qi or energy is of unlike kinds – wind and water – it is a diversity and not a unity, and requires much study, by observation and experiment, to understand; it controls man yet may in some contexts be controlled by him; rather it *is* man and may change when he does, as he does by it.

The word *yang* originally meant sunshine or light, *yin* meaning shadow or darkness. *Yang* later was asserted as a cosmic principle – masculinity, activity, heat, brightness, dryness, hardness – *yin* its counterpart – femininity, passivity, cold, darkness, wetness, softness. Qi expresses itself as this duality and the fang shih claim a knowledge of the interdependence and shifting recombinations of dark and light.

One significance of this development is that the father god and mother goddess of primordial times, thought to have given birth to the world, were replaced by or reinterpreted as completely impersonal forces of nature, whose cycles might be studied and understood.

This advance is the deepest element of Chinese thinking and its most important contribution to the world.

The Book of Changes is considered to be one of the Six Classics, the Lui Yi or "liberal arts." These books constituted the cultural legacy of early Chinese history and were the basis of the education of aristocrats in the Iron Age (Early Chou dynasty). Five hundred years later, as feudalism began to disintegrate in the seventh century BCE, the aristocrats and their teachers lost their positions and merged into the general population. Wandering from town to town, many made their living by teaching the classics and conducting rituals according to ancient ways at weddings and funerals. These were the *ju* or literati.

Kung-Fu Tzu, the man whose Latinized name is "Confucius," lived in the ancient fifth century (551-479 BCE). Kung Tzu or Master Kung or The Master grew up in poverty, became a wandering teacher, then entered government service and achieved high rank by the time he reached fifty. Political intrigue forced his resignation and exile from his home province. For thirteen years he traveled near and far hoping to realize his ideal of social and political reform. He never succeeded. As an old man he returned to his home state of Lu and died.

The Master's account of himself is contained in his *Analects* II, 4: "At fifteen I set my heart on learning. At thirty I could stand. At forty I had no doubts. At fifty I knew the Decree of Heaven. At sixty I was already obedient to it. At seventy I could follow the desires of my mind without overstepping the boundaries of what is right."

Important aspects of Confucian teachings include a love of learning; a belief that everyone is capable of learning and that all men have an equal potentiality for moral growth; that education should be available to everyone, and that education breaks down class and other artificial distinctions; that the focus of education should be the transmission and enlivening of cultural inheritance as support to the moral enlightenment of man; a dismissal of mere self-seeking or profit-seeking; a belief that the central human virtue is human-heartedness or humaneness (*jen*), which is "to love others" (XII, 2); that humaneness expresses itself in filial piety and reverence and sensibility and the "golden mean," as well as gravity, impartiality, and wise tranquility; that a government of men must lead by moral example and by virtue rather than by threats and fear; and that nothing, not even hope of doing good, should compromise one's commitment to the Way. To devote oneself to the study of the Way and to attempt to bring it into being for one's own generation is the highest calling of the superior man.*

At a deeper level it may be said that Confucianism involves an acknowledgement of the facticity of the world just as it stands (and perhaps some confusion between natural and social being). The superior man disregards the outward success or failure of his actions and sets himself to do what he thinks right without regard to any consideration other than his moral compulsion. This is sometimes expressed in the concept of "doing for nothing," a rejection of utilitarian calculation. The superior man overcomes anxiety as to the outcomes of his action and achieves his happiness in the calm of unfolding personal development and unity of moral conscience.

Later developments of the Master's teachings include Mencius' (371-289 BCE) assertion of the essential goodness of man and introduction of mysticism into Confucian thinking; Hsun Tzu's (298-238 BCE) realism, skepticism regarding the supernatural, and refocus on ethical questions; the *Chung Yung* or "Doctrine of the Mean," by tradition a work of The Master's grandson, Tzu-ssu, but more likely a product of later times, in which the Tao is asserted as a metaphysical principle; the amalgamation of the Yin-Yang school and Confucianist metaphysics by Tung Chung-Shu (179-104 BCE); the consolidation of all Confucian traditions in the Han dynasty; and the advent of so-called Neo-Confucianism in the Tang dynasty (modern seventh through tenth centuries), a late phase in which Taoist and Buddhist ideas merge with an early conception of science.

¬ Some Confucian symbols

The world-chariot, the universe-symbol, the ideogram for righteousness, portraits of the Master, the fundamental changes; the Temple of Heaven, and designs around concentric circles; the image of a dragon, a willow tree, a sundial, also of jewels – especially jade.

¬ Some Confucian beliefs

The importance of ritual. When offered a first cup of tea, the guest should assume a grave attitude; when offered a second, an air of respectful contentment. "Sacrifice implies presence; sacrifice to the gods as if they were right in front of you." "If you do not sacrifice with your whole heart, it is better not to sacrifice at all." "Humaneness is, to subdue oneself and return to ritual." But ritual can degrade and become mere ceremoniousness – mere words with no meaning and no heart – "If a man is not humane, he no longer hears any music."

Rectification of names. The first priority in government is to give things proper names so that each thing can be fulfilled as what it is. "Let the prince be a prince, the minister a minister, the father a father, and the son a son." In a properly ordered society, there is nothing new and no need for any new words.

Basic moral position. Education is the basis of everything and should be universally offered; it breaks down class distinctions and forms the outline of a person's goodness. The essence of morality is human-heartedness and righteousness. The way to practice humaneness is not to do anything to anyone that you yourself do not wish. All action should be "doing for nothing." To know *ming* (fate, destiny, decree) is to disregard the external success of one's actions and accept the inevitability of the world, just as it is. To know *ming* is to be free from anxiety and find true happiness.

¬ Some Confucian ideology

Confucian thinking degrades over time into an arch-conservatism. Family relationships and existing power hierarchies are endowed with magical qualities and transcendental significance – thus to oppose the father or the ruler is to fight Heaven and make oneself an outcast. Confucianism has too often been the apologist for the existing order and thus has seemed the enemy of progressive thinking – despite Confucius' emphasis on education, breaking down class distinctions, and progressive social agenda.

Confucius' ideas did not catch on until nearly 500 years after his death. This fact may help to explain why his recommendations are so different than the actual policies adopted in his name centuries later. One of the most famous passages in the *Analects* goes to this subject. "Exemplary persons should pursue harmony, but not conformity." Harmony requires differences – as with tasty dishes that combine many different ingredients that may even be bland on their own but together are delicious; as with opposite traits in the personality that help to offset one another; as with different regions of the nation, so that wind can correct water, north can correct south, and each tendency can be matched and steadied by its counterpart.

The progressive attitude veers towards conservatism when people lose the confidence that they can respond to change and find new ways to create harmony; instead, they try to preserve harmony by opposing all change.

¬ Taoism

According to tradition, Lao Tzu ("Old Master") lived in the early sixth century BCE and was an older contemporary of Master Kung. Lao Tzu became a kind of patron saint of Taoism, though little or nothing is known about him. He was a native of the state of Ch'u in Honan province and wandered alone for most of his life.

As Confucianism represents the social impulse in Chinese civilization, Taoism represents the recluse. The desire to be pure, free from ties, to test one's strength against nature and fate, to ignore tradition – to value above all the self and hold oneself accountable to oneself alone – to wander in the countryside and avoid cities – to despise things and possessions and value life itself: these and similar ideas are expressed in early Taoist thinkers such as Yang Chu (c. 380 BCE).

A book called the Lao Tzu (after Master Lao) or Tao Te Ching (Book of the Way and the Power) is datable to roughly 300 BCE and represents the second phase of Taoist thinking. The book is a paradox in that its subject is the unnameable: "The Tao that can be named is not the eternal Tao; the name that can be named is not the abiding name. The Tao is eternal, nameless, and uncarved..." (ch. 1). This book conceives that the Tao does not describe anything but instead is that by which things are described. The Tao is the basis underlying all change and is comprehensible as law: the law of change; the law of reversal; the law of moderation. At least this much *does not change*. "To know the invariables is called enlightenment" (ch. 16). One's enlightenment is also one's power (*te*), and the word 'natural' means following one's power with no arbitrary effort. In Taoist thinking, words like 'natural,' 'spontaneous,' 'centered' and 'simple' have nearly identical sense.

Confucian thinkers sought to increase knowledge and to spur progress in city life by sponsorship of new initiatives; Taoist thinkers sought to undo these improvements and return human society so far as possible to the countryside and its most primitive state. Taoists uphold an ideal of ignorance in opposition to Master Kung's ideal of knowledge: let people be simple and ignorant and rooted back into the ways of the earth; for then they will be happy; then the father will be a father and the son will be a son.

Chuang Tzu (369-286 BCE) is said to have been a recluse who shunned human society and preferred the enjoyment of his own free will. A book of his sayings, named after him, and probably compiled in the modern third century, teaches a doctrine of naturalness, ignorance, and simplicity, while upholding the ideal of emotion purged by reason. The so-called Neo-Taoism of the third and fourth centuries (*hsuan hsueh*, "dark learning") develops these themes by use of the central concept of *wu* ("nothingness"), conceiving freedom and happiness as "abiding in nothingness."

Religious Taoism also developed in the modern third century and incorporated the writings of Yang Chu, Lao Tzu, and Chuang Tzu into its official canon. It shares with its philosophical forerunner a vision of humanity in harmony with nature and the search to find one's niche in the cosmic order. Much further, however, it strives to attain power over nature and release from the power of death. By practice of hardships, meditative and dietary and physical disciplines, development of scientific grasp of primal energies, it preached a form of transcendence out of the mundane world. Religious Taoism spurred the development of Chinese martial arts and of Chinese medicine, particularly acupuncture, and lent to them its vocabulary of Confucian and Taoist concepts.

The Tao is origin to Yang and Yin; primordial breath (*qi*) awakens the spirit (*shen*) of human beings and stirs their vital essence (*jing*). The balance of elements in the greater cosmos provides a model for psychological balance, and practice of meditation, exercises, and varied regimens help to bring this about.

Gods of the Taoist pantheon include the Jade Emperor (Yuhuang) and the God of Literature (Wenchang) who probably derive from local cults; these figures were reinterpreted to reflect basic forces such as the Primordial Chaos or the Prime Mover.

Taoism bears many resemblances to Japanese Shinto practices and may be ancestral to them: both are rooted in forest and mountain nature worship, reclusiveness, and local cults, and both spurred development of medicinal practices and martial arts such as gung fu and kendo.

¬ Some Taoist symbols

Lao Tzu riding a bull through the Gateway to the West; the Yin-Yang symbol; the Butterfly; also small triangular or rectangular flags; also a zigzag shape with seven stars, representing the Big Dipper (or the "Bushel," the Chinese equivalent); images of dragons and phoenixes; images of the Flaming Pearl; also the number 5000 (as in "The Book of Five Thousand Characters").

¬ Some Taoist beliefs

Yang Chu. Desire to maintain personal purity. Retreat. "The world is a swelling torrent, and nothing can be done to change it." Each one for himself. "Though he might have profited the world by plucking out a single hair, he would not have done it." He despises things and values life. See the usefulness of the useless. Preserve life, avoid injury, escape.

Lao Tzu. To discover the invariable laws underlying all natural change – that is understanding. Regulate living according to these laws – that is happiness. Reversal is the movement of the Tao – to go further and further is to revert to the beginning; extreme qualities transform themselves into their opposites; there is a continuous reversion of each thing back to its starting point – ultimately to non-being or nothingness; therefore, "blessing leans upon calamity" and "those with nothing will acquire, those with much will lose" and "diminish a thing and it will increase." If you want to attain anything, start with the opposite. E.g. to be strong, admit weakness; to preserve selfishness, open it to sharing; thus also the reverse. *Wu-wei* – having no action – non-action – means acting without artificiality or arbitrariness; sometimes this means "not over-doing" – sometimes it means simplicity, not to have too many desires or to know too much. Be like a child. Wisdom is like innocence and ignorance.

Chuang Tzu. Transcend the terrestrial plane – the point is not to escape society but to escape terrestrial thinking altogether. Escape – not to mountains or the forests – but to pure being. Defeat emotion by reasoning. Not to be affected by events. He is one with the Tao – he is nameless like the Tao itself. He takes the higher level point of view. Store the universe in the universe; then there is no chance for it to be lost. In order to have knowledge, discard knowledge; but first you must attain it, in order to discard it afterwards; forgetfulness is a great achievement.

¬ Some Taoist ideology

Taoism as a principle of social organization opposed Confucian thinking about education, virtue, family obligations and offered a new hierarchy based on the distinction between the sage and the common people. Lao Tzu: "the sage treats them all as children" and "he does not make them enlightened, but keeps them ignorant."

Taoism represents the view that the norms for language, knowledge, ethics and society are grounded in and continuous with principles inhering in natural processes of change. *Wu-wei* – having no action – extends to government, which makes Taoist political philosophy align with classical liberalism in advocating limited government and open markets.

Confucianism (by contrast) develops a progressive, educational and humanistic ideology, focused on human being and human potential and human community.

Confucian progressive policies created a Taoist conservative reaction. There is a link between Taoism and the sentimentalist school, just as the European Enlightment preceded Romanticism – in both cases an emphasis on reason and bringing reason to social problems engenders a counterwave praising raw impulse, common sense and getting back to nature. Romantic ideas in both contexts disparage intelligence and intentions about "improving society."

Taoists tend toward anarchism, mistrustful of hierarchical social structures and particularly of governments (Chuang Tzu argues that the proponents of benevolence and morality are usually found at the gates of feudal lords who have stolen their kingdoms).

Taoism in practice has been the state religion of a variety of dictatorships with expressly anti-progressive social policies, resting on obscurantist – mystical and confusing – public statements encouraging political dis-engagement and exaltation of leaders.

¬ Buddhism

The Buddha, whose personal name was Siddhartha Gautama, lived in North India in the sixth century BCE. His father, Suddhodana, and mother, Queen Maya, ruled the Sakya clan, which is why Siddhartha is sometimes referred to as Sakyamuni ('Sage of the Sakyas'). Siddhartha married Yasodhara, the daughter of another local chieftain. Yasodhara bore the young prince a son, Rahula. Yet at age 29, while his child was still an infant, Siddhartha left his family and kingdom never to return and became a wandering ascetic in order to solve the problem of human suffering. He met famous teachers and submitted to rigorous ascetic practices. None satisfied his craving. He continued his search by his own lights for several more years. One evening while sitting under a tree – since known as the Bodhi tree or Tree of Wisdom – at age 35 he attained enlightenment and was afterwards known as the Buddha, the Enlightened One. He spent the balance of his long life teaching this enlightenment to all classes of men and women and died at age 80.

As Rahula Walpola points out in his study *What the Buddha Taught* the Buddha is unique among founders of religion because he claimed merely to be a human being and nothing more and did not even rest his claims on earlier tradition but instead purely on the clarity of his ideas. The Buddha asked his listeners to doubt everything he said, to examine carefully each claim, to take nothing on faith but instead test each proposition by reflection and experience. He did not talk about prayer, faith, creation, sin or judgment. He made no claim about the supernatural or immortality or commandments or miracles. He classified all these ideas under the heading "subjects which tend not to edification." He regarded them so because whatever they may be, they do nothing to alleviate the problem of suffering. His teaching and solution to the problem of suffering is known to history as the *Four Noble Truths*. The following is one way of stating these truths:

1. *Suffering*. There is suffering. (This is the disease)
2. *Arising*. The cause of suffering is desire. (This is the cause of the disease)
3. *Cessation*. Extinguish desire, and suffering ends. (The disease is curable)
4. *The Path*. Desire may be overcome by meditation. (This is the cure)

What is meant by *suffering* (Pali 'dukkha'; Sanskrit 'duhkha,' pain, sorrow, misery), *desire* (Skt. 'tanha,'   craving, thirst, clinging), *extinction* (P. 'nirodha,' 'nibbana'; Skt. 'nirvana,' reality, truth, extinction), and *meditation* (Skt. 'samadhi,' concentration, mental discipline, mental culture), is the substance of Buddhist teaching. The Fourth Noble Truth, in particular, sometimes called the Middle Path, also the Noble Eightfold Path, is the subject of many volumes and much controversy.

The Buddha appears to have taught a straightforward and pragmatic doctrine without reference to gods, demons, past or future lives, or supernatural forces of any kind, but instead focused very narrowly on the driving problem of suffering. He rejected the Vedic ritualism and practice of animal sacrifice that preceded him – likewise Hindu caste and gender divisions – equally he does not offer himself as a political leader but as a teacher and founder of a monastic order – a community in retreat rather than a political entity itself.

The Buddha is credited with developing traditional Hindu practices of meditation, known to history as the four absorptions (Sanskrit *'jhana'*), a graduated series of increasingly deep meditative states, and the four planes (Skt. *'ayatana'*), conceived as increasingly distant locations in the topology of consciousness, by teaching a new form of meditation, insight meditation (Skt. *'vipasanna'*). Insight meditation is conceived as a kind of experimental method by which information is gathered about states presently occurring in the body and the mind. It is regarded as a means of witnessing the foundation or constitution of consciousness in short-lived purposive impulses, and thus a grasp of the very craving or clinging that *makes* consciousness.

The Buddha held that moral self-discipline grows out of the concentration and equanimity practiced in insight meditation; he also held that a kind of wisdom derives from the calm of meditative practice, allowing one to stand aloof from experience and extinguish clinging within one. One should neither hope nor fear nor clutch, but let slip the moments of experience. Out of liberation grows a compassion that draws us to serving others.

This austere view has played a relatively small role in the development of Buddhism: within two centuries of Buddha's death at least nineteen schools were formed with much elaborated and widely varied doctrines. All these but one are referred to collectively as the Hinayana, or lesser vehicle: the most important of these is The Way of the Elders, or Theravada Buddhism. The nineteenth school and dominant form of Buddhism for most of the world is referred to as Mahayana, or greater vehicle.

There is no easy way to characterize the differences between these schools – in general the Theravadins and other Hinayana thinkers emphasize intellectual insight whereas Mahayana Buddhism emphasizes compassion. Questions in dispute include the constitution and persistence of the self or ego, whether enlightenment is gradual or instantaneous, and whether enlightenment once gained can ever be lost afterwards. In the Mahayana tradition, the Buddha is regarded not merely as a human master and model but as a supramundane being who multiplies himself in a series of incarnations. Mahayana philosophy develops a complex teaching regarding the insubstantiality of existence, its 'emptiness' or 'nothingness' (Skt. *'sunyata,'* Chinese *'wu,'* Japanese *'satori'*), as for example by its great exponent Nagarjuna (c. 150-250).

Buddhism reached its zenith in India in the third century BCE and died out altogether in its homeland by the twelfth century of the Common Era.

Buddhism entered China in the modern first century and rapidly grew in influence. Buddhism became the state religion of China in the Sui dynasty (581-618) and remained in favor during the Tang dynasty (618-907). Main concepts of Sanskrit origin were translated into a Taoist vocabulary and mixed with traditional Chinese concepts of breath, change, golden mean and reversal. The most important product of this union is the Ch'an school, better known in the West by its Japanese name, Zen (Skt. *'dhyana,'* meditation). Ch'an has exercised an enormous influence on all subsequent Chinese philosophy.

The traditional origin of the Ch'an school is that the Buddha possessed an esoteric teaching communicated to his most trusted disciple, which was passed down by generations to Bodhidharma, who is supposed to have been the twentieth-eighth Patriarch in India, and who arrived in China around the year 525, where he became the founder of the Ch'an school. This secret teaching appears to combine notions like those of Nagarjuna regarding emptiness with Taoist doctrines concerning the unnameable: thus the first principle is inexpressible because, once stated, it becomes the second principle. The Ch'an school is sometimes referred to as "The Philosophy of Silence." This school taught a notion of sudden enlightenment that breaks through illusion by effacing all the distinctions in which experience is constituted, and most particularly the illusion of being a substantial person or self, as means of extinguishing craving such as Buddha conceived. Various means were employed to help the aspirant leap to enlightenment – including beatings and sudden shouts – but especially by use of puzzling sayings known as gongon (Jp. *'koan'*) such as "Listen to the sound of one hand clapping" and "Riding an ass to get to an ass" and "Before one has studied Ch'an, mountains are mountains and rivers are rivers; while one is studying Ch'an, mountains are no longer mountains and rivers are no longer rivers; and after one has mastered Ch'an, mountains are again mountains and rivers are again rivers." These sayings were designed to jar the mind loose from convention and bring about recognition that reality is ultimately incommunicable.

¬ Some Buddhist symbols

Images of the Buddha (as a child, as a young man, as the Enlightened One, as reincarnated); of the Wheel of Life (*dharmachakra*, a symbolic representation of *samsara*); of Avalokitesvara (aka Kuan Yin, Kannon, Kanzeon, Quan Te Am, Chenrezig, Padampani, Lokanat, Lokesvara); also of Bodhisattvas of different kinds; *mandala* (skt. 'circle') symbols (diagram representing the universe); also the Tree of Enlightenment (Bo or Bodhi tree, Fig, Pipul or Aswattha tree); also the image of an open hand.

¬ Some Buddhist beliefs

Dependent origination. All phenomena 'exist' in the context of the network of other phenomena and the many causes and effects that bind them; all things are conditioned and transient and have no separable or independent status; there is no individual 'self.' The being of an individual is made up of a series of causes and effects and is therefore in motion, ever-changing – yet in the most important sense the individual is his or her own *karma*, effective action, works, deeds, choices – not simply action but also thinking and speech.

The Noble Eightfold Path. View, resolve, speech, conduct, livelihood, effort, mindfulness and concentration are censurable; they can decline or be improved; the right way is the middle way, non-extremism; neither self-indulgence nor self-mortification.

Karma. There is no otherworldly salvation or escape; there is no path that everyone can take; there is no formula for enlightenment; no one attains wisdom; every belief must be tested by individual reflection and experience; the task is develop one's diamond focus, do good works, and pursue the path; each one is his own refuge; each must become his own witness.

¬ Some Buddhist ideology

Buddha refused to take the hereditary office of king in the feudal state ruled by his family clan, the Shakyas, and instead joined the *sramana* movement of homeless spiritual wanderers who sought escape both from the dictates of the *brahmins* and from all bonds in the material world. Buddha ultimately rejected the *sramana* path and defended the middle way of non-extremism.

Buddhism retained and developed the *sramana* idea that opposed the traditional caste system of ancient India. Like the homeless wanderers who were his earlier colleagues, Buddha sought to replace the idea that one has to be *born into* a brahmin (spiritual) caste with the idea that one *makes oneself* into a brahmin (spiritual) being by one's intentions, actions and character.

After his enlightenment, Buddha did not actively proselytize for any specifically religious cause (he did not discuss 'religious' issues – religious ideas "tend not to edification" – likewise he even persuaded adherents of other traditions to remain loyal to them). Buddha confined himself (like a physician) to the relief of suffering. Buddhism spread slowly in his lifetime (fifth century BCE) and splintered into 19 sects by the second *Sangha* Council (383 BCE). The Mauryan King Asoka (260-218 BCE) initially sought to spread Buddhism around the world; this led to the development of Greco-Buddhist

Art and the Gandhara culture and later migrations in the Southern tradition (*Theravadins*, The Way of the Elders) and the Northern tradition (*Mahayana*, The Greater Vehicle). Asoka, however, also experienced an awakening and reversed his policy of proselytism and expansion, instead developing a new universal policy of toleration (*Edicts of Asoka*):

"All religions should reside in all places, for all of them promote self-control and purity of heart." (*Rock Edict 7*)

"It is good that religions are in contact. We should all listen and pay respect to the doctrines from other peoples. We should all be well-learned in the good doctrines of other religions." *(Rock Edict 12)*

That we should pay respect to the *good* doctrines of other peoples seems to suggest an element of criticism. Asoka also shows us something about the difficulty of the policy of toleration by his first edict, which appears to prohibit the traditional Vedic practices that preceded Buddhism in India:

"Here in my domain no living beings are to be slaughtered or offered in sacrifice." *(Rock Edict 1)*

Asoka also calls himself "Beloved-of-the-Gods" and brings the innovation of talk about reincarnation to Buddhism (*Rock Edict 1, 11*).

None of these views can be attributed to Siddhartha, who upheld the social ideal of a small egalitarian community, governed under direct democracy.

¬ The Three Ways

The 'three ways' of Confucianism, Taoism, and Buddhism are often depicted in Chinese art as a quiet conversation between three figures: the Confucian is dressed as a scholar, the Buddhist in the robes of a monk, and the Taoist, in his garment of leaves, as a forest ascetic.

Deities from all three traditions sometimes are sometimes portrayed together in Chinese temples – Confucian ancestor worship, Taoist 'red-faced gods,' the Buddha of Boundless Life (Amitabha), the Healing Buddha (Bhaysajyaguru), the future Buddha (Maitreya, Mi Lo Fo), and Avalokitesvara, Goddess of Mercy – and a synthesis of the three traditions was created in the Ming dynasty (1368-1644) on the principle "three teachings harmonius as one" as complementary aspects of self-cultivation. Li Shiqian, a scholar from this period, is credited with the saying "Buddhism is the sun, Taoism the moon, and Confucianism the five planets." Syncretism, the combining of discrete faiths, also occurs widely (Din-e Ilahi, the Druze, Sikhism, Chrislam).

The history of the West can perhaps be dated from ~4500 BCE, which is the transition from Mesolithic times to Neolithic times – from a temporary camp to a village of farmers – in the meeting ground between the Greek islands and the fertile crescent. Two populations, arriving from opposite directions north and south, encountered one another in Anatolia – present-day Turkey – in what archeologists call the Chalcolithic Near East – stretching from the Caucasus to Jerusalem – 'chalcolithic' indicating copper-and-stone working, a middle stage between the Stone Age and the Bronze Age. The innovations of this period include the domestication of the horse, the discovery of the wheel, and new epochs of metallurgy.

The northern population – a people we call the Indo-Europeans – was a nomadic people originating in the central Asian steppes or, alternatively, in the farming culture of the Danube. They are sometimes referred to as the Kurgan people and sometimes as the Danubians. They called themselves the *Arya*, the nobles, which is the root of the modern term 'Iran.' The Arya originated in a cold northern climate without a word for sea, with common references to snow, beech, bee, wolf. Half-settled, half-nomadic, these people had oxen, pigs, and sheep; they worked leather and wove wool; they ploughed the land and planted grain. The Arya culture was a horse culture and is likely the source of the myth of the Centaur, fierce warriors with the body of a horse and the trunk of a man. The Arya migrated in three separate waves – east, south, and west. In each case, they conquered an indigenous people (in the east, the *Vainu* people and the *Dasyus*; in the south, the *Pelasgians*; in the west, the *Ertebolle*). In each case, they created new languages, as their own tongue, Indo-European, merged with the language of conquered peoples (in the east, Sanskrit, Avestan, and Hittite; in the south, Minoan, Greek, Thracian, Phrygian, Illyrian and Italic; in the west, Celtic, Germanic, Slavonic and Baltic). The Arya worshipped deities ancestral to India, Iran, Greece, Rome, and Celtia – i.e. Europe as far west as Ireland.

The southern population – a people we call the Semites – was a nomadic people aboriginal to the Arabian Peninsula, dominant in North Africa from at least 4500 BCE onwards. The languages of Semitic peoples, including the Cushites, Hamites, Capsians, Akkadians, and Egyptians derive from Africa – e.g. Hebrew, Aramaic (the language spoken by Christ), and Arabic – they are an offshoot of the Afroasiatic family, including over 200 languages still spoken today. The Semitic people migrated north, overwhelming their enemies and establishing the kingdoms of Kish, Erech, and Ur. God-names of the Egyptians, Akkadians, the ancient Hebrews, Hamites and Cushites are related – also devotional practices and sacrificial rites.

The historical record of the West opens with the city-states of Mesopotamia in the twenty-sixth century BCE, beginning in Sumer.

Sumer, directly in the center of the Chalcolithic Near East, appears to be the birthplace of civilization – civilization implies urbanization – and is neither Indo-European nor Semitic. It was conquered and reconquered both by Indo-Europeans (e.g. the Elamites and the Zagros tribes) and Semites (e.g. by Gilgamesh in the twenty-sixth century and by Sargon the Great in the twenty-third). Thus the interaction between these two peoples dates from Neolithic times, producing many kinds of merged forms through the centuries, and continues today.

The West, the Western world, Western civilization, Western thought, Western culture – these terms are all controversial – they have been and are still the subject of much argument. Some writers make Egypt the source of all Western culture; some include Europe, the Near East, the Middle East and India as divisions of the West; some include the Indo-Europeans and exclude the Semites; some include Europe and its colonial extensions; some disparage the term and recommend abolishing it. Jacques Derrida used to refer to 'the West' as "the white man's mythology."

The expression 'Western thought' points to a compound of a fantastic number of influences – e.g. incorporating religious traditions and secular traditions – incorporating science and faith – at once Graeco-Roman and Judeo-Christian – often at odds with each other and often synthesized. The term is problematic but does appear to identify a valid unit of study.

I accept the convention of *three* great ancient traditions – the West, India, and the East – considering them separate units of study despite their complex interaction – India is East and West at once. This strategy makes Socrates a Western thinker, Buddha an Indian thinker, and Confucius an Eastern thinker.

¬ Prehistory into history

Early history is divided into broad periods according to the hard materials from which cutting tools and weapons were fashioned – stone, copper, bronze, iron, in that order. As the knowledge of the past increased, these long periods were subdivided in different ways – the Stone Age becomes old, middle, and new – Paleolithic, Mesolithic and Neolithic. These transitions took place earlier in some places, later in others, but there are some constants running throughout all archeological findings. River deltas play an important role – the first forms of agriculture appear at the Euphrates, the Nile, the Indus, the Yellow River – city-building and the advent of farming occur together. Agricultural societies destroyed their Stone Age predecessors in the ancient Near East, but also in ancient China and Mesoamerica.

The transition from Mesolithic times to Neolithic times quickly followed by advances in metallurgy happened in Sumer and Egypt before there was anything like Europe or India or China. Dates for Sumer are as early as ~7000 years before the modern era. Agriculture and large building construction appear in the Nile valley as early as 6000 BCE.

Sumer and Egypt make a contribution to history unlike Babylonian science, Hebrew theology, or Greek or Chinese rationalism. The student of these first Valley cultures discovers their focus on something even more elemental (relative to prehistoric times), i.e. the idea of death.

Egyptian hieroglyphic writings such as the 'Pyramid Texts' (2600-2300 BCE), the 'Coffin Texts' (2000 BCE), and the *Book of the Dead* (1600 BCE) are alike concerned with preparing for death, preparing the dead, and ideas about the afterlife.

Sumerian cuneiform writings date from as early as 3000 BCE. The reign of mighty kings such as Agga, Enmebaragesi and Gilgamesh is thought to date from roughly 2700 BCE, but the Epic of Gilgamesh is thought to have been composed around 2100 BCE. Gilgamesh, ruler of Uruk, drives his people too hard. The people appeal to the gods to give Gilgamesh a companion, someone he can fight with, so the people may find rest. The gods comply and create Enkidu, who becomes Gilgamesh's companion and friend. They set out on many dangerous journeys and conquer giants such as terrible Huwawa and the Bull of Heaven. The Sky Father Enlil, also called Lord of Winds, angry that the friends have slayed Huwawa, takes Enkidu's life, sending him to the underworld. Gilgamesh had not understood what death meant until losing his friend. This loss is too great and he refuses to accept it and he will not allow Enkidu to be buried. He travels to the end of the world, beyond the waters of death, to find everlasting life and rescue Enkidu – and along the way he meets ancestors and sages from ancient times, such as Utnapishtim (later called Noah), who tell him that his quest is hopeless. Gilgamesh ends his quest full of bitterness, unhappy, unsatisfied, "tears streaming down his cheeks," still asking his question that finds no answer.

The *Epic of Gilgamesh* is among the earliest known writings of any kind but may still be accounted a work of probing spirit. It offers a detailed account of human experience; it puts forward the key value of friendship; it is also a deeply pessimistic work that refuses to be consoled. It is hard to characterize the difference between Egyptian ideas about death – e.g. filling the gravesite with food and weapons so that the dead may eat and protect themselves – and these Sumerian ideas, which dismiss the fantasy of eternity, directing us to enjoy *this* life, and portray human grief without evasion.

¬ India

The innovations of the Neolithic period include the cultivation of wheat and barley, the domestication of goats, sheep, pigs and cattle, fired pottery and polished stone tools. These advances occurred first in the 7th millennium

BCE in the Near East and gradually spread outwards to Europe, Africa and Asia. Copper-working followed the same path – from the Near East, outwards in all directions – from 4500 through 2500 BCE – reaching Egypt, Greece, Germany, Russia, Iran, Afghanistan, and Pakistan to the limit of the Indus river. The causes of these changes are the subject of much controversy.

A mainstream position today is called the 'Kurgan Hypothesis' – so named for the northerners from beyond the Black Sea – also called the Danubians or the Arya or the Starcevo people – who traveled south after 4500 BCE and conquered every people they met. Evidence for this hypothesis includes thousands of burial sites with 'barrow' graves, mostly containing males holding weapons; also thousands of habitation sites, utterly destroyed after flourishing undisturbed for many centuries. There is no evidence of competition between households in pre-Indo-European Neolithic cultures. The Kurgans brought this conflict and destroyed their predecessor cultures. They were a horse culture, had mastered the wheel, made bronze weapons, and, where they settled, were farmers.

The Kurgan migration east seems to have resulted in religious traditions in Iraq, Iran, and India that shared a fire sacrifice, or burnt offering, performed by priests and accompanied by special chants or songs. All three societies were likewise caste systems.

Proto-Indo-European, also called PIE, is a hypothetical common ancestor of all Indo-European languages, originating (according to various estimates) from between 10,000-5,000 BCE, and divided into unconnected 'daughter dialects' by 3000 BCE. One such daughter dialect must have been spoken by the Kurgans.

The Mohenjo-Daro or Harappan civilization, named after the large cities in the region unearthed by archeologists – sometimes called the Vainu or Dasyu culture, after the names of its most ancient tribes – covered a very large area of the Indian subcontinent, including what are today the Punjab, Haryana, Sindh, Baluchistan, Uttar Pradesh, Rajastan and Gujarat. This civilization arose contemporaneously with the Nile and Mesopotamian cultures, well before the arrival of the Kurgans. The Harappan civilization was attacked and conquered by the Kurgans. The result is what archeologists call the Indus Valley civilization. Linguistically, Kurgan merged with Vainu, producing the new form Sanskrit. Kurgan religion and Kurgan society – fire sacrifice and caste hierarchy – merged with Vainu religion and Vainu society – worship of Kama and egalitarianism – producing Hindu religion and society. Thus the foundational basis for what is today considered Indian culture – e.g. its language and religion – came originally from *outside* India. Indian civilization is as much a subject of debate in India as Western civilization is in the West.

Sanskrit, Hittite and Avestan – the ancient languages of India, Iraq and Iran – are the oldest attested members of the Indo-European language family, dating back at least to 2500 BCE. Sanskrit terms are often recognizable in English cognates: *pitar* (father), *matar* (mother), *bhratar* (brother), *svasar* (sister), *deva* (divine), *naman* (name).

Sanskrit was preserved in an oral tradition and a teacher-disciple tradition before it was written down. Sanskrit literature is vast, including *Vedas* (perhaps as early as 2000 BCE), the *Brahmanas* (1000 BCE), the *Upanishads* (1000-300 BCE), the *Mahabharata* (600 BCE), the *Ramayana* (500 BCE) and the *Bhagavad Gita* (400 BCE).

Sanskrit is the vehicle of much of India's spiritual writing. Jainism, probably India's oldest religion, which taught that salvation is one's own responsibility, speaks words like *nirvana* and names like Parshva (877-777 BCE) and Mahavira (Vardhamana, 599-527 BCE), by tradition the twenty-third and twenty-fourth spiritual leader or 'Fordmaker' (*tirthankara*) respectively, which suggests a very early date for this tradition – by tradition Rishabha ('Bull') is the first Fordmaker (he is also called Adinatha, 'original lord') who founded what is called the Solar Dynasty, the mythological beginning point for India. Adinatha is a son of Manu, the first man, who worshipped the Sun, called variously Surya, Aditya, and Arka. Adinatha's eldest son is Bharata, who gives India its traditional name (*Bharatasvarta*, 'Bhararta's realm'). Jainism, emerging out of these stories, is a religious consciousness centered in ideas about *samsara* (the flow of experience), *dhyana* (meditation), *shramana* (self-reliance), and *ahimsa*, non-violence, from which comes *moksha* (liberation).

This ancient school of self-reliance had an ancient counterpart, the Vedic religion, which taught reliance on sacred texts such as the *Vedas* and *Brahmanas*. This is the *santana dharma*, the Eternal Religion, i.e. Hinduism. Early Buddhism defines new key Sanskrit concepts such as *duhkha, tanha*, and *vipasanna* and the ancient atheistic philosophies of India, such as the *carvakas* (radical materialists) and the *lokayatas* (skeptics), which offered skepticism about such things as gods, the soul and reincarnation, coin Sanskrit terms for premise, syllogism, analysis, conclusion, and comparison.

For the student of religion and philosophy, the most significant ancient Sanskrit writings are the *Upanishads* – there are more than a hundred such writings – eleven of which are known as 'major teachings' – the word *upanishad* means literally 'sitting under' (*sad*, as in English sit, sat; *ni*, as in English beneath, nether) – sitting for a lesson, sitting at the feet of a master.

More than a thousand years separate The *Epic of Gilgamesh* and the *Upanishads*. The former work communicates amazement at the stark fact of death and a spirit of inconsolable grief. The latter work is equally preoccupied with the idea of death, but has meanwhile developed a completely new attitude toward it.

The *Katha Upanishad*, for example, tells the story of the boy Nachiketas and his conversations with Death. Nachiketas sees that his father is only a poor man and cannot sacrifice anything of great value to the gods. He bothers his father about this repeatedly and, in anger, his father gives him to Death. Nachiketas has to wait three nights in the Dark Place before Death arrives. This is considered a great discourtesy and Death offers to recompense Nachiketas in order to remedy the injustice – Nachiketas may ask Death any three favors he wishes. The boy asks Death to restore him to his father and let him be welcomed back with love; and this is done. The boy asks Death how men should honor the gods; and Death teaches him the fire sacrifice. At last the boy asks Death to solve the mystery of death. "For when a man dies, a doubt arises, because some say 'he is' and some say 'he is not.' How can this be – tell me the truth." Death says that "even the gods had this doubt from ancient times" – "the law of life and death is mysterious" – "please ask me for something else, take wealth, children, pleasure, land, or become the ruler over the vast earth, I will grant all your desires, but do not ask me the secrets of death." But the boy is undismayed and forces Death to speak. Death begins to explain himself – he tries to explain suffering – he quotes an ancient saying that even the boy has heard – "A man is born, he suffers, and he dies" – all life is suffering. Suffering, *duhkha*, is the problem; and Death says that *maya*, illusion, is the cause of suffering; *vidya*, knowledge, pierces illusion; knowing is the path to *moksha*, liberation from suffering. The term *brahman* indicates absolute reality – the thing that you get to when you overcome illusion – when you know – then you *are* and you have slipped past the reach of Death.

There is a passage in the *Chandogya Upanishad* in which another boy, Svetaketu, asks his father about *brahman* (usually translated 'God'). The father teaches his son that *brahman* is a compound of existence (*sat*), consciousness (*chit*), and bliss (*ananda*) – thus the compound term *satchitananda* – often translated as 'reality' – i.e. in this tradition reality itself is defined in terms of the release from suffering. The boy keeps asking new questions about 'God' and 'reality' and finally the father answers "it is the true, it is the self – it is you." *Atman* is the self, the soul, the observant witness. The conversation ends with the formula '*Brahman = Atman.*'

This is the basic formula of Hinduism – the expression '*Brahman = Atman*' – i.e. the self is ultimate being and ultimate being is the self – a claim about the world and about the self but also a means of conceiving the paradigmatic relationship between the problem of suffering, knowledge, and release from suffering.

Relative to the *Epic of Gilgamesh*, this new position is more like optimism than pessimism. Death is not too great a loss to bear; it is not even clearly a loss at all; at any rate this new answer to the problem of suffering is to rethink it or redefine it or reinterpret it. To interpret is to diverge from orthodoxy – thus very quickly many different views appear and the discussion begins. 'Sitting at the feet of the master' becomes 'thinking for oneself' and 'thinking for oneself' becomes 'working through the arguments' for and against.

There is nothing exactly corresponding to 'Hinduism' without any further qualification (the word 'Hindu' itself is derived from *Sindhu*, a river in Northwest India; the ancient Greeks referred to the people who lived beyond this river as 'Hindus,' and the name stuck). The contemporary essayist Pankaj Mishra has shown that 'Hinduism' is an invention of the eighteenth century – conceived as a rival of monotheisms – losing its spirit of tolerance with this change – and covering over fundamental differences (*An End to Suffering*, 2004). By tradition there are six 'orthodox' (*astika*) schools, since they all accept the authority of sacred texts – all are concerned with overcoming *maya*, attaining *vidya*, and achieving *moksha* – yet each approaches these fundamental problems in distinct ways.

the six schools

Logic (nyaya) – the real is discoverable via logic – the good via *samadhi*, mental culture
Mathematics (samkya) – reality discoverable via mathematics – good via detachment
Exegesis (mimansa) – reality shows itself in the *Vedas* – good via action, *karma*
Atomism (vaisesika) – reality is composed of atoms – we discover the good in science
Self-discipline (yoga) – reality appears in meditation – good emerges from composure
Monism (vedanta) – reality is undivided – it is us – good shows itself in *samadhi*

These six are recognized as *astika* ('it exists') schools. More of what exists shows itself in the Hindu pantheon, which typically includes the trinity *Brahma*, the creator, *Vishnu*, the Preserver, and *Shiva*, the destroyer. Myriad other gods are recognized, some for the forest, for springs, for the household, some in totem forms in the shape of animals, some in human forms, some as natural elements – Fire, Wind, Sun, Moon – some as weather gods and fertility gods and protector gods, messengers, warriors, laughing gods, gods of love. Some are compounds of all of the others – such as Indra. The great variety of cults must derive from great the variety of villages and cities in India – this teaches the idea that there is an irreducible local element in every name of god. Despite this there is a broad theme in the Indus Valley tradition, which is the presence of death, suffering, and the desire to worship something indestructible; to put desire beyond the reach of death by attaining knowledge; and the sense that the attainment of knowledge and ultimate release achieve a kind of unification or oneness with the cosmic order. This position is sometimes referred to as *cosmos-piety*, an ancient version of pantheism, i.e. the belief that God is the universe.

The problem of attaining some measure of understanding, then losing it, thus of having to regain liberation over and over again and thus be 'reborn' is sometimes referred to as *samsara* – the world of change and becoming – whereas attaining composure and perfect release is called *nirvana* – the world of being and completion. Nagarjuna (c. 150-250), born into a Brahmanical family, student of the *Vedas* and the *Upanishads*, the six *astika* schools, and also the *nastika* (unorthodox, literally 'it does not exist' schools – i.e. Jainism, the Carvakas, and Buddhism), became the preeminent thinker in the Buddhist tradition after Siddhartha Gautama himself, principally by working through the problem of *samsara* and *nirvana*.

Nagarjuna refers to his position as the "theory of no theory" – historians gave it the name *madhyamika* (literally a superlative formed from the word 'middle' and thus 'middle-est' or 'supremely middle') – a view that steers between the opposites of realism (the world is real) and nihilism (the world is an illusion). Nagarjuna taught that enlightenment is not so much a change from one condition (*samsara*) to another (*nirvana*) but an experience in which both extremes cease dominating the mind, so that we begin to live a life in a transformed state.

Nagarjuna explains that these extremes are not entities but merely interpretations of our experiences and as such are both nothing (*sunyata*), i.e., merely concepts; and since they are empty or nothing, every life encounter ignites the same possibility to serve as a basis for the transformation that supersedes both extremes.

Nagarjuna makes emptiness (*sunyata*) the central concept of philosophy. Not only our interpretations, but phenomena in general have no substance, no "own-nature" or "self-nature" or underlying essence, because their coming-into-being depends on conditions over which they have no control; they have a "dependent origination" and therefore are "nothing." Experience of whatever kind is transitory – it vanishes – so that we have to beware building on it as a solid foundation – to do so will only bring us sorrow and obscure our vision. That it is transitory is not a reason to despair – the transitory is a lamp to the everlasting which no words can express and which pervades everything temporal – a reference from the here and now to the ground of being and fundamental fact of existence. The world and everything in it that we identify and call out is a source of pain, sorrow, frustration, because all of it has an origin in our actions (*karma*); what we call heaven and hell are in reality the feeling-tones of our actions; the insight that everything is "empty of being independent" is the discernment or realization or breakthrough that empowers our liberation.

Adi Sankara (788-820), among the great thinkers in the Hindu tradition and the dominant figure in the school of absolute monism (*Vedanta*), was aware of, and sought to transcend, all previous thinking, whether Hindu, Buddhist, or strictly materialistic; he was a student of sacred writings but explicitly rejected relying on them; instead he attempted to arrive at his conclusions by a course of strict reasoning. Like Parmenides long before him and Descartes long afterwards, he discounted the evidence of his senses. He held that doubt requires a ground on which doubt arises; he held that contradiction requires a ground of consistency; he held that negation rests on a fundamental assertion; and he held in general that all things relative rest on a still more fundamental absolute, without which they vanish and have no being. This background of absolute existence is Brahman, which is behind all proof as the basis of proof, which is beyond doubt because it is the basis of doubt, and which is real in a way that makes everything else unreal. Thus the main problem in *Vedanta* is the odd fact of phenomenal world – the world of plurality, doubt and suffering – the problem of *samsara* (the world of change and becoming; the cycle of birth and death) or *maya* (the veil of illusion): and the answer is the insight that the world is a dream, real as long as one is ignorant, unreal the instant one awakens.

Sankara saw his mission as reforming the *santana dharma* but he also professed a higher allegiance to truth. He advocated an ethic in which human beings are duty-bound to recognize humanity in themselves and in everyone – – every other human being – we are called to uphold the dignity of the other person in compassion and benevolence, but also in tolerance and open-mindedness – an ethic that states explicitly that it is not a form of escapism but instead a practical attempt to make life livable. This is how he saw the Hindu path – this was his earnest attempt to cultivate and live this ethic – but he never claimed to have reached the end in seeking knowledge. Sankara often calls himself a fool and a sinner; he never says 'this is the only way.'

The authoritative work on the history of Indian thinking is the *Sarva Darsana Samgraha* or 'Collection of All Philosophies' by Madhava Acarya, who is thought to have lived around the year 1380. Acarya emphasizes the diversity inherent in Sanskrit writing, beginning with the 'song of creation' in the *Rigveda* (10. 129), which throws doubt on the idea of creation; atheistic and materialist ideas alongside devotional passages in the *Upanishads*; arguments against all forms of religion in the *Digha Nikaya* and other works attributed to Siddhartha, as well as arguments for a fantastic variety of religious positions developed in and combining the six schools. Acarya offers sympathetic accounts of diametrically opposed systems. He sees himself as the historian of a culture of discussion, in which minds drawn to different positions work through arguments about action and peace, speaking up and keeping silent, the conception of the world as a delusion and opposing ideas of the spiritual nature of the world, and many conflicting conceptions of reality and freedom. He explains that all these positions can degenerate into unarguable dogmatisms and, in other cases, that they elevate the mind and provide themes for searching meditation.

¬ The Olympian tradition

Western civilization rests on the foundation of Greek philosophy. Greek philosophy rests on the foundation of Greek religion. In Plato's words, "Homer is the educator of all Greece." The classical scholar Werner Jaeger summarizes the result of many generations of thinking in a famous passage of his work *Paideia*: "The work of Homer is inspired by a comprehensive philosophy of human nature and the eternal laws of the world-process, a philosophy which has seen and judged every essential factor in man's life. He contemplates every event and every character in the light of his universal knowledge of the underlying and eternal truth."

Jaeger concludes (in brief) that Homer teaches the Greeks, and that the Greeks teach the world, to think.

If we begin to look at the Homeric religion we quickly see many of the elements discussed above: a contemplation of death and wresting with the problem of suffering, which appear e.g. especially in the *Gilgamesh* epic and in Hinduism and Buddhism; a deeper look into the mechanism of the world, and the discovery of impersonal forces of nature, also found e.g. in the *Book of Changes*; a concern with worldly honor (in Greek, *timè*, honor, penalty, compensation), which is also a focus of Confucius' sayings in *The Analects*; anthropomorphism and wild multiplication of the gods, as also developed e.g. in Hinduism; worship of nature, as found e.g. in Taoism; and, as is common, sacred texts.

Herodotus says that Homer and Hesiod were the first to name the gods and tell their stories for the Greeks. But he also researched the question and discovered that Greek religion derives from many other traditions. The worship of Dionysus, the cult of Orpheus, and Aesop's fables come from India; Cronus and Rhea and the race of Titans have Hittite and Babylonian origins; Zeus ('bright sky') is a weather-god from Anatolia; and most of the Olympians have an Egyptian or Libyan source. The distinguishing feature of Greek religion is that it is not mainly about gods but is about *heroes*.

It is typical in religious traditions and mythologies that the focus of interest is on the gods – the creation of the world, laying out the sky and the foundations, the creation of all living beings, great powerful forces that hold us captive and dominate us – also the world of the sea, of plants and animals, many of which can speak and have human or superhuman powers. This is not the case in Greek religious culture, where everything is oriented towards the central hero. The Greek scholar Jasper Griffin puts this point in his study, *Homer* (1980):

"The replacing of the colossal, the vague, and the bestial with the human image and the human scale is the most vital and most lasting of all the achievements of Greece, both in literature and in art. In the *Iliad* this achievement is already complete."

In making the hero the central figure of worship, Greek religion re-imagines both the problem of suffering and the conception of divinity. Aristotle says that religion is simply "to honor the gods." The gods demand honor from men in the form of sacrifices, offerings, and temples. Honoring is something men already do among each other. The difference is simply that gods "have more virtue, *timè*, and strength than men" – as well as the fact that they do not die (*Iliad* IX, 498). The gods merit more honor than men because they are perfect models of the things men try to honor in each other. Thus the gods become the standards and witnesses of human deeds. The gods are sometimes enemies of great men who reach too close to the divine; they are sometimes jealous of human pleasures and triumphs; and in particular their gaze is most attracted to great suffering. Because human beings are doomed, but still act and live, even sometimes reaching heroism, human life becomes poignant and draws the passionate interest of the immortals. In effect this says: accepting the destiny of suffering ennobles and transforms the mere necessity of enduring it; suffering shows the subtle human compound of fragility and greatness; a kind of beauty emerges out of suffering and disaster – *because suffering is the focus of divine interest.*

Griffin tries to summarize the significance of this change in religious life in psychological terms:

"The Homeric poems do not tell us that the world was made for man, or that our natural state is one of happiness. They do say that it can be comprehended in human terms, and that human life can be more than an insignificant or ignoble struggle in the dark. The human soul can rise to the height of the challenges and the suffering which are the lot of all mankind. That spirit, chastened but not despairing, which sees the world without illusion and confronts it without self-pity or evasion, was the gift of Greece to the world, and is the deepest element of thought in Homer."

The Olympian religion is about heroes – about confronting death – but is also about seeing the whole – that is why it is 'Olympian' – a vision from on high, as from the summit of Mt. Olympus. This idea comes out in a scene in Euripedes' play *Bacchae* in which the two old men Cadmus and Teiresias, dressed in fawn-skins and Dionysiac costumes, are about to join a celebration for the gods, while young Pentheus, self-willed and arrogant, mocks the god Dionysus and refuses to join in. The chorus intercedes with the force of *sophia* (wisdom) and *sophrosunè* (temperance) and *dikè* (justice), arguing with Pentheus, pleading the cause of *all* the gods, and hoping to save Pentheus from ruin:

> We do not trifle with the gods
> We are the heirs of customs
> Hallowed by age and passed down
> By our fathers; no logic can topple them,
> Whatever subtleties cleverness invents.
> For all the gods desire honor from all of us;
> No one is excluded from this worship.

(*Bacchae* 200-208)

Pentheus is unmoved and, in the end, he is destroyed. Euripides appears to be saying: men owe due honor to all the gods – all the great powers that stalk the world – all the great realities that define human life, as death, birth, sex, grief, joy, war, sickness, mind, ecstasy, skill – these and many more – to narrow down this comprehensive vision or to despise any one god is injustice; life is many things, not one; life is fragile and great, comic and tragic all at the same time.

¬ Monotheism

Many generations of historians have tried to comprehend the change in the tone of experience in the enormous transformation of Western civilization from the pagan world to the believing world. There are many elements of continuity through this transition but also something radically new – new in Judaism, new in Christianity, and new in Islam – likewise this new element has traversed a troubled history that continues to define our world.

There was something like faith in *many gods* before the new faith in *one God*. Faith in the first sense is something ordinary: faith is courage – faith is the heart – faith is what we are able to do. Faith in the new sense is something extraordinary: faith is otherworldliness – rapture, martyrdom, the longing to be forgiven for unspeakable sins. The 'pagans' worship the gods by offering sacrifices, by telling stories about them, by fearing them and hoping for their help. There are rituals, but no doctrines, laws or instructions. The 'believers' are all 'people of the book.' The *Torah* (the 'law'), also called the *Pentateuch* (the 'five scrolls' – Genesis, Exodus, Leviticus, Numbers and Deuteronomy), are Israel's 'sacred books' or 'scriptures' – as the *New Testament* is for Christianity – as the *Qur'an* is for Islam. Sacred books lay down divine commandments concerning how people are to worship and live. The words of God supersede merely human speech. They indicate the transit from this world to the next – as in India the school of self-reliance is left behind and the *Vedas* become everything – the change from faith in ourselves to faith in otherworldly power.

With the advent of the Christian era, classical philosophy lost its central position in culture and became "the handmaiden of theology," and much of classical philosophy was recast in support of monotheism. Nietzsche said that Christianity was "Platonism for the masses." The point he is trying to make is actually much more general. The great spirits of all *three* Western monotheistic traditions developed their core doctrines as interpretations of Plato or Aristotle. Philo Judaeus of Alexandria (20 BCE - 50 CE) is a follower of Plato; the great Jewish theologians Saadya Ben Joseph (882-942), Moshe Ben Maimon, known as Maimonides (1135-1204), and Hasdai Crescas (1340-1410), among many others, are Aristotelians. The great Church fathers

Athanasius (297-373), Augustine of Hippo (354-430), Anselm (1033-1109), Thomas Aquinas (1225-1274), among many others, follow either Plato or Aristotle; and so do all the great figures of Arabic philosophy and theology, such as al-Kindi (800-866), al-Razi, known as Rhazes (865-925), al-Farabi (died circa 950), Ibn Sina, known as Avicenna (980-1037), and Ibn Rushd, known as Averroes (1126-1198), among many others. An exception may be made for al-Razi, who says that Plato is "the *shaykh* of philosophers," but that higher up is "Socrates, our true *imam*."

¬ Judaism

The *Torah* is written in Hebrew. The term *torah* means 'teaching' or 'instruction,' also 'scribe,' as in the person who copies the teaching down. According to tradition, Moses is the author of the *Torah*. Recent scholarship (beginning in 17th century rationalism and culminating in what scholars call "the higher criticism") asserts that the *Torah* is largely a compilation of works by four authors, dating from the period of Solomon and through the exile in Babylon. The four texts are:

The Jahwist (or J) - written around 950 BCE. The J work derives from the southern kingdom, also called Judah. It is named according to its frequent use of the name 'Yahweh' ('Jahve'). The oldest part of the J text is Exodus 15: 1-21, also called "The Song of the Sea," which is thought to have a Canaanite origin. The J text includes the Eden story and Abraham's departure from Mesopotamia. The setting of the J text begins somewhere around 1850 BCE, yet the text often reflects the circumstances of the time in which it was written (perhaps 900 years later). Scholars often characterize the J text as anthropomorphic, since Yahweh sometimes appears in the form of a human being (e.g., Yahweh appears to Abraham at a place called Mamre, near Hebron, in the form of a travelling stranger, *Exodus* 18:1).

The Elohist (or E) - written around 850 BCE. This text is from the northern kingdom, also called Israel. It is so named because it often uses the plural form 'Elohim' (this was also the Hebrew term for gods worshipped by other peoples; Yahweh sometimes appears as one of the Elohim). The E text is focused on the story of Moses. Scholars regard the E text as taking the first step towards a transcendent, imageless form of worship. The E text also tells the story of God's command to Abraham to take his son Isaac to Mount Moriyya and sacrifice him there, the Lord's reprieve, and Abraham's sacrifice of a ram in Isaac's stead (*Genesis* 22: 1-10).

J and E were combined after 722 BCE and began to be recited at tribal festivals throughout the region.

The Deuteronomist (or D) - written around 650 BCE. Dating from the time of King Josiah of Judah, thought to be the author of the last part of the Torah, i.e. Deuteronomy, as well as the Book of Joshua and most of the Old

Testament up to 2 Kings. The D text refers to God as Yahweh Elohaynu (translated "the Lord our God." This text brings in many reforms, including a separation between temple (as a place apart) and life (the secular realm); a judiciary independent of the cult; a constitutional monarchy, which made the King subject to the law and the equal of every other citizen; and various attempts to rid the tradition of superstition. This text also emphasizes the idea of the chosen people and a generally hostile attitude towards Israel's neighbors. Babylon destroyed Jerusalem and burnt Solomon's temple in 586 BCE.

The Priestly source (or P) - written after the Babylonian exile, sometime around 550-400 BCE. So named because it focuses on religious laws and the authority of priests. The P source includes the Creation hymn in the first chapter of Genesis, the expulsion from Eden, the wanderings of Cain, the "Holiness Code" (a collection of laws originating in the seventh century) (*Leviticus* 17-26), and the "Tabernacle Document" (a description of the Ark of the Covenant and the tent in which it was housed) (*Exodus* 25-31; 35-38; 40). The P source refers to God as Elohim. The P source develops a kind of theology of exile. Israel is not a people because of where they live, but because they live in the presence of a God who accompanies them wherever they happen to be. P makes Israel *a nation of priests* – everyone in the community is expected to live as if he or she is a priest serving in the Jerusalem temple – the real temple has been destroyed but our actions rebuild the symbolic temple – God is said to be holy (*kaddosh*) but the Israelites are enjoined to be holy also. P commands Israel to honor everything living.

The Old Testament contains three parts: the Law, the Prophets, and the Writings. The Law is the *Torah*, i.e. the Pentateuch, the first five books. The Prophets include the Former Prophets and the Latter Prophets and the Book of the Twelve. The Writings begin the *Psalms* and end with *Chronicles*. The *Psalms* are thought to be the oldest part of the Bible altogether. They were compiled from older collections for use in the Temple in Zerubbabel (*Ezra* 5:2). Some derive from Egyptian sources and some even from Sumer (third millennium BCE).

As a collection from these many dates and sources, the Old Testament does not contain a single orthodox message but is an interweaving of distinct themes. There are at least three creation stories (*Genesis* 1, *Genesis* 2, *Isaiah* 40). There are three different versions of the Ten Commandments (*Exodus* 20, *Exodus* 34, *Deuteronomy* 5). Note for example that the Fourth Commandment – "Remember the Sabbath day, to keep it holy" – is explained as honoring the day the Lord rested after completing the Creation (*Exodus* 20: 8-11) but also as a memory of the exile in Egypt (*Deuteronomy* 5:15). It is easy to point out discrepancies and contradictions. This complex document portrays Yahweh as creating, regretting, punishing, hardening hearts, killing, cursing the sinner and his son, grandson, great-grandson, even his great great-grandson; sending famines, floods or plagues. He permits or even commands many horrible things (e.g. summary execution, rape, torture, pushing off a cliff) but also makes laws protecting animals, strangers, the accused, even convicted criminals.

The American religious scholar and author Jack Miles imagines that these contradictions flow from trying to remake a polytheistic tradition into a monotheistic cult. He thinks that he can trace sources relating to the god Eloh, who is calm and benign, the god Yah, jealous and changeable, the serpent goddess Mot, the kindly but mysterious god Magen, and the ferocious, unquenchable and violent god Sab. Miles draws a number of conclusions. First: the Bible portrays the Jews as flawed human beings wrestling with a perplexing God. Second: "Protracted exposure to a God in who several personalities coexist and alongside whom no other god is ever portrayed … must foster a way of thinking about the self as similarly composite and similarly alone." Third: this God "has no opponent but himself" and, although none can escape him, neither can he escape himself. He is trapped within his own contradictions. "He is a tender solicitous husband and a sword-in-hand butcher." "His is the restless breathing we still hear in our sleep" (*God: A Biography*, 1995).

In a Confucian world, in ancestor worship, people offer up prayers to their departed ancestors. But the Taoist school invites people to look to themselves. In India there is a tradition of self-reliance alongside reverence shaped by age-old customs. Thus in China and in India, there is a tradition and a counter-tradition, and their contests help define national histories. In Judaism, a world of tribal idols precedes the epoch of imageless worship – Jahve precedes the Elohim – individualism standing out against exalted status. There is a manyness which gradually becomes a people, as something like manyness precedes achieving personal individuality. In Judaism, this division is unresolved. It shows itself in the names of God, which include *Ehye* and *The Rock* and *The Holy One of Israel* before resolving to Adonai and Elohim.

¬ Names of God

YHVH
Yod-Heh-Vav-Heh (YHVH); the Name (Ha Shem); related to the root Heh-Yod-Heh (the verb *to be*); frequently shortened to Yah (Yod-Heh), Yahu or Yeho (Yod-Heh-Vav), as in Yehoshua (Joshua, meaning 'the Lord is my Salvation'), Eliyahu (Elijah, meaning 'my God is the Lord'), and Halleluyah ('praise the Lord').

Adonai
Translated 'Lord' – what is read when the name YHVH appears in the text – or the phrase 'the Name' (Ha Shem) is substituted.

Elohim

Masculine plural of a word that is feminine in the singular (Eloha). The same word refers to princes, judges, other gods, and other powerful beings. This name is used in scripture when emphasizing God's might, creative power, and attributes of justice and rulership. Compare Elohai (my God), Elohaynu (our God), and El Elyou (God most High).

El Shaddai

Translated 'God Almighty' in the King James Bible (KJB) – literally is 'God of the Mountains.'

YHVH Tzva'ot.

KJB and the Revised Standard Version (RSV) translate as 'Lord of Hosts' The word *tzva'ot* means 'hosts' in the sense of a military grouping or an organized array or more simply a large group. This name refers to God's leadership and sovereignty. This name is used rarely in scripture. It does not appear in the *Torah*. It appears in the prophetic books and in the Writings, especially in *Psalms*.

Shekina

The feminine aspect of God; the veil. Literally the term means 'dwelling' or 'settling.' It was used to indicate the dwelling place of God and, after Solomon, the place of the Ark in the Temple in Jerusalem. The reason why Solomon plays a role in this history is from *I Chronicles 17, 4-5:* "Go and tell David my servant, Thus saith the LORD, Thou shall not build me a house to dwell in. For I have not dwelt in an house since the day that I brought up Israel unto this day; but have gone from tent to tent, and from one tabernacle to *another*" (KJB). The implication here is that God needs no temple and does not want one. Later in the story, God tells David that David's son, Solomon, rather than David, will build the temple. Rabbinical consensus today puts the construction of the temple at 835 BCE, but there are also estimates from the 10th century BCE.

The term *shekina* is also used to indicate the nests of birds (somewhat like the Greek term *ethos*, whose original use had to do with the haunts and niches of animals, and which by analogy was extended to habitual conduct and character). A thing is partly where it dwells and what it habitually does.

The reference in the above quote to tents suggests a period of transition between tribal worship and temple worship – religious practices of nomadic versus settled peoples. The Greek word *skene*, English *scene, scenic, scenery*, was used to translate *shekina* in the first translation of the Bible into Greek – the Greek word indicates a stage or a tent. The Hebrew term may be the basis of the Greek term. Some scholars attribute *skene* with an Etruscan or Phoenician origin. This word could be Indo-European or Semitic.

The transition from tents to the Temple marks the passage between tribal worship and temple worship; the destruction of the Temple (586 BCE) marks the transition from temple worship (in which sacredness is located in a resting place for the Ark) to private worship (religious 'feeling,' worship in the diaspora, the theology of exile) (in which the worshipper invokes sacredness by acts of consecration).

The term *shekina* strings together the idea of femininity, of a residence or resting place, of veiling or hiding or not showing oneself. These are all, sometimes, divine attributes. The *Talmud* and the Hasidic tradition develop many ideas about the *shekina* and the feminine aspect of God. (As God begins to create the first human being – the Adam – he says "Let us make the earth-creature in our own image." The text goes on: "Then God created it in God's own image. Male and female God created them" (*Genesis* 1: 26-27). The text appears to be saying that God created Adam as male and female. Reflecting on this text, Rabbis have wondered whether this is a signal that God is equally male and female – as the tradition of the *shekina* seems to imply. The *shekina* is the divine presence in the world, its indwelling, and is coextensive with the people of Israel; but it was considered to be specially present in the Jerusalem Temple.

[   ]
The orthodox rarely pronounce any of God's names. The usual practice is to substitute letters or syllables, so that Adonai becomes Adoshem or Ha-Shem, Elohaynu and Elohim become Elokaynu and Elokim, and so on. This is considered a sign of respect and an attempt to obey the third commandment (RSV: "You shall not take the name of the Lord your God in vain: for the Lord will not hold him guiltless who takes his name in vain" *Deuteronomy* 5:11). However, this practice was not followed in very ancient times, but came about in the following way. The name was permitted for everyday greetings and discussions until the destruction of the temple in 586 BCE (*Mishnah Berekhot* 9:5). The tradition afterwards was to allow priests to say it (*Mishnah Sotah* 7:6) and then (after the death of a famous High Priest, Shimon Ha' Tzaddik around 300 BCE) only the High Priest on the Highest High Holiday – Yom Kippur – the Day of Atonement – celebrating the atonement for false worship (worshipping the Golden Calf) (*Mishnah Sotah* 7:6, *Mishnah Tamid* 7:2). Finally, after the destruction of the Second Temple (70 CE), the Name was made unspeakable, on all occasions and for everyone.

¬ Translations of the Bible

Jewish tradition divides the Bible into three parts. The *Torah* (first five books), the *Nevi'im* (the Prophets) and the *Ketuvim* (the Writings). The entire document – the Hebrew Bible or Old Testament – is called the *Tanakh*.

This word (Tanakh) is an acronym formed from the initial Hebrew letters of the Tanakh's three traditional subdivisions: Torah, Nevi'im and Ketuvim - hence TaNaKh. This appears to be the origin of making acronyms.

The *Tanakh* was translated in Greek more than two hundred years before Christ. This translation came to be called the *septuagint* and is done in what is called Koine Greek, or common Greek, which was the world language of this period of history. The *Septuagint* was done in stages between the 3rd and 1st centuries BCE in Alexandria.

The word *septuaginta* means 'seventy' in Latin and derives from a tradition that seventy Jewish scholars translated the Pentateuch (Greek for 'five scrolls') (and other parts of the *Tanakh* and even some writings that were not part of later traditions) from Hebrew into Greek for Ptolemy II Philadelphus, 285–246 BCE.

Protestant Bibles follow Jewish tradition and exclude additional books added by the translators of the *Tanakh* into the *Septuagint*. Roman Catholics include some of these books in their canon and exclude others. Eastern Orthodox Churches use all the books of the *Septuagint*.

The New Testament was written in the same language as the *Septuagint*, i.e. Koine Greek. The earliest writing in the New Testament dates from the year 54 (Paul's letters). The *Gospels* date from 75 to 100.

The Vulgate is a Fifth Century (modern era) translation of the *Septuagint* and the *Gospels* into Latin, and largely the result of one person, St. Jerome, who was commissioned by Pope Damasus I in 382 to make a new translation of the ancient texts. The Vulgate became the definitive and officially promulgated version of the Bible of the Roman Catholic Church, and ultimately took the name *versio vulgata*, which means 'the published translation.' There are 76 books in the Vulgate Bible: 46 in the Old Testament, 27 in the New Testament, and three in the Apocrypha.

The Englishman William Tyndale (1492-1536) was a scholar influenced both by Erasmus (1436-1536) and Luther (1483-1546). In 1530 he made the first translation of the *Torah* into English. Tyndale renders the divine name as 'Iehovah.' In his note to this edition he wrote: "Iehovah is God's name... Moreover, as oft as thou seeist LORD in great letters (except there be any error in the printing) it is in Hebrew Iehovah." Tyndale was executed by religious edict for making this translation; his translation lived on as the basis for the KJB.

Pietro Colonna Galatino, also known as Petrus Galatinus (died after 1539) was an Italian Friar Minor, philosopher, theologian, and Orientalist. Galatino translated parts of the Bible into Italian and may be responsible for the modern term 'Jehovah.'

By another theory, an unknown sixteenth century German Christian scribe, while transliterating the Bible into Latin and the consonants of YHVH with the vowels of Adonai, came up with the word Je Ho VaH – this became the basis for the English word 'Jehovah,' the proper name of the God of Israel. In his Dictionary of the Bible (1863), the Bible scholar William Robertson Smith summarized the arguments for and against this name, and concluded that Moses himself never pronounced this name or anything like it (Jove, Ieve, Ieoa), but substituted 'Adonai' in place of the unknown name.

Rabbi Jacob ben Asher (1270-1340), a German-Spanish scholar, lists 70 different names of God. The King James Bible (aka the KJB), which dates from the year 1611, translates all of them, as well as YHWH, as 'Jehovah.'

¬ Some Jewish symbols

The Star of David, the Lukhot Habrit (an image of tablets with rounded top edges on which were written the Ten Commandments), the Menorah (a seven-branched candelabrum), the Lion of Judah (heraldic Lion associated with Judah and the duty to serve others ("my brother's keeper," *Genesis* 4:9)), the mezuzah (a doorpost casing containing a line from the Torah, *Deuteronomy* 6:9), and a symbol formed from the letters Cheit and Yod (meaning "life" and having the numerical value 18).

¬ Some Jewish beliefs

Messiah. A savior or liberator who will come and inaugurate the Messianic age, uniting the tribes of Israel and bringing a reign of global peace. "Then the earth will be filled with a knowledge of God, as the waters cover the sea" (*Isaiah* 11:9).

Sheol. The abode of the dead, a place of darkness to which all the dead go, both the righteous and the unrighteous, regardless of moral choices made in this life, and completely cut off from God (*Genesis* 37:36). Sheol is an underworld place in the earth, akin to Hades or Tartarus, whose gateway lies in the west. It has a ruler, seven gates guard its approach, and a river flows around it. This is the "Land without Return." Traditionally this word has been thought to be an Assyrian or Babylonian loan-word, but this has been disputed recently. The concept of Sheol marks Judaism with a worldly, rather than an otherworldly focus, akin to the lament in the *Epic of Gilgamesh*.

b'tzelem Elohim. In Latin, *Imago Dei.* Human beings are created in the image of God. They have inherent worth, independent of their station in society or fate in life. This is an assertion of irreducible human value, power to do good, free will and responsibility for one's actions. "And let us make mankind in our image, and as our likeness (*kid'muteinu*)." Image implies a likeness to sensible things, likeness is more general, including one's character.

¬ Some Jewish ideology

The call from God. God calls to Abram, "*Lek leka,*" which translates as "be take yourself," "Go out from your country and your people and your father's house" (*Genesis* 12:1). A rabbinical teaching on this line interprets it to mean, "Go forth to find your authentic self, to learn who you are meant to be." Abram, later called Abraham, is the *man called by God.* This is not the idea that man should make himself – not the idea of humanism – not the idea of standing on one's own, of self-conscious achievement – not "know thyself" but rather "fear God." Judaism is not about man, but about God; not about pride, but sin; not about mind, but about heart.

The call to Justice. Judaism makes the transition from polytheism to monotheism and from reverence before awesome power to reverence before ethical principle. This transition occurs over centuries and, as argued by Jack Miles and many other authors, is never completely resolved.

John Shelby Spong, an American bishop of the Episcopal Church, has written extensively about this change. In his words: "Some transition moments on this journey can be studied easily. It was the prophet named Hosea, writing in the eighth century BCE, who changed God's name to love. It was the prophet named Amos who changed God's name to justice. It was the prophet we call Jonah who taught us that the love of God is not bounded by the limits of our own ability to love. It was the prophet Micah who understood that beautiful religious rituals and even lavish sacrifices were not the things that worship requires, but rather "to do justice, love mercy and walk humbly with your God." It was the prophet we call Malachi, writing in the fifth century BCE, who finally saw God as a universal experience, transcending all national and tribal boundaries." Spong's writings about the prophets follow Karl Jaspers' conception of the "Axial Age" and the "Great Transformation" – an historical period stretching between 900 and 200 BCE – that works through changes from competition to cooperation, honor to dignity, shame to guilt, and mere power to real strength. The change is encapsulated in the slogan "no peace (*shalom*) without justice (*tzedek*)."

The Jewish people accomplished this transition after its enslavement in Egypt; after its captivity in Babylon; after being humbled by Assyria, Persia, Greece, Rome and Byzantium; after its occupation by Umayyads, Abbasids, Fatimids, Seljuks, Crusaders, Turks, Mamluks and Ottomans; through a long series of military defeats, exiles and persecutions that did not end even with the Holocaust. A signal moment in this history occurs in 167 BCE, when Antiochus IV Epiphanes, ruler of the Seleucid Empire, issued what amounts to the first officially sanctioned religious persecution in history. The practice of Judaism was outlawed in all of Judea. The Temple was shut, the Sabbath forbidden, and Jerusalem was renamed Antioch in Judea.

Karen Armstrong comments: in response, for the first time, "an apocalyptic piety entered Judaism which looked forward to a final victory of the righteous at the end of History. Subsequently this type of faith appeared in all three of the monotheistic traditions, whenever a cherished way of life came under attack, as happened in Jerusalem under Antiochus Epiphanes … When the present looked hopeless, the faithful found comfort in visions of a triumphant future" (*Jerusalem*, 1996, p. 114).

The prophets teach that doing justice brings us closer to God. The call from God is the call to justice, and the call to justice brings God into the world. But the world is a place of suffering, and suffering does not make its victims compassionate. Suffering attacks a person's sense of the meaning of things, his commitment to his core values, his confidence and energy. A person in pain is not curious about his surroundings but instead is focused on his troubling inner world. We do not expect people who have suffered grievous wrong to be generous or gracious or kind; it seems more natural to us for such people to be the opposite of these good things. The good will is injured by misfortune, as Aristotle taught. And just as an individual can become blunted into a lesser being through mistreatment or trauma, so a faith, emerging from a history of persecution, becomes embattled, defensive, ready to strike, and cut off from its own sources of wisdom and healing. And thus the State of Israel, founded shortly after the catastrophe of the Holocaust, a phoenix rising out of ashes, rather than brightening the world with the light of justice, powerfully focused by its heritage of suffering, instead becomes merely another nation among others and even an occupying power and a source of new suffering; so that the drama is certain to continue.

The Promised Land. God calls to Abram, "Go out from your country and your people and your father's house and go to the land I will show you. And I will make you a great nation, and I will bless you … so Abram went, as the Lord had told him … and came to the land of Canaan. At that time, the Canaanites were in the land. Then the Lord appeared to Abram and said: "To your descendants I will give this land"" (*Genesis* 12:1-7). An important part of the ideology or socially constructed reality of a people or nation – what Plato calls a "noble lie" – is the belief that the state's land belongs to it even though it was likely acquired by conquest; thus also that citizenship is rooted in something more than the accidents of birth. The underlying assertion seems to be that people need powerful and inspiring myths to help them achieve a cohesive society. Interestingly, the Genesis narrative does not attempt to resolve the contradiction between God's promise of land to Abram and the fact that another people are already living there. The Israelites struggle mightily to subdue the land, but also quickly lose it. According to Jewish tradition, even when it is *not* in Jewish occupation, which is most of recorded history, the land of Canaan never loses its status as "the Promised Land."

¬ Christianity

Early Christianity, which began as a part of Judaism during Jesus' lifetime (died c. 30), gradually became distinct from Judaism. It continued to revere the Hebrew Bible, generally using the Septuagint translation that was already in general use (completed 200 years before Jesus' birth). Jesus' followers were called 'Nazarenes' and 'Galileans' by their opponents but called themselves 'the disciples' (meaning 'learners' or 'followers of the teaching.')

Early Christianity is also called the 'Apostolic Age' after the first twelve apostles or leaders of the church. The First Council of Nicaea (325) is accepted as the end of this period.

Jesus and his original followers were all Jews. The followers of Jesus composed a sect within Judaism marked by their belief that Jesus of Nazareth was the long-awaited Messiah (*Acts* 2:22-36), and that the Kingdom of God had come or would soon come, in fulfillment of prophesy (*Acts* 19:8).

Early Christians appear to have been influenced by the Jewish sect called the Essenes, who today are considered Gnostics or forerunners of Gnosticism. The Essenes practiced baptism, believed in a New Covenant, were messianic and believed themselves a remnant of the faithful preparing the way for a new reign of God. They used terms that were later important in Christianity, such as way, saint, preach, and charisma. John the Baptist was likely an Essene.

Early Christians were also called Ebionites. The Ebionites believed that ancient Jewish customs such as circumcision and the Passover and study of Hebrew should be continued by the new Christian religion. The Ebionites were later disparaged as 'Judaizers,' i.e. not true Christians, after the Council of Nicaea.

The Ebionite movement was centered around Jerusalem and led by James the Just, who Paul refers to as Jesus' brother (*Galatians* 1:19). They held faithfully to the *Torah* and Jewish law. Another early Christian movement was centered around the Apostle Paul (Pauline Christians). The Paulines maintained a similar faith, differing only in practice; they moved away gradually from Jewish practice; ultimately they condemned it. Gentile (non-Jewish) Christianity became the orthodox version and outgrew all previously Jewish Christian sects.

The term 'Christians' (from the Greek *christos*, 'anointed') occurs only three times in the New Testament. The disciples were called 'Christians' in Antioch (*Acts* 11:26). The term also appears in *Acts* 26:28, used by Herod Agrippa II. In the First Epistle of Peter, it is said that believers should not be distraught if they are called by this name (*1 Peter* 4:14-16). Ignatius of Antioch was the first 'Christian' to call himself by this name and made the first documented use of the term 'Christianity' (Greek Χριστιανισμός), sometime around the year 100. In Greek he is referred to as Theophorus – 'God-bearer' – he became an Apostolic Father of the Church and was the third Bishop of Antioch.

The Roman centurion Cornelius is traditionally considered the first Gentile convert. His conversion, as documented in *Acts* 10, carries great significance. Both Peter and James referred to Cornelius in arguing for the inclusion of Gentiles in the Jerusalem Council. His conversion is broadly considered to have been the beginning of Christianity as a world religion, separate from Judaism. Armenia was the first nation to adopt Christianity as its official religion. This occurred in the year 301. Rome followed in 313.

¬ Sources

Scholars today consider the basic sources for Christianity to be the lost Gospel (called the "Q document") (50-55 CE), Paul's letters (54-58), the Gospel of Mark (75), as well as the later synoptic gospels Matthew (80) and Luke (85).

The "Q document" is thought to have gone through three editorial phases – an Aramaic phase, a Jewish-Christian phase, and a Gentile phase. Q (so-called for the German tern *Quelle*, 'source') brings us to the shadowy period between Jesus' life and the writing of the Gospels. Its original is in Aramaic and it documents actual words of Jesus or records of them from within twenty or twenty-five years of his life (Edward Schillebeeckx, *Jesus*, 1981).

Both Paul's letters and the Q document are thought to have some connection with Rabbi Hillel (80 BCE – 30 CE), a famous teacher who taught a doctrine of brotherly love and formulated a version of the Golden Rule ("What is hateful to yourself, do not do to anyone else. This is the whole truth of the *Torah*. The rest is commentary"). Hillel taught in a *beth hamidrash* – a house for searching – *lidrosh* is to investigate and *darash* is to search – the term *midrash* is roughly 'exegesis' (but also covers an interpretative tradition beginning in the third century). Hillel's grandson Gamaliel was also a famous Rabbi and continued his school; one of his students was Saul of Tarsus (St. Paul). The Q document includes many famous passages: Love your enemies; The Golden Rule; The Lord's Prayer; Judge not, Lest ye be Judged; Beware of false prophets; Ye shall know them by their fruits; and the Beatitudes (from 'The Sermon on the Mount,' *Matthew* 5-7).

There is no virgin birth and there is no resurrection story in the Gospel of Mark or in the Q document. Mark takes it for granted that Joseph was Jesus' father and that he had brothers and sisters. He regards Jesus as a prophet.

The fourth Gospel, John, dates from somewhere near the year 90 and has an important context in the conflict between the Ebionites, led by James, and the Pauline Christians, and especially over the question from John "Does he [Jesus] intend to go to the Dispersion and teach the Greeks?" (*John* 7:35)

In John we see the struggle between Jewish orthodoxy, which looks inward and has no proselytizing drive, and Jesus as a new meaning in the world, Jesus as the Son of God (*John* 1), Savior of the World (4), the Holy One of God (6) – someone who can say "I and the Father are One" (10:30) and "I am the Son of God" (10:36). In John, there is no temptation in the wilderness; no agony in the garden of Gethsemane; and no cry "Why have you forsaken me" from the cross. In John, what Jesus says is much less the focus than who Jesus is – Jesus is hardly human, Jesus is divine, Jesus is God – which makes the break with Judaism complete. John is fighting for this vision of Jesus rather than for Jesus the prophet from Nazareth. Thus John disparages the Jews in many passages and it seems clear that his target is the Jewish orthodoxy that condemns the heresy that man could ever be God. John records the excommunication from the synagogue of Jews who take this new stance (9, 12, 16) and also harangues Jews who believe in the new message but cannot find the courage to say so publically (12, 19). The context is a battle between two groups of Jews. There are heated words. The unanticipated consequence is religious hatred culminating in the Holocaust.

There are two ancient sources for Christianity outside the Christian community: Josephus, writing in *Jewish Antiquities* (18.63), which dates from 93, and Tacitus, in his *Annales* (15-44), which dates from 115. Josephus calls Jesus a wise man and doer of marvelous feats, "a teacher of such men who receive the truth with pleasure," who drew over to him many Jews and many Greeks, but who also drew the ire of the men of highest standing among the Jews. Tacitus mentions the Christians as being hated for their depravity and notes that a man named Jesus was the founder of this deadly superstition, which now is come to Rome, "where all disgusting and shameful practices collect and flourish on all sides."

In later times, the historical Jesus becomes a cloudy figure. A vision more like John's prevails. The emphasis is magic, miracles, divine status and language that interpreters take either figuratively (as a way of helping the reader understand Jesus' ideas and mission) or factually (as straight reporting of facts).

Belief or faith, in the sense of assent to statements that we do not completely understand, appears to be important in Christian teaching, but there are problems with translation that may also contribute to this topic. Mark says: "Lord, I believe, help thou my unbelief" (*Mark* 9:24-25). The Greek word here is *pistis*, which means, 'trust, loyalty, engagement, commitment.' Some scholars argue that Jesus was not asking people here to *believe* that he was God but that he wanted their *commitment*. He wanted them to tend to the poor, feed the hungry, abandon pride, cut family ties, follow him and put their trust in God. St. Jerome translates the Greek *pisteuo* (roughly 'I trust') with the Latin term *credo* ('I give my heart'). The KJB translates *credo* as "I believe." This begins to look like intellectual assent.

Some important sources here are C.H. Dodd, *Historical Traditions in the Fourth Gospel*, 1965; Rudolf Bultmann, *The Gospel of John*, 1971; Wilfred Smith, *Belief and History*, 1977; *Faith and Belief*, 1979; Emil Schurer, *The History of the Jewish People in the Age of Jesus Christ*, 1986; E.P. Sanders, *The Historical Figure of Jesus*, 1993; John Watson, *Jesus and the Jews: The Pharisaic Tradition in John*, 1995; John Dominic Crossan, *The Historical Jesus*, 1991, *The Birth of Christianity: Discovering What Happened in the Years Immediately After the Execution of Jesus*, 1998; Karen Armstrong, *The Case for God*, 2009.

One third of the human race is avowedly Christian. Thus what began as a small Jewish sect in the mid first-century became the single most important influence in world history.

Christianity is many people, many cultures, many histories – many arguments and ideas – among which are, freedom rather than slavery; trust in God over self-reliance; monotheism over polytheism; and love even above the law. Christianity traverses many histories from magic to ideology, in which religiosity has gradually less significance as an attitude towards the sacred, and gradually more weight as intellectual loyalty to a doctrinal statement.

¬ Some Christian symbols

The cross and crucifix, the ichthys (sign of the fish), the alpha-omega sign, the staurogram or tau-rho symbol, the chi-rho symbol, the good shepherd, the dove, the lamb, the crown of thorns, the sacred heart, the sign INRI (Jesus King of the Jews), images of Jesus, the Stations of the Cross, images of the holy family, images of Mary, images of the Apostles, images of the saints.

¬ Some Christian beliefs

Divinity. Christianity becomes the belief that Jesus is the Son of God.

Resurrection and life everlasting. Christians consider the resurrection of Christ to be the central tenet of their faith and the most important event in human history (*I Corinthians* 15). Jesus demonstrates a power over life and therefore the power to grant or withhold from others the gift of eternal life.

Sacrifice and redemption. Sacrifice is a way of honoring God and asking for divine assistance. Christianity conceives humanity to be in a condition of sin and death from which it seeks salvation; salvation comes by Jesus' substitionary death, resurrection and atonement for the human condition. "He himself bore our sins in his body on the tree, that we might die to sin and live to righteousness" (1 *Peter* 2:24). He did for us what we cannot do for ourselves.

Politics. Jesus appears to take an apolitical stance in his comment "Render unto Caesar the things that are Caesar's, and unto God the things that are God's" (*Matthew* 22:21). The context is Jesus' being asked whether he pays taxes. If he answers yes, this would signal that he accepts the Roman occupation and opposes the Jewish resistance. If he answers no, this would signal that he is a rebel and thus risk immediate arrest by the Roman authorities. He dismisses the question. In John's conception, when Jesus is before Pilate, he says "My kingdom is not of this world. If my kingdom were of this world, my servants would have been fighting, that I might not be delivered over to the Jews. But as it is, my kingdom is not of this world" (18:36). Christianity has by this an otherworldly focus rather than undertaking a political reform. Christianity has therefore sometimes preached an apolitical yet social gospel, aid to the poor and opposition to governments that wage war. Paul instructs Christians to submit to the state, pay their taxes, wield the sword when requested and help preserve the social order that God has ordained (*Romans* 13:1-7). Christianity has by this sometimes preached a conservative gospel, restricting personal choices and freedom of action, imposing narrow limits on education, and especially restricting women's lives. Thus Christianity has inspired both liberation theology and Christian fundamentalism – humanism and authoritarianism – blue state and red.

Identity. Perhaps a defining line of demarcation here concerns the self and ideas about personal identity. Leftist Christianity offers the model of religiously-inspired principles that help a person flourish and become herself or himself. Christianity *per se* is not the issue, nor is it important that a person identify as a Christian or even as a religious person. Bonhoeffer held that to be a Christian has nothing to do with being religious; it is simply "to be" (*Prisoner for God*, 1959). This tradition rejects fundamentalism as a transparent attempt to bolster deeply insecure and fearful people. Rightist Christianity offers the different model of God-centered, God-fearing, obedient and pro-selytizing, in-gathering caretaking, based on the idea that human beings have no legitimate identity apart from God. A person does not choose a tradition or make his or her own identity. Tradition chooses us and we become what God has made us (Alasdair MacIntyre, *Whose Justice? Which Rationality?*, 1988).

Exclusivity. Christianity achieved an unparalleled victory over all its rivals, not only against Judaism and rival mystery cults of its day, but doubly again over Rome: first by supplanting Rome's traditional religion, centered around worship of the emperor, but also over Rome's traditional tolerance for the variety of its subject peoples' devotions. Christianity was initially encouraged and later, from the 5th century, enforced. It became the one and *only* truth.*

¬ Islam

Muhammad (Mohammed, Muhammed, Mahomet) is regarded by his followers as a prophet of God (Allah), last in the series that includes Adam, Noah, Abraham, Moses, David, Solomon, John the Baptist and Jesus.

Muhammad was born in the year 570 in the Arabian city of Mecca. His father Abdullah died before he was born. His mother Amina died when he was six years old. Muhammad was sent to live with his maternal uncle Abu Talib, chieftain of the Banu Hashim, a distinguished family clan and part of the Quraysh tribe. The Quraysh became guardians of the Meccan sanctuary, the Ka'ba, five generations earlier, under the leadership of Qusai bin Kalib, said to be the first king of Arabia; Qusai traced his lineage back to Noah.

The Quraysh play an important role in Islam. They are Muhammad's native tribe; the Quraysh also led the initial resistance to Muhammad's leadership; Muhammad dethroned the Quraysh during his lifetime and became the ruling Caliph himself; the Quraysh regained supremacy after Muhammad's death and founded the three main historic Muslim dynasties, the Ummayads, Abbasids and Fatamids, who ruled as Caliphs.

Descendants of the Quraysh family still preside over the Ka'ba (an Arabic term which is the basis for the English word 'cube'), which is something like presiding over the Vatican or the Great Wall of China or Lhasa in Tibet. The Ka'ba, also called the House of God (*Bayt Allah*), also called the Black Stone (*al Hajar ul Aswad*), is thought to be carved from a fallen meteorite and to be very ancient. By tradition the Ka'ba was erected by Adam, the first man. It is said that the flood destroyed the edifice and that Noah rebuilt it.

The shrine was forgotten for centuries until Abraham rediscovered it. In Islamic lore it was here that he offered his son Isaac for a sacrifice and where Isaac was spared (Arabic *Ismail*).

Many gods are represented in the *Bayt Allah*. The god not represented in the Ka'ba is *El* – also known as 'Creator God,' 'King of Gods,' 'Lord of the House,' *Jahve, Jehovah, Allah*, and *Jah* (also the basis of names such as Joshua, Jeshua, Yeshua (Jesus)). *Allah* may not be represented in any way – it is not permitted to make a drawing of him or (in some traditions) even to pronounce his name – this again is considered a sign of respect. In Arabic, the period preceding Islam is called the *Jahiliyyah* – 'the time of ignorance.'

In Muhammad's lifetime, Persia and Byzantium took turns conquering and reconquering Jerusalem and all its surrounding territories – including Arabia – which helps explain why, in addition to local cults and moon worship and ancient Judaism, Muhammad also had a chance to learn about Christianity (from the Romans) and Zoroaster (from the Persians). Muhammad had no formal education and as an orphan in a large household he had to learn to fend for himself. He became a sheepherder, camel driver, a conductor of caravans through the desert and, ultimately, a merchant, like his uncle; this gave him the chance to travel widely and to learn about the customs and worship of people from Carthage to Damascus.

There is a tradition that when Muhammad was a young man and was making his first visit to Syria, he encountered a Christian monk named Bahira who foretold that he would become a great teacher. At the age of 26, he married Khadijah, a princess of the ruling Quraysh clan – she was also called al-Tahira (the Pure One) – a woman 15 years his senior – but Muhammad did not take to family life easily and had a restless spirit. After his marriage he met his wife's cousin, Waraka, a member of a small group of enthusiasts who called themselves the *Hanifs*, or 'those who turn away' (from polytheism). The *Hanifs* taught a strict monotheism and a consecration of life in preparation for the Day of Judgment. They denied the existence of tribal gods and preached that salvation was only possible on the basis of *islam*, submission, to the One, to Allah, to the true God who appeared to Ibrahim in historic times and created both Judaism and Christianity. The *Hanifs* held that Ibrahim (Abraham) was the first *hanif*; that his message had been lost through the ages; and that it was their task to reawaken this spirit through meditation, asceticism, and frequent prayer.

It is said that Muhammad liked to wander the caves in the mountains encircling Mecca, especially around Mt. Hira, to find some quiet, to meditate and reflect. According to tradition, it was in the foothills of Mt. Hira that Muhammad first heard the message sent by Allah, the Merciful, whose angel Gabriel (*Jibril*) appeared amidst the rocks and bade Muhammad speak the words that stand at the beginning of the *Qur'an*: "Recite (*iqra'*) in the name of the Lord who first made men from clots of blood." Several years after his first revelation, Muhammad began preaching a message of strict monotheism and surrender to God very like that taught by the *Hanifs*, also using as they did the Arabic term for surrender (*islam*) to indicate the new revelation he hoped to bring to his time and place. The record of his teaching, the *Qur'an* (recitation) was completed by 632.

This new message of *islam* was, like Christianity and the preaching of the *Hanifs*, a proselytizing faith. Muhammad's first convert to the new revelation was Khadijah, his wife, but he made few converts from the tribes of Mecca (some were moon-worshippers, some worshipped ancient gods such as Ishtar, some were Jews, some were Christians, and some were Parsis).

Muhammad's preaching put him in direct opposition to the ruling Quraysh dynasty. Responding to Muhammad's challenge, the Quraysh put the prophet's life in danger. Muhammad and his followers migrated to Medina (then known as Yathrib) in the year 622. This historic event, the *Hijra* (migration, journey) marks the beginning of the Islamic calendar (622 CE = 1 AH). Muhammad was welcomed into Yathrib and quickly became an arbiter and judge. The city was renamed in his honor – Madinat un-Nabi – City of the Prophet, shortened to Medina, "the City."

The feud is an important element of tribal society. Every adult male in a tribe has to be ready to take up arms in its defense; an attack on a member of the tribe has to be avenged by the entire group; also, any member of a tribe may be attacked in revenge for an offense committed by one of his tribe members. Tribal life, with its system of collective responsibility – also its strategy of surprise attacks on innocents based on a principle of collective guilt – is a dominant theme of cultural life in the Arabia. The prophet brings a new message to his people, but he is also caught up in its ancient customs. The cultural template of feuding is a kind of overlay at odds with the universalist ambitions of Islam.

Muhammad ruled in Medina eight years and, his party growing to more than 10,000 followers, he set upon Mecca at the head of a large army and conquered that city. During the next ten years he was many things: prophet and preacher and recipient of the *Qur'an*; general of a conquering army; head of state; also husband to 13 wives. In 632, a few months after returning to Mecca from a brief visit to Medina, where his preaching first struck a chord and began to be heard, Muhammad fell ill and died. By this time, the whole of the Arabian Peninsula had converted to Islam. By 750, Islam had spread to Spain, all of North Africa, and to the entire Middle East as far as the Indus river. The Turks (~1100), the Mongols (~1250), the Ottomans (~1350) and the Mughals (~1520) successively conquered and extended the House of God – *dar al Islam* – the growing Muslim empire. Converts from the Mughal epoch in India brought Islam as far east as Indonesia, which is today the world's most populous Muslim-majority country.

¬ the Five Pillars

Muhammad is the author or transcriber of the Muslim holy book, the *Qur'an*, a text that makes frequent reference both to the Hebrew scriptures, the *Torah*, and Christian writings, or *Gospels*, and also to the ancient Zarathustrian works, the *Avestas*. Muhammad calls all three of these peoples "the people of the Book" (*Ahl al-Kitab*). He encourages his followers to argue with this people and try to win them over to Islam, but also demands that his followers show courtesy and respect to everyone among "the people of the Book," except in the case that he does evil. Muhammad thought that he was bringing a special revelation for the Arabic-speaking peoples from the same God who first made a covenant with the children of Israel and also sent Jesus to the Christians. In the *Qur'an* he says "We believe in that which has been revealed to you. Our God and your God is One. To Him we submit" (29:46). Muhammad made appeals both to Jews and Christians to join him in his new revelation and did make converts from both groups. He also failed to make converts from both groups and shows some signs of anger towards them. He advises his followers not to make friends among these outsider peoples (5:51) and establishes the practice of imposing a religious tax or penalty (*jizya*), payable by everyone in the Caliphate who resists becoming a Muslim (9:29). He warns that those who do not submit will be consigned to hell (5:10); that they will drink boiling water and wear garments of fire (14:17, 22:19). There are passages that suggest a hostile attitude and passages that suggest a friendly one. "There can be no compulsion in religion" (meant to answer the question whether parents should force their children to convert to Islam)(29:46; 2:256) – but also "You must strike terror in the hearts of the unbelievers" (8:60). It is easy to point out discrepancies and contradictions – as with Judaism, as with Christianity – the record on these questions is mixed.

Jalaluddin Muhammad Akbar, called Akbar the Great, the Mughal emperor of India (1542-1605) ruled over a diverse population of Hindus, Buddhists, Muslims, Jains, Sikhs, Parsis, Jews, Christians, holy men, atheists and freethinkers of many kinds. Akbar ascended the throne at age 13 and immediately faced the problem of religious intolerance, martyrdom, racism and sectarian war. Thinking the problem through, he laid the foundations of the modern secular state and the ideal of the religious neutrality of the state.

He said "no man should be interfered with on account of what he thinks" and that "the reliance on tradition" leads to war. He held that civil society must rest on "the pursuit of reason." These are his exact words: "The pursuit of reason and rejection of traditionalism are so brilliantly patent as to be above the need of argument. If traditionalism made any sense, the prophets would merely have followed their own elders, and not come to us with new messages – yet all of them propose to teach us new things."

A recent writer, Ahmed al-Tayeb, who is also the president of Al-Azhar, the oldest university in the world (founded 975), has said on this point: "God created diverse peoples. Had he wanted to create a single *ummah* (religious community), He would have done so. But He chose to make them different. Every Muslim must fully understand this principle. A relationship based on conflict is futile" (*Egypt Today*, vol 26, no 2, February 2005).

At the same time, many Muslim writers call for a harsh attitude towards believers in other religious communities – even harsher against atheists and agnostics – citing passages in the *Qur'an* such as 3:85 ("If anyone desires a religion other than Islam, it will never be accepted of him, and in the hereafter such a one will be in the ranks of those who have lost all good"), 8:17 ("It is not us who slay the unbelievers but Allah, who tests believers by this trial"), and much of chapter 56 ("Whether you slay or are slain in Our cause you will wed with the Houris(celestial virgins))" and "you will eat and drink pleasantly for what you did" and "you will have boys like hidden pearls" and "you will find good things, beautiful ones, pure ones confined to the pavilions that man has not touched before, not even jinni"). The modern Egyptian writer Sayyid Qutb published his influential work *Milestones* in 1964 and touched off the current wave of fundamentalism that plays such a large role in Islam today.

These controversies seem very distant from the simple and powerful faith that Muhammad sought to introduce to a population of illiterate moon worshippers who still resisted the message of monotheism. Muhammad's original vision of Islam makes five, and only five, demands on believers. These are called "the five pillars" – the five sacred duties of every Muslim – the basis of the faith. They are:

The *shahadah* (the first pillar – the Prime assertion – the basic creed or tenet of submission (*islam*)). This is the profession of faith: "There is no god but Allah and Muhammad is his His prophet." ['ašhadu 'al-lā ilāha illā-llāhu wa 'ašhadu 'anna muḥammadan rasūlu-llāh]

The *salah* (prayer) is performed facing towards the Ka'ba in Mecca. Salah is intended to focus the mind on Allah; it is seen as a personal communication with Allah, expressing gratitude and worship. According to the *Qur'an*, we pray "to restrain ourselves from shameful and evil deeds." Salah is to be performed five times a day.

The *zakah* (alms-giving) is the practice of charity, and is obligatory for everyone who has something to give. It is considered to be a personal responsibility for Muslims to ease economic hardship for others and eliminate inequality.

The *sawm* (fasting during Ramadan) is considered a kind of repentance and extends to food, drink and sex. Muslims are also expected to refrain from violence, anger, greed, lust, obscenity and every other kind of dissolution not just during Ramadan, but throughout the year (the Jews' fast is called *Ashura*, the ancestor of Yom Kippur, the Day of Atonement; in Christianity this period is called *Lent*, and ends with the Easter feast).

The *hajj* (pilgrimage) to the holy city of Mecca is the fifth and last pillar. The pilgrim is required to walk around the Ka'ba seven times. The hajj is obligatory to all who are able-bodied and can afford it. It is a kind of re-enactment of Muhammad's escape from Mecca, transit to Medina, and triumphant return.

This creed makes no room for priests, clergy, saints or any sort of intercession between God and man. The believer fulfills his duty by obeying five rules: profession, prayer, almsgiving, fasting, and pilgrimage. To become a Muslim, a non-Muslim must repeat the *shahadah,* in Arabic, three times in front of witnesses. There are beliefs, and if a person has questions, there are traditions of interpretation.

It is noteworthy that in pre-Islamic times – in the *Jahiliyyah* or 'time of ignorance' – the state of society in which the Arabs found themselves before the revelation of the holy *Qur'an* – Mecca was an open city. Pilgrims arrived from all over the world, speaking many languages and following many different religious teachings. There are traveller's accounts about the city in many languages from ancient times. Mecca today is a closed city, surrounded by signposts that read "No entry for non-Muslims."

The *Qur'an* (or Koran) is written in Arabic and divided into chapters (*suras, surahs*) and verses (*ayah*, plural *ayat*). The text has approximately 80,000 words, 114 suras and 6200 ayat. These suras are arranged by length – longest to shortest. All but two suras begin with the words "In the name of the merciful, the compassionate." The *Qur'an* notes that it is written in Arabic (sura 12.1). However, scholars have discovered 275 words of foreign origin in this text – e.g. from Hebrew, Aramaic, Greek and Syriac.

The contemporary scholar Ibn Warraq notes that, beyond matters of language, the *Qur'an* includes borrowings from several traditions, including talmudic Judaism, apocryphal Christianity, the Samaritans, Zoroastrianism, and Pre-Islamic Arabia (*The Origins of the Koran*, 1998).

There are two accepted versions of the text – one from Asim of Kufa and one from Nafi of Medina (both from the ninth century). The latter is used mainly in Africa.

Robert of Ketton translated the *Qur'an* into Latin in 1143. Ricoldo da Monte Croce wrote a text called *Against the Saracen Scriptures*, which translates much of the original text again (1243). Martin Luther translated this book into German (1542). Many Western scholars have written about the text. A few are: Juan of Segovia, Nicholas of Cusa, Pico della Mirandola, Guillaume Postel, Adam Olearius, Jean Chardin. George Sale translated the text into English in 1734. There is a long and respectful tradition of Koranic study in the West. Islam is not a new discovery in Western Civilization – it is a continuing theme in it – not alien, but intimate.

Part of the difficulty of interpreting the text is that in some passages Muhammad is the speaker and in others – most – God is the speaker through his angel, Jibril. Muhammad asks God a question in sura 114; Muhammad is angry with a man and curses his wife in sura 111. Muhammad also seems to refer to the natural world in a way that God would not: "I swear by the afterglow of sunset, and the night and all it enshrouds, and by the moon when she is at her full" (84.16). God is often referred to in the third person. Angels sometimes speak for themselves (19.64).

Ibn Warraq credits Islam with moral advances in its teachings about generosity, respect for parents, and the importance of free will (18.28: "The truth is from your Lord. Let him then who will, believe; and let him who will, be an unbeliever"). He also observes moral decline, e.g. intolerance, the call to violence and murder, lack of equality for women and for non-Muslims, the acceptance of slavery, barbaric punishments and "contempt for human reason." He documents the change in Islam also seen in other episodes of religious history, from traditions of tribal ritual to an emphasis on belief.

The philosopher Al-Kindi (writing around the year 830) criticizes the text as "jumbled together, full of discrepancies and contradictions, and thus not at all worthy of being called a revelation from heaven." This comment goes to the issue raised in all interpretation of sacred writing, e.g. in Judaism and in Christianity, whether speech is figurative or factual; between those who look for poetry, and those who demand obedience.

¬ Some Muslim symbols

The color green, symbolizing nature and life (the inhabitants of paradise wear garments of fine silk dyed green, *Qur'an* 76:21), the crescent and star, the word 'Allah' in Arabic script, the *Shahadain* (the words of the first pillar, the *shahadah* in Arabic script), the *Kalima-e-shahadah* (the Islamic creed made into a geometric emblem), images of the Ka'ba, images of an eight-pointed star.

¬ Some Muslim beliefs

The Mahdi. Approaching the Last Day (*yaum al qiyama*), the Hour (*al sa'ah*) and the end of time, when Israphel (Raphael) will blow the trumpet sounding the end, a man from the family of the prophet will appear. The redeemer, the Mahdi, will rule of the earth for a period of years, and finally rid the world of wrongdoing, injustice and tyranny.

Last Day, Judgment and Resurrection. On the Last Day, when the world will come to an end, the souls of the dead will be resurrected and face judgment. Those who are condemned will burn in hell (*jahannam*) and experience a fire in their hearts; those who are blessed will enjoy the pleasures of paradise (*jannah*) and enjoy a divine bliss in their hearts. The Mahdi and Jesus (*Isa*), who play important roles in the endtime, will convene the judgment. Faith alone, or certitude about the unseen (*iman*), is sufficient for salvation.

Qadar. The Arabic term *qadar* indicates destiny, fate, decree. Human beings have free will and thus bear responsibility for their actions, whether to their shame or credit. Nothing they do is preordained, and Islam has no concept of predestination, or divine decree in this sense. The idea is rather that from a standpoint outside of time, God already knows how a life unfolds and has already written it down on the Preserved Tablet (*al-lauh al-mahfuz*). Thus the expression "it is written" does not indicate that the outcome was decreed in advance. Thus divine omniscience and human freedom are made compatible.

The Nabi. Allah has sent prophets (*nabi*) to every nation to provide mankind with guidance. The fundamental message of all prophets is the same: God is one; beware the judgment to come; the good life is rewarded with bliss, sin is punished by hellfire (*Qur'an*, 16:36).

In one sense we can talk about ideology as the worldview in which a faith tradition is born and in which it has its life. In another sense the term 'ideology' fits the circumstance in which a faith is transformed into a political program. Both these senses apply to Islam.

Regarding the first, much of pre-Islamic Arabia is preserved in Islam and re-appropriated in the new context. All five pillars continue practices originating in the *Jahiliyyah* or 'time of ignorance' – e.g., the important place accorded the shrine of the Ka'ba for prayer and as a site of pilgrimage – in this sense Muhammad is a reformer who finds new ways to reenergize and interpret long-held beliefs and practices of his community. Thus he says "God has established for you [the Arabs] the same religion enjoined on Noah, on Abraham, on Moses, and on Jesus" (*Qur'an*, 42:13). Islam appears in a social, spiritual and cultural world – a tradition – gradually evolving out of moon worship and culminating in monotheism.

Islam becomes an 'ideology' in the latter sense, as a political program, at the outset of its history, in its developing creation of *shari'a* or Islamic law. The *Qur'an* and traditions such as *hadith* contain a vast array of laws, held to be sacred, regulating most of the details of public and private life. It sets down rules governing charity, marriage, orphans, fasting, gambling, vanity, infidelity, polygamy, incest, divorce, modesty, censorship, inheritances, prostitution, alcohol, collecting interest, proper education, family life, and female dress. Yet if a law is *sacred*, changing it risks heresy. Various historical movements, beginning with Hanifism itself and culminating in traditions like Wahhabism and Qutbism and newer forms of Islamism and Islamic fundamentalism, seem bent on outdoing one another in calling for a return to the purity of the original doctrine, and for rejecting pretended improvements. The British-American orientalist Bernard Lewis writes that the pattern of calling for a return to the pure doctrine emerges from Islam's rapid conversion from spiritual revelation to military program. "Islam is a military religion, with fanatical warriors, engaged in spreading their faith and their law by armed might," in which warriors show their prowess as much by the severity of their principles as by horsemanship and skill in wielding a sword. Weber described Islam as a "warrior religion" and Samuel Huntington said that Islam is "steeped in blood."

The *Qur'an* wrestles with the problem of doctrine becoming more severe, e.g. at 2:106: "Whenever we abrogate a verse or cause it to be forgotten, we exchange it with a better one; don't you know that God can do anything?" At a certain point in questioning, where contradictions appear and responses like these, which proclaim infallibility and at the same time a kind of gradual revelation that appears to overturn previous revelation, the tradition has developed the formula of *bila kayfa*, which translates as "don't ask why."

Islam is often thought to be the most perfectly monotheistic work among the three Abrahamic traditions. There is no god but God and Muhammad is his prophet.

Islam offers in a new concentrated form the tension in Abrahamic faiths compressing many different localities and cultural differences and submerged personalities down into one compact form. It makes us raise the question: why monotheism? – why one and not many? – why reduce all gods into one?

Commentators in all three Abrahamic traditions argue that monotheism brings a kind of order into the welter of "primitive" gods. Zwi Werblowsky, a scholar of comparative religion at Hebrew University in Jerusalem, argues that polytheism does not actually disappear under the new order of monotheistic worship, but instead the old gods are "bedeviled" (they are turned into demons) or become angels or ministering spirits. Islam is fierce monotheism but also refers to five kinds of spirits (Jann, Jinn, Shaitans, Ifrits, and Marids). The text also refers to Iblis (Satan) and his sons Tir, al-Awar, Sut, Dasim and Zalambur.

The American novelist and playwright Gore Vidal (1925-2012) attacks the idea of monotheism as "the great unmentionable evil at the center of our culture." He argues that this conception is anti-human, anti-woman, anti-freedom, a break on emotional and moral progress and a harsh dictator, jealous and demanding of total obedience. Totalitarianism is the only politics it recognizes, because any other threatens its authority. "One God, one king, one Pope, one master in the factory, one father-leader in the family…"

Do we understand God better as one person – Jahve – or better as Eloh, Yah, Mot, Magen, and Sab – or as the Trinity – or, as the *Avestas* describe, as a duality, Ahura Mazda and Angra Maynu – and why is the number associated with God even important?

We can perhaps ask this same question about ourselves. The Nobel laureate in economics Amartya Sen makes the point that he can only really count as *one person* though a violent suppression of his manyness – Asian, American, British, Hindu, Secularist – and he takes on the project of keeping his view of himself complex, rather than allowing himself to be flattened out into one aggressive ethnic identity or religious identity or national identity or political or cultural identity. He argues that it is an individual's responsibility to keep watch over himself and not allow himself to be cut down to *one* thing or one loyalty. This is perhaps a way of getting at one side of the question.

Schizophrenia or other dissociative conditions result from failures in psychological integration, individuation and gradual consolidation of the different aspects of the personality into a mature adult – *not* making the transit from persona to ego to self, in Jung's terminology, or what Erikson calls the stages of psychosocial development – thus *not* being able to resolve manyness down to one stable form. The analogy with society seems to point in the same direction. "A house divided cannot stand" as we read in *Mark* (3:25), and as Abraham Lincoln reflected in 1858: "A house divided against itself cannot stand. I believe this government cannot endure, permanently, half slave and half free. … It will become all one thing or all the other." These ideas are perhaps ways of getting at the other side of the question.

One God, many gods; one self, many voices; one people, many factions. The transformation from manyness to oneness can be a flattening-out and a conformism that suppresses complexity. It can also be a resolution that gradually brings order to a chaotic mess.

Whether *one* is greater or less than *many* is a question without any useful general answer. We have to understand something about the context. A patient who has banished a part of himself that he cannot face, and who is thus cut down to a fragment of himself, is 'unified' under duress. A people cannot endure by enslaving another people. Better to be *more* in such cases, rather than less. Yet multiple personality disorder is an opposite example, or a political constitution for a *democratic* state that is also a *religious* state. Better to be *less* in such cases, rather than more.

Everything is one reality and the fundamental character of the universe is unity; or there are irreducibly many realities and the universe is fundamentally plural.

There is some common ground in psychology, religious studies and in metaphysics where we are looking at problems that emerge with conflicting elements, and where it is uncertain whether monism, i.e. the dedication to a principle of unity, or pluralism, which normalizes variety, represents a better solution.

However – reaching back to the beginning of this reflection – we see that monism and plurality are "essentially political discourses," to use Karen Armstrong's phrase – the stakes in this conflict have to do with the self and how people look at themselves, how to conceive the state and perhaps even the universe, but ultimately *whether we are left to this problem ourselves* or whether we should cede authority to some group or someone else *to resolve this problem for us*.

The Abrahamic traditions are alike in offering conflicting messages on this issue. All three celebrate freedom and all three claim a prerogative for dictating what is so. In Islam this tension is encapsulated in sura 2 and sura 8: "There can be no compulsion in religion" (2:256) and "You must strike terror in the hearts of the unbelievers" (8:60).

¬ Religious freedom

Islam was once a vast empire stretching from Africa to India that promoted learning of all kinds and preserved the heritage of ancient Greece.

We know something about Socrates and Plato and Aristotle today largely because of Arab scholars – Aristotle was Arustutal, Plato was Aflatun, Socrates was Suqrat. Al-Kindi (800-866), al-Razi, known as Rhazes (865-925), al-Farabi (died circa 950), Ibn Sina, known as Avicenna (980-1037), and Ibn Rushd, known as Averroes (1126-1198) all made pioneering contributions to philosophy, as well as medicine and scientific research. Omar Khayyam, whose dates are 1048-1122, is among the great mathematicians and poets in human history. Al-Biruni, writing in the eleventh century, Rashid Al-Din, in the thirteenth, and Ibn Khaldun, writing in the fourteenth century, all made pioneering contributions to history; the Christian historian Arnold Toynbee called Khaldun's book *Muqaddimah* "the greatest work of its kind that has ever yet been created by any mind in any time or place." From its inception in the seventh century and for hundreds of years afterwards, Islam flourished.

Crucially, this impressive success came from *openness* – from a curiosity about other peoples and an attempt to learn from them – the very word "philosophy" in Arabic is an import from the West (*falsafah* (philosophy), *faylsuf* (philosopher), *tafalsafa* (to philosophize)). Islamic civilization at its zenith shows curiosity, confidence, gathering knowledge and building for the future – the opposite of fear, despair of worldly things, superstition and demonizing whatever is unfamiliar.*

Another way to see into the power of Arabic culture at its zenith is to shine a light on its impact on Western history, for example by looking look at words in the English language that derive from Arabic roots. All these English words derive from the Arabic language:

Admiral	Assassin	Hazard	Sherbet
Alcohol	Basil	Magazine	Sofa
Alcove	Carafe	Mask	Syrup
Algebra	Caraway	Masquerade	Talc
Algorithm	Coffee	Monsoon	Tambourine
Amber	Cotton	Myrrh	Tariff
Arsenal	Ghoul	Saffron	Zenith
Artichoke	Giraffe	Sequin	Zero

Christian Europe suppressed or destroyed most of its share of the Greek cultural inheritance as pagan heresy. Justinian (emperor 527-65) suppressed the schools of Athens and banned nearly all ancient learning. At the same time, Arabia preserved this heritage and significantly added to it. Thus St. Thomas (1225-1274) refers to the Arabs as "a bestial people living in the desert," yet his exalted world of divine order is largely a Greek world preserved by Arab scholars.

The Yale professor of Near eastern languages Franz Rosenthal writes: "the Arabian environment in which Islam had its roots was in contact with Hellenistic civilization. This generated in Islam a certain affinity with classical culture. ... This effort was *not* influenced by the negative motive of undermining Islam or doing away with its way of life or fundamental beliefs. On the contrary, the principal aim of all but a very few Muslims concerned with the Greek heritage was to breathe new life into their religion. ... It was significant for the development of modern Europe that the coming of Islam made final the break with classical antiquity in the West and that in subsequent centuries Europe was confronted with the material prosperity of Muslim civilization and considered it an ideal worth either emulating or fighting" (*The Classical Heritage in Islam*, 1965)

This contrast between openness and devotion to learning, and close-mindedness and harsh censorship, has been reversed in more recent history – Islam is in retreat and Europe is advancing – the question being, why? How did this happen? What happened in the West and what did not happen in Islamic culture?

In a word, the difference is 'Enlightenment' – we live in a world shaped by the Enlightenment – capitalism, democracy, the nation-state, and the Enlightenment arose together in Western history. Thinkers have proposed a variety of narratives explaining the causes of this change in Europe and its absence in other places, e.g. the Church's role in shaping ideas about marriage; feudal property laws; urbanization; a growing secular presence – especially in education – to counteract narrowly religious education; the increasing role of science and technology in society; and humanism.

The historian and economist James Q. Wilson (1931-2012) offers this view: "In an old world where knowledge came from libraries, and scientific experiments were rare, freedom was not so important. But in the new world, knowledge and all that it can produce come from the sharp challenge of competing ideas tested by standards of objective evidence. In Istanbul, center of the Islamic world, Muslims printed no book until 1729, and thereafter only occasionally. By contrast, the West became a world in which books were published starting three centuries earlier and where doubt and self-criticism were all-important...The central question is not why freedom of conscience has failed to come to much of Islam but instead why it came at all to the West. Though Westerners will conventionally assign great weight to the arguments made by the defenders of freedom, such as the ideas of Milton, Locke, Erasmus, and Spinoza, these were probably not decisive – though they were important – ...What made religious toleration and freedom of conscience possible in England was not theoretical argument but political necessity. It was necessary, first in England and later in America and much of Europe, because rulers trying to govern nations could not do so without granting freedom to people of different faiths. In the words of the historian of science Herbert Butterfield, toleration was "the last policy that remained when it had proved impossible to go on fighting any longer.""

Kenneth Clark's great work *Civilization* claims that "the great thaw" in Europe – which set a process in motion that led to the Enlightenment – began around the year 1100. Europe at this time was still dominated by tribal warfare. There was little or no national history or stable government. European nations had not yet made governments in which one set of leaders could be replaced, in some orderly fashion, with a new set. The advent of democracy, changes in economic life that created capitalism, pressure against religious fanaticism, the printing of books, changes in the status of women in society, changes in marriage and property laws, a spirit of empirical inquiry and scientific experimentation, respect for diversity and a culture of toleration were still a very long way off. These accomplishments take up approximately one thousand years of Western history.

America in the seventeenth and eighteenth centuries had many religions and some tolerance for dissenting views, but the colonists did not face the problem of religious freedom until they tried to form a national union. The thirteen colonies, in order to become a nation, had to decide how to manage the extraordinary diversity of the country. The colonists did so largely by writing a constitution that was silent on the question of religion, except to ban any "religious test" as a requirement for holding federal office. Jefferson said that the government had to "erect a wall between church and state." For this reason American politics, like its European model, has been a largely secular matter. This is not an accident. Politics made it *necessary* to establish a truly free conscience.

Iraq, Syria, Saudi Arabia, the United Arab Emirates, Lebanon, Iran, Egypt and the other great nations of the Muslim world are today roughly where England stood in the eleventh century. Democracy, equality for women, freedom of expression and a free press, a critical questioning of traditional institutions and customs and morals, a confidence in reason and in the individual, optimism, pragmatism – also a sense of political necessity to establish a free conscience – we have only the first signs of these things and their fruition remains a very long way off.

Iraq was once the center of great ancient civilizations. It was conquered by the Mongols and the Ottoman Turks, then occupied by the British during the First World War. It became a League of Nations protectorate; it was torn apart by internal wars among the Shia, Sunnis, and Kurds; then it was divided by military coups. Then it waged a decade-long war with Iran that left brutal dictatorships on both sides. Syria, a land with often-changing borders, has been occupied by Hittites, Egyptians, Assyrians, Greeks, Romans, Mongols, Turks – even by the French. After Syria became a self-governing nation in 1944, it was, like Iraq, divided by a series of military coups, repeated wars with Israel, and then, in 1991, with Iraq. Lebanon, which was once part of Syria, became an independent nation at the close of World War II, but soon fell under Syrian domination again – under which it is still struggling at present –

a land divided by tribal warfare – Marionites, Druze, Sunni, Shia, Kurds, Armenians and many other groups – traversing what seems like an endless history of wars and economic collapses.

Despite all this fighting and struggle among rival parties for political control, to date no *political* will has emerged to create a democratic state and a free conscience. Most of the basic conditions that lead to enlightenment are still far off. The main obstacle to this progress appears to be theocracy itself.

Theocracy creates its rule of sacred law, governing virtually every aspect of daily life. This is exactly what Justinian forced upon the Roman world around the year 550. This practice was *not* followed at the same time nor for centuries after in the great cities of the Middle East. Today, effectively, there is no separation of church and state in the Islamic world – save in a few places, such as Turkey, where it is under severe attack – and thus it appears that Islam and the West are trading mistakes.

In Islam there is an official religion and thus a closed market for religion. In the West there is no official religion and thus an open market for religion. The West reconciled religion and freedom, and did so by making the individual the focus of society. Islam elevated religion above the value of freedom, and did so by making the individual subordinate to society.

This is a struggle between cultures – between values of freedom and community – between liberty and piety – between progress and sanctity. Yet we can also see the same struggle *within* every such culture – between personal liberty and family values. The same cultural and historical forces are at work in all societies and, as William James held, institutional religions are cultural and historical artifacts. This means that the contest between cultures, and the contest inside culture, is *not* the crucial factor. Conflict is a given and the attempt to suppress it will always fail. The determining factor is the nature of the institutions in which the conflict is carried on. We can only be human if our institutions let us.

Institutions can enslave or liberate; they can lord over us or free up a space for living. But even in the best of circumstances and with liberating, democratic institutions – institutions that do not resolve our problems for us but instead create a forum in which we can do this work for ourselves – the trick is to keep finding ways to prevent these institutions from hardening and dying. Religion is likely a human universal, but freedom is not.

¬ The Abrahamic faiths

For most of its history, the Roman Empire practiced a policy of universal toleration, often protecting faiths that they despised and believers who despised them. Gibbon's *The Decline and Fall of the Roman Empire* describes the religious harmony of the ancient world under this policy. Gibbon also tries to understand how this humane consensus fell apart and what it means.

"A single people refused to join in this common intercourse of mankind." The Jews, enslaved first by the Egyptians, then by the Assyrian, then the Persian Empire, held fast to their stark worship, and refused to associate their faith with "the elegant mythology of the Greeks." Gibbon claims that the Jews first introduced the "spirit of inflexible and intolerant zeal" into the West; that this same spirit in Christianity derives from the Jews; that Christianity taught this spirit to the world; and that this same claim of *exclusive possession of the truth* continues and is made even more extreme in Islam. Gibbon attributes the success of exclusionary faith to several causes: to the pure and austere morals of great leaders in these causes; the union and discipline of their followers; the belief in miracles; and, especially, the promise of a future life (ch. 15). Whatever it may have been previously, religion becomes preoccupied with the happiness of a *future* life. And this idea is fatal to the exercise of reason. It "resolves every question by an article of faith, and condemns the infidel or skeptic to eternal flame" (ch. 40). To accept this tyranny over our minds, this distraction from our earthly business, this subjection to superstition, can only be due to indolence, servility and weakness of character (ch. 38, *General Observations*).

Christianity began as a persecuted sect in the early empire. But its promise of a future life won the day. Constantine's (274-337) conversion of the empire to Christianity (Edict of Milan, 313) initially took the form of a renewed policy of toleration, yet gradually required the active suppression of old forms of worship. His successor Julian the Apostate attempted and failed to reverse this course by returning the empire to the Olympian religion.

Gibbon judges these changes harshly, but he is of two minds about their ultimate significance. During the same period in which the splendid works of classical antiquity were "eclipsed by a cloud of ignorance," vast numbers of people were lifted out of their "original barbarism." As religious zeal spreads around the world, so do great discoveries in the arts, technology and commerce. "We may therefore acquiesce in the pleasing conclusion that every age of the world has increased and still increases the real wealth, the happiness, the knowledge, and perhaps the virtue, of the human race" (ch. 38, *General Observations*).

Historians since Gibbon continue this debate and describe the triumph of monotheism oppositely: as the victory of freedom over slavery and of insight over superstition; as the victory of barbarism over classicism and religion over philosophy. It is said that the pagan world was a shame-culture and that the believing world is a guilt-culture: in the former, the worst thing that can happen to a person, the overt sanction, is 'what people will say,' i.e. humiliation, being mocked, or losing face; in a guilt-culture the worst thing that can happen to a person is an uneasy conscience, i.e. to be divided against oneself, to be at fault, to find no peace. It is said that the pagan world was a results-culture and that the believing world is an intentions-culture: in the former, what matters is that one succeeds, whatever one's intentions – thus forgetting one's duty is as shameful as refusing it; in the latter, what matters is one's intentions, whatever the outcome – thus manslaughter is less culpable than murder, because one didn't 'mean' it, because it was involuntary. The change from shame to guilt, and from results to intentions, shows a new psychological awareness – a more accurate view of human nature – but also ushers in an epoch in which people are held less responsible for themselves, and more the plaything of larger forces.

The transformation from polytheism to monotheism brings with it a rise in asceticism, mysticism, and pessimism; a gradual but very evident loss of self-confidence, hope, planning for the future, and trust in normal human effort; an impatience with *mere inquiry*, merely gradual progress and uncertain results; fear of subjecting cherished ideas to scrutiny; a demand instead for *absolute truth* and infallible revelation; also an indifference to the welfare of the state, because the state is merely 'terrestrial' or this-worldly; and thus a conversion of the soul to God. This is why the state of society from the end of antiquity to the beginnings of the Renaissance is called 'the Dark Ages.'

It is important to distinguish Judaism, Christianity, and Islam as faiths from the political causes to which they have been put in history and presently. Orwell, for example, imagines a future in which human beings are tortured to the point where they no longer can see the truth. Huxley imagines a future in which people are drugged to the point where they don't care about the truth. But Spinoza discovers another danger – that of religion, rather than pain or pleasure, when it becomes the instrument of tyranny. "In despotic statecraft, the supreme and essential mystery is to hoodwink the subjects, and mask the fear, which keeps them down, with the specious garb of religion, so that men may fight as bravely for slavery as for safety, and count it not shame but highest honor to risk their blood and lives for the vainglory of a tyrant" (*Theologico-Political Treatise*, 1665).

Abrahamic monotheism offers this complex legacy of knowledge or ignorance, freedom or tyranny: of fanaticism and progress at once.

+

The 'three ways' of Confucianism, Taoism, and Buddhism are depicted as a quiet conversation. Judaism, Christianity and Islam are three different ways – three ardent causes – there is little quiet between them – and much change.

¬ The Great Mother

The archeology of North Africa, Europe, the Middle East, the Fertile Crescent and India is a seamless whole and points to an epochal change occurring in human history within the fourth and third millennia BCE. This is the advent of the Bronze Age. The most accepted and consistently debated explanation for this change is called the 'Kurgan Hypothesis' – so named for the northerners from beyond the Black Sea, who spoke an early form of Indo-European, who traveled south after 4400 BCE, and who conquered every people they met. The Kurgans were a patriarchy.

On a wider scale the important event here is not the Kurgan invasion but the advent of farming. Agricultural societies destroyed their Stone Age predecessors in the ancient Near East, but also in ancient China and Mesoamerica. The consensus of historians, developed over several centuries of work, is that patriarchy seems to occur at a certain point in all early agrarian societies.

There are as many common characteristics of the predecessor societies as there are for the victors. The victors are warlike peoples, weapons-makers, sun worshippers, with rigid caste systems, who celebrate the birth of a boy over that of a girl. The predecessor societies are matriarchal or matricentric or matrilineal, moon-worshippers, egalitarian, who celebrate the birth of a daughter more than a son, and whose primary deity was female. The worship of The Great Mother is connected to a mother-kinship system and ancestor worship in which the sexual identity of the head of the family has a divine counterpart.

Authors such as Sir James Frazer, Max Müller, F.M. Cornford, Jane Ellen Harrison, Marija Gimbutas, Robert Graves, Rianne Eisler, Gerda Lerner, Merlin Stone, among many others, have tried to fill in the details of life in ancestral times when religion centered around female cult-figures. The most important finding of all this work goes to the root concept of religion itself – *religare*, to tie or bind; to be tied to something; to belong – that the mother-child bond stands at the origin of worship. All persons claim a matrilineal descent to the common ancestress, the Great Mother, the foundation of cultural and personal identity.

Farming implies urbanization, close proximity and competition, and technological changes of the Bronze Age run parallel with linguistic, economic and social upheavals, as well as religious change. The stable, egalitarian, matricentric cultures of the Stone Age were succeeded by the patriarchy, and the Female principle became an undercurrent in overt worship of weather-gods and warriors; the old woman is succeeded by the brahmin, the seer, prophet or priest. Worship of the Great Mother is suppressed from this point on in the history of religious culture, and the Father God is ascendant. Waves of female-centered spirituality (e.g. of the *Shekina*, of the White Goddess, or of Mary) remain in the undercurrent; the overtone is God the Father. But the Female principle is far older, as attested by widespread finds of 'goddess' figures, even among the earliest traces of human culture.

¬ The Great Forgetting

Whales and dolphins risk their lives to save injured companions; killer whales follow sick companions into shallow water and beach themselves with them; elephants attempt to revive slain comrades and even refuse to leave them behind; chimpanzees rush to defend a weak combatant; chimpanzees console the sick and injured by putting their arm around them; chimpanzees who receive favors from others, such as the sharing of food, yet who fail afterwards to act in kind, produce indignation in their companions, and are in turn shunned and attacked. These and innumerable like examples illustrate the truth that the same process of natural selection that has produced existence struggle and vicious competition, yet also symbiosis and sharing responses, likewise shapes human behavior, and thus also human morality and religion. It is typical of mammals to play and to nurture, to trade and to repay, and such principles as reciprocity, mutual obligation, and punishment of transgression are as much a part of animal behavior as they are of human behavior. Darwin first pursued this line in *The Expression of the Emotions*. The same theme has been developed more recently in works like Alexander's *The Biology of Moral Systems* and de Waal's *Origins of Right and Wrong* and Bonner's *The Evolution of Culture in Animals*. Bonner, for example, does not think that culture involves genetic inheritance or, therefore, Darwinian evolution by natural selection, but that the ability of any animal to create culture is a direct product of just such an evolutionary mechanism. Darwin thinks that he can find *precursors* to the desire to worship in the behavior of many animal species, and thinkers like Alexander and Bonner follow this course. This opens a line of inquiry outside of studies of human life that offers a much broader perspective than the one followed in these pages.

Even within the perspective adopted here – studies of *human* life – there is an obvious and startling error so overwhelming that it is almost always overlooked. This is what the writer Daniel Quinn aptly named the "great forgetting." The "great forgetting" is the simple idea that when we think about religion and culture and history we confine ourselves to the period beginning with the late Stone Age, as if human beings did not exist prior to the advent of farming, as if the world were empty of humans until the peoples of modern culture made their appearance only a few thousand years ago. Quinn also notes another odd fact, which he says is among the most amazing occurrences in human history. For nearly all of the expanse of time beginning in the Neolithic epoch, all thinkers and guides of cultural traditions held that the life of human beings on this planet amounted to a short span of time, measured in thousands, if not hundreds of years. When the great thinkers of the seventeenth, eighteenth, nineteenth and twentieth centuries were finally compelled to acknowledge that this assumption rests on a profoundly important error, *absolutely nothing happened.* Traditions continued – even though their foundations were laid during the great forgetting – their foundations were not shaken but instead persisted unchanged. Thus "the great remembering" was "turned into a nonevent."

Quinn – like great predecessors such as Frazer, Tylor, Evans-Pritchard, Montagu, Lévy-Bruhl, Boas, Braudel, Radcliffe-Brown, Lévy-Strauss and many others – wants to draw our attention to the fact that human beings have moved outwards from their African homeland for more than a hundred thousand years – by some accounts, for *millions* of years – and have since reached every corner of the world. Thus religion-making and culture-making and history-making are unimaginably ancient and have many more significances than are usual and familiar.

What do the Tepe Sialk paintings (~9000 BCE) tell us about religion, culture, and history? What do the cave-paintings of Altamira and Lascaux (~26,000 BCE) tell us? What do the 'goddess' figures tell us, some from "Upper Paleolithic" times (~45,000 BCE)? But all of these are *late* creations of the human species.

Before Neolithic times, before there was farming, before the beginnings of the historical world, there was the *tribe* – the tribal village, the tribal law, the tribal elders, the tribal lore – before the great change from village to city and hunting to farming and tribute to global commerce. In the present world there is an awesome force pulling society backwards to the life of the tribe – religious fanaticism – and an equally awesome force pulling away from the tribe towards a planetary society and consciousness – global capitalism. This division is the most evident and troubling fact of world history and raises *the* question of our study.

There is always the danger that a given culture will equate itself with humanity. If a culture remains isolated and never encounters a competitor, it *is* humanity – but in our time this isolation is rare. Yet even *within* culture there is the danger that one voice will shout down all the others. Religion is bound up with powerful and extraordinary people who become leaders and spiritual guides – someone in the culture who is accounted to be especially wise. The sage or shaman may be an elder, the ancient one or great mother. The sage may be a rainmaker, storyteller, musician, herbalist or poet – a magician, wizard or healer – someone who reads signs, who keeps the law, who preserves the history of the people – the prophet who calls us to prayer. Yet religion is also bound up with collective life, and may be accounted as the spontaneous worldview embedded in language and culture. Folklore, poetry, myths, rituals, pithy sayings, proverbs and tales, taboos, moral ideas, turns and structures of language show the mentality of a people. In this sense religion is the world outlook, the framework or communal consensus – what everyone believes. There is a belief-system implicit in everyday talk and lived practices. The 'science of religion' studies the web of belief – the record of what is accepted by the whole community, even when beliefs contradict one another – and the web of relations – every kind of relation people can have with one another, whether of respect or humiliation, loyalty or betrayal.

Some writers argue that exploring religion from the perspective of ethnological study results in parochialism and cultural particularism, so that we have to give up the project of reaching outside local belief to get at the truth. Others argue: if you are part of the tribe, then you speak the tribal language, you are part of the tribal culture – thus it is pointless to talk about reaching *beyond* anything.

Perhaps the best argument for the tribe is that it has lasted – perhaps for a stretch of time measured in *millions* of years. Every religious tradition carries the insignia of an ancient tribe. Interestingly, Quinn argues in *The Story of B* that belonging to a tribe has never inspired religion – religion comes from *losing* the tribe – not fitting in, getting lost along the way, becoming separated, being alone. Without the tribe, we are lost, and look for rescue. Thus Quinn preaches what he calls "antisalvation" – which is, roughly, a return to the tribe – then there is nothing to search for.

Others argue: no single voice comprehends the whole of culture; thus it is a good thing that there are many cultures; and this result gives us a kind of foundation in the human condition for uncertainty and wakefulness; for not remaining in one place or in one fixed idea, but searching.

+

Religion as signaling belonging and religion as a search for meaning – tribalism and religious fanaticism vs. globalism and laissez-faire capitalism – religion as the charismatic figure and religion as the spontaneous worldview – these are highlights from the source material to try to explain and understand.

Religion is ancient. Human beings from tens of thousands of years ago worshipped by dance and sacrifice. At a certain point in history, worship became belief and action for a cause. This is a main finding from the sources.

Religion activates identity. It becomes a way of bolstering an insecure identity. It can also dethrone pride and inspire a loving humility. This is part of the source material: the psychology of ignorance and of understanding.

Religion brings peace but also is a cause of war – or an excuse for war – religions are cultural artifacts, historical forces, traditions that claim us or that we explicitly choose – religion as zealotry and religion as illumination. The philosophy of religion tries to survey all this ground and get to know it.

(8) explaining religion

I present below four approaches to religion, which interpret it as instinctive behavior. These are: the account from evolutionary biology; neurotheology; the claim that religion is a human universal; and structuralism. I present four approaches that interpret religion as learned behavior: hermeneutics; the theory of language-games; the economic account of religion; and game theory. I present one account according to which religion is expressly chosen. This is from Paul Tillich's 1957 work *The Dynamics of Faith*. This list is not meant to be comprehensive, any more than the above survey of religious life is comprehensive – both are meant to be represent- ative and to show enough of the phenomena to raise the essential questions. Working through the outlines of the history of religions, seeing some of the diversity of culture in religious life, examining arguments meant to help us understand religion, and bringing all these voices into communication with each other, we begin to model philosophy as enlightened humanity in conversation with itself. Philosophy today looks for this enlarged perspective and a truth-content that survives a planetary scrutiny.

evolutionary biology

The philosopher Daniel Dennett claims that Darwin's idea of natural selection is "the single best idea that anyone has ever had" (*Breaking the Spell: Religion as a Natural Phenomenon*, 2006).

Darwin conceived natural selection to be a process by which favorable heritable traits become more common in successive generations of a population of reproducing organisms, and unfavorable heritable traits become less common. Natural selection acts on the *phenotype*, or the observable characteristics of an organism, such that individuals with favorable phenotypes are more likely to survive and reproduce than those with less favorable phenotypes. If these phenotypes have a genetic basis, then the *genotype* associated with the favorable phenotype will increase in frequency in the next generation. Combined with ideas about mutation, fitness, selection and variation, the theory of natural selection provides the primary explanation for adaptive evolution.

Useful adaptations that equip organisms to thrive in some or other environment tend to be preserved in the struggle for existence. Applying this thinking to religion, religion may be taken to represent a *useful* adaptation that has persisted because it lends its adherents some or other important advantage in the life struggle. Religion on this account is a collection of beliefs and behaviors that changes individuals or brings people together and coordinates their activities. A religion succeeds in the struggle for existence – e.g. against competing religious offers – because its creed helps adherents adapt to environmental challenges. Thus for example religion provides a kind of welfare state and common front against famine, natural disasters, disease, poverty, social disintegration, economic failure, enslavement or war or other taxing changes in the environment.

On this kind of assumption, Christianity (for example) outgrew its status as an illicit mystery cult and grew into a world religion – whereas competitor cults of the time such as Mithraism, Gnosticism, Manichaeism, Mandaeism (among others), after initial expansion, all ultimately died out – arguing that Christianity was better adapted to the changing world of the early Empire.

Natural selection has outfitted animals with a pain reaction – getting to close to the fire, we pull away reflexively – this is a useful prompt to avoid potential life threats. In higher animals and particularly mammals, life threats also elicit stress. When a rabbit is cornered by a lion, its brain signals its adrenal glands to flood the rabbit's nervous system with adrenalin (epinephrine), whereupon its blood vessels contract, its air passages dilate, its heart rate increases, oxygen and glucose supply to the muscles increase rapidly – in general the body prepares for action in an emergency situation – stress increases and the animal is primed to fight or flee. But the stress response also has many negative and even debilitating effects, particularly in humans; prolonged stress tends to compromise the immune system and leads to panic disorders and dysfunctional responses to environmental cues. One of the most common hypotheses put forward by biologists regarding the contribution of religion to fitness – to success in the struggle for existence – is focused on the uniquely human problem of *knowing that one is going to die*. Humans became self-aware and grasped their mortality; and this awareness threatens to keep people in a generalized condition of stress throughout life; nature, therefore, has a motive to relieve us of this debilitating (forbidden) knowledge. The problem is to maintain self-awareness, including the awareness of impending death, without being overwhelmed by stress. This signals the usefulness of the spiritual function – the religious response – as an evolutionary adaptation that compels our species to feel, believe and act as though our 'spark' or 'spirit' or 'soul' is safe and destined to live eternally.

Another approach to religious history and culture from the standpoint of evolutionary biology derives from the biologist Richard Dawkins (*The Selfish Gene,* 1976) and his theory of mimetic evolution. A "meme" is an idea or practice that can replicate itself from one brain into another. Just as some genes grow more common and others less common, so some memes grow more common (ritual cleansing, confession, forgiveness, promise of a future life) and others less common (animal sacrifice, bloodletting, initiation into the mystery rite, exorcism of demons).* Dawkins compares memes to mental viruses that have a kind of parasitical relation to the host mind. From this perspective, the beneficiaries of religion are not human beings (believers) but memes (beliefs). Some ideas are good at keeping themselves alive; others are less able to catch fire and spread.

Dennett uses the same terminology but thinks that human beings are the beneficiaries of the process. One group of people prospers under the influence of a dominant religious idea – another group fails because its religious idea slows or obstructs adapting to new conditions. The anthropologist Jerrod Diamond's book *Collapse* uses this same principle to explain the success and failure of villages, nations, even civilizations. Societies die because they fail to adapt – they hang on to outmoded ideas – they refuse to learn from their mistakes – but if enough people choose to learn, to profit from the opportunity to learn, then by itself *this positive choice* makes the difference. This choice can be supported or opposed by the leading religious concept of the society. Diamond shows how religious prohibition among medieval Greenlanders, Easter Islanders, the Maya and the Anasazi prevented these societies from adapting to change – and oppositely how religious optimism served to preserve societies such as Tokugawa Japan, the New Guinea highlanders, and the Tikopia in the Solomons.

Most of the scientific literature on religion tries to explain religiosity in light of evolutionary benefits for the individual or the group; other models draw analogies between the religiosity phenotype and adaptive animal behaviors; thus Dawkins' approach of looking for effects on "memes" is unusual. Another branch of research bypasses ideas about individual experience, ideas about cultural learning (or religious upbringing), and even ideas about the *survival* of human creations such as concepts or practices. Instead it tests hypotheses directly linking religiosity with physiology.

An interesting example of this kind of study is the work being done by the research group led by Dimitrios Kapogiannis and Aron Barbey. The hypothesis in this case is that religiosity is modulated by neuroanatomical variability. The study group defined four factors in relation to religiosity: religious upbringing, religious behavior (as exhibited in going to church or reporting a sense of intimacy with God), fear of God, and a generally pragmatic attitude coupled with agnosticism.

The study likewise identified several neuroanatomical structures of interest such as the prefrontal cortex, the precuneus, the temporal lobe, and the orbitofrontal cortex, all measured by cortical volume (via magnetic resonance imaging of the brain, with several large study groups with diverse upbringings and diverse attitudes about religion). The findings: variability of religious upbringing was *not* correlated with variability in cortical volume in any region of the brain; variability in religious behavior *was* correlated with increased volume of R middle temporal cortex; fear of God *was* correlated with decreased volume of L precuneus and L orbitofrontal cortex; and the pragmatic/agnostic cluster *was* correlated with increased volume of the R precuneus. These findings suggest a proximate cause for religiosity or its lack in *differences in regional cortical volumes of the brain*. The conclusion of the study group was that religion emerged in our ancestors with the development of novel cognitive processes; later, doubt about religion becomes possible with the development of still newer structures. Given our strong sense that religion has its main significance at the level of individual commitment, and at the level of the faith community, these results are striking. It is at least possible that religion has nothing to do with any of our intuitions about it.

neurotheology

Neurotheology is a relatively new discipline that attempts to synthesize findings from cognitive science, neurology, experimental and developmental psychology, anthropology, archeology and linguistics. This school approaches religious studies with a materialistic, experimental, reductive, scientific point of view. This new school proposes to revise our thinking about religion but also concerns such topics as morality, metaphysics (the theory of being or of what is real), social identity (the socialization process, roles in society) and personal identity. Researchers working in this discipline today include Scott Atran, Michael Gazzinga, Pascal Boyer, Vilayanur Ramachandran, Sara Lazar, Andrew Newberg, Antonio Damasio, Jonathan Haidt and Deborah Kelemen.

The background in this case begins with speculations in antiquity that religious feeling may be correlated with a specific part of the brain. Hippocrates, Galen and Rhazes have some notes on this subject. Jean-Martin Charcot (1825-1893), the father of modern neurology, hypothesized a link between "religious emotionalism" and epilepsy. The possible relation between schizophrenia and certain kinds of religious ecstasy – both cases correlating with increased supplies of the neurochemical dopamine (the D2R protein) in the brain – has been the subject of scientific papers since the 1950s. The British author Aldous Huxley coined the term "neurotheology" in 1962 in hopes that science would one day make medically assisted visionary religious insight possible. In 1975 neuropsychiatrists Norman Geschwind and David Bear documented a peculiar form of epilepsy whose symptoms included patients reporting intense religious experiences. With advances in neuroimaging, such as CAT scans (computerized axial tomography) in the 1970s, the invention of PET scans (positron emission tomography) in the 1980s and of fMRI scans (functional magnetic resonance imaging) in the 1990s, a body of evidence has grown up correlating temporal lobe epilepsy with patients' reporting religious imagery and mystical experiences. Another body of evidence has grown up linking neurological conditions that result in changes in the parietal lobe – the part of the brain that orients us in space – with patients' reporting powerful feelings of being connected to a larger whole (the ability to transcend oneself, the sense of merger, a boundless sense of well being).

The overall research program in neurology is to understand the neural basis of cognition, emotion, memory, language, perception – of human powers of mind – as well as the various disease conditions of the nervous system. Applied to religious studies, and supported by the growing research linking neurological conditions with esoteric states of mind, the problem is to understand the neural basis of religious thinking, without assuming that there is a specific religious organ or mode of function in the mind. The object of this science is not to describe religiosity or to validate it, but to explain the occurrence of religious thoughts and their contents.

Some ideas in this school include: that human psychology is shaped by natural selection; that religion is merely *one* domain, among many others, in which very different socially transmitted ideas result in very similar recurrent cultural themes; and that the explanation for this similarity has little to do with social life, geography, cultural transmission, history or language, but is a consequence of having the type of brain that we have; a consequence of instinct, of what comes naturally to us; of the deep structure of the mind.

The mind in this conception has no single belief network. It is more like a toolbox with many sorts of tools. Just as color and shape are handled by different parts of the visual system, so myriad distinct networks contribute to the behavioral system – which domains remain separated in human cognition. One of the strangest findings in this school is the discovery that there are several unconscious guidance systems (e.g. perceptual, evaluative, motivational) at work simultaneously in shaping behavior. Thus actions undertaken unconsciously precede the arrival of conscious will – *action precedes reflection*. The assumption of conscious primacy has to be given up – yielding to the reverse assumption of blindly adaptive processes that have accrued through natural selection – instinct rather than learning.

The explanatory idea in this case is that mental representations that have evolved to perform a certain function will perform that function once activated. The source of the activation is irrelevant. The function is 'blind' about its source. It has no 'memory' about it that might cause it to behave differently depending on the source. Past evaluations predispose us to make similar choices in new situations; past goals become active and guide our behavior; past perceptual and emotional reactions motivate our searches and discoveries.

The unconscious, pre-reflective contribution to behavior is referred to as "tacit knowledge" – generally not available to conscious inspection – a basket of implicit ideas and principles of explanation running independently of one another. This kind of knowledge is unconscious but can be detected via experiment; decades of work in this field (e.g. by John Bargh and his colleagues at Yale University) demonstrate that, underneath human variation – differences in culture, language, religion, climate, upbringing, economy, social mores – people are remarkably identical at the level of tacit knowledge.

Tacit knowledge comes in clumps, variously called *programs, modules, schemas,* and *operators*. At some level these must be networks of nerve tissue devoted to specific functions; thus they are neural mechanisms or lines of neurological development; and in each case there is a point of origin on the evolutionary timeline. These include affect programs, social interaction schemes and cognitive modules.

Affect programs include 'surprise' and 'fear' – reactions human beings share with reptiles – as well as 'guilt' and 'grief,' which may be unique to human beings. Like echolocation or an active sonar device, we send out bursts of affect to test the environment, trying to fine tune and speed up the basic decision of fight or flight. We make our way through an environment by means of an emotionally charged positioning system. This is a kind of defense system, or a security and precaution network – e.g. dedicated to preventing potential hazards such as poisoning or contamination. These networks trigger specific behaviors such as checking the environment and washing.

Social interaction schemas include 'detecting predators,' 'seeking protectors,' and 'reciprocating in kind' – which appear to reach back very far in evolutionary time – as well as very new patterns such as 'welcoming strangers' or even 'showing mercy.' Part of the social interaction schema has to do with detecting *agents* versus mere objects; as it were, this function is a human-specifying and human-defining function; likewise it has to do with establishing and maintaining relationships with agents beyond their physical presence; e.g., social hierarchies that include temporarily absent members. These same networks form the background for something like 'group feeling' or 'coalitional psychology' or 'principles of social cohesion' – e.g., detection of kin or in-group members and feelings such as loyalty (thought to have evolved from cross-group or sub-group competition); inclusion functions based on kin-detection that motivate trust and cooperation and lending of aid; also submission patterns, behavior signaling respect and feelings such as respect and awe relative to leaders (thought to have evolved from primate hierarchies).

Cognitive modules include something like a 'causal operator' (a function that searches for causes and effects) and a 'holistic operator' (a function that searches for wholeness in the midst of diversity). These functions represent a kind of hard-wired metaphysics: they determine what is real and define patterns of explanation.

The main idea in this school is that *religiosity is an emergent property of ordinary powers of mind*. Affect programs, social interaction schemas and cognitive modules define a few basic moral principles – purity, loyalty, exaltation of leaders – also a rudimentary metaphysics – the distinction between objects and agents, the distinction between causes and effects. Religious thinking recruits or exploits or hijacks or extrapolates these same systems, particularly under the stress of calamity. Thus philosophy, religion and ethics have the same activating source. They arise from the very immediate problem of surviving in an environment.

Neurotheology interprets belief in supernatural entities as an *accidental* output, or byproduct, of affective, social and cognitive systems normally employed in the work of warding off danger, establishing coalitions and detecting perceptual cues. The hypothesis is that these systems go into a hypertrophic, exaggerated or dysfunctional mode – in response to stress, e.g. in an attempt to understand disease, disaster or death – also because they are directed outside their routine sphere of application. A search network focused on environmental hazards and cleanliness goes into overdrive and produces an obsessive-compulsive fixation on purity, arriving at ideas such as original sin, virgin birth, unclean spirits, lurking devils, pollution, corruption, untouchability and baptism.

The normal ability, beginning in childhood, to establish and maintain society with agents who are not physically present – imaginary friends, loved ones who have passed away, heroes and heroines from storytelling – in effect a process of honing social skills by constant practice with imaginary partners – spins itself into myth-making and communication with angels, saints, demigods, sprites and gods. The social interaction schema also works via the general tendency to interpret misfortune in social terms – a predisposition to perceive events generally as manifestations of *intentionality* – a tendency observable especially among small children (a phenomenon dubbed "intuitive theism" by Boston University cognitive psychologist Deborah Kelemen) but also among tribal people and people suffering from paranoid delusions.

The idea of the self emerging from these studies is not any kind of fixed entity – it is more like a collection of dynamic processes – likewise this school does not identify any *unique* origin for religious belief. The guiding idea is that many different cognitive, social and affective systems are at work in everyday experience, and all of them can and have played a role in myth-making: in some cases conjuring up a new kind of entity; in some cases assigning responsibility in the natural world on the model of human relations; in some cases evoking a feeling of disgust or danger or warning in unfamiliar circumstances. What these cases have in common is a redirection of completely ordinary human powers of feeling, socializing and thinking, from real-world applications, into fantasy, under the stress of powerfully eruptive existential crises.

anthropology

The paleoanthropologist Richard Leakey expresses what he believes is the current consensus regarding the defining characteristics of human beings in the following brief list.

104

1. Locomotion on hind legs: forelimbs free for other functions.
2. Prehensile hand: making of tools, development of technology.
3. Enlargement of brain relative to body size.
4. Development of speech and language.
5. Development of social interactions and culture: prolonged youth; division of labor in society; controls on sex and aggression.
6. Individual artistic and spiritual expression.

This conception is current and represents the best judgment of the scientific community today. The neurobiologist Gordon Shepherd, director of the *SenseLab Project* at Yale University – a comprehensive attempt to understand the neuron and the synaptic organization of the brain – comments as follows: "Forelimbs became free to work on the environment in new and novel ways. The prehensile hand led to tools and technology. The parallel development of speech and language gave rise to adaptable modes of communication and ultimately to symbolic thought. A prolonged childhood provided the basis for complex social organization and an enduring culture. Finally, humans express themselves as individuals. The ingredients here include emotion, motivation, and imagination; their testing ground is play; they realize themselves to the fullest in the supremely human qualities of artistic expression and spiritual experience."

Note that Leakey and Shepherd point to religiosity as a basic trait of *individual* human beings. On this reading religiosity is not properly a social or cultural fact but instead something welling up from the psyche. Andrew Newberg of the University of Pennsylvania speculates that there is something like an aesthetic-religious continuum based on a kind of progressive activation of the ability to discern wholeness – sensing beauty and feeling excitation at one end of this spectrum; conceiving the sublime and achieving something like hyperlucidity at the other – a continuum between feeling and thought – between the (passive) experience of being overwhelmed and the (active) realization of meditative calm. These ideas suggest something like an aesthetic-religious impulse or capacity or responsiveness. The claim is that this is something people do – this is a defining category of being human – we know, or we can feel, that something is sacred.

The anthropologist Donald E. Brown's 1991 work *Human Universals* takes a somewhat different perspective – religion on his account has a social, not a psychological explanation – Brown also claims that *every human society without exception has practiced religion.* Brown spells out what he means by 'religion' by describing many sorts of cultural phenomena – birth rites, funerals, storytelling, genealogies, medicinal lore, social conventions, moral rules and taboos, mystical beliefs – all referencing magic, the supernatural, fate, spirits, life after death, life before birth, goblins, ghosts or mythopoetic ancestors. Brown holds that, starting with our common biology and the shared problems of the human situation, human societies end up at many common solutions. These include music, poetry, dance, jokes, insults, marriage, funerals, hospitality, modesty; ideas such as good, evil, right, wrong; man, woman, parents, child; past, present, future; responsibility, shame, reciprocity, hope; also 'religion.'

Brown makes a distinction between different kinds of human universals – what he calls *emic* universals versus *etic* universals (derived from the words 'phonemic' and 'phonetic'). *Emic* universals are features that are overtly or consciously represented in the culture and *etic* universals are features that are present but are not called out overtly or made conscious by people in the culture. For example, every language has a grammar, but not all cultures develop an explicit (or written) grammar of their language. Again, all people have blood types, but not all cultures develop the explicit idea of a blood type. Blood type is a fact about all people (an *etic* universal), but the cultural practice of distinguishing between blood types is rare (it is not an *emic* universal). Gender is an *etic* universal and an *emic* universal – we observe it in all cultures and it is explicitly called out in all cultures. Religion, Brown says, is an *etic* universal, but not an *emic* one. That is, religion exists in all societies, but in many societies people do not know that they are practicing religion. They have no word for it.

The Indian sociologist S.N. Balagangadhara's 1994 work *Asia, the West and the Dynamic of Religion* and the British historian Richard King's 1999 work *Orientalism and Religion* both try to refute the claim that religion is a human universal. Western scholars (they argue) have imposed a template derived from Christianity on spiritual ideas of many kinds. Balagangadhara argues that Christianity gives people the idea that religion is "an explanatory account of the cosmos" but (as he also argues) in many cases (from around the world and in different epochs of history) so-called 'religions' do not even attempt to explain anything. He concludes from these reasonings that religion does not exist everywhere and in all histories – religion is not a human universal – because religion necessarily has to do with doctrines and creeds.

Much of the history of anthropology is devoted to the reverse conclusion. Herodotus (484-425 BCE), Plutarch (46-120 CE), Abu al-Biruni (973-1078), Montesquieu (1689-1755), and contemporary thinkers like Ruth Benedict (1887-1948) and Margaret Mead (1901-1978), argue for a *universal* religiosity, drawing their examples widely from world culture.

Karen Armstrong's well-regarded books such as *Beginning the World* (1983), *The History of God* (1993) and *The Great Transformation* (2006), dispute the claim that religion equates to doctrine, arguing that religion is largely about practice, not belief. She argues that the focus on explanation, belief and doctrinal purity is a very recent invention – a defensive response by faith traditions to the challenge of science – that has no relevance to ancient religiosity. This supports the claim that religion is a human universal.

The American anthropologist Paul Radin (1883-1959) takes a Darwinian perspective, argues for a universal religiosity, and interprets shamanic phenomena from a neurological point of view – combining biology, anthropology and neurological studies. The shaman is a kind of "neurotic-epileptic" who suffers from a "special and diseased mentality" but who also has "power to cure himself" – the shaman takes flight and looks for helping and answering spirits, but spirits come of their own accord, as possession, like the flashes of disease – these 'cures' by magic, symbolic action and storytelling are normalized through being passed down by "more normal individuals" and shape the cultic practices we call 'religions.' Radin argues that religion is universal because neuroticism is.

structuralism

Thinkers such as Georges Dumézil, Claude Lévy-Strauss and Mircea Eliade, who call themselves 'structuralists,' hold that the unity and common structure of the human mind helps to explain the unity and common structure of 'mental' phenomena. The structuralists approach religion as a kind of blueprint of the human mind.

The human mind confronts experience on the strength of a few basic facts: every human being has a body that moves around in the world, that grows and decays; every human being has a mind, which is something like a three-dimensional screen or 'sensorium' that operates through a fourth, or temporal, dimension; the mind becomes more powerful and reaches an apogee of performance and also grows less powerful and ultimately darkens; and the body is distinct from the mind. Structuralists argue that all human beings, in all cultures and in all periods of history, begin reasoning from these "inevitable premises." Once a person begins thinking, he or she will arrive at these premises. And in reasoning from these bases it is also inevitable that the thinker – whoever, wherever, and whenever – will arrive at a few basic results.

These include the idea of the soul or its equivalents, which is supposed to exist independently from the body; the idea of deity, power, spirit or force, which is like a soul, and which exists independently of any body; the idea of a beforelife and an afterlife; the idea of life judgment; the idea of reward and punishment; and many related ideas such as prayer, offerings, sacrifice and other kinds of transactions with the spirit realm; shame, guilt, purity, defilement, cleansing; loyalty, betrayal, damnation and blessedness. The basic conditions of mind are also the basic themes of world storytelling.

A religion is a system of thinking – a collection of ideas – generated by the human mind. Thus it may be considered a kind of mirror image of the mind that thinks it. The similarity of unrelated religious traditions and of religious ideas worldwide derives from their underlying universal mental imprint.

Our biology, neurology, common human nature, and basic intellectual framework appear to implicate us in religiosity, religious practice, religious thinking and belief – *homo sapiens* is *homo religiosis* – Karen Armstrong has written that "as soon as we became recognizably human, men and women started to create religions" – there is a preponderance of evidence to support this view, but it is still debatable whether this is more a blessing or a curse. The "new atheist" Sam Harris accepts the idea that mankind thus far has been hugely impacted by religion, though generally *for the worse*; Ms. Armstrong argues that we should not identify religion with its worst manifestations, but see its complexity. She writes: "like art, religion is difficult to do well and is often done badly; like sex, it is often tragically abused … but it is also about the quest for transcendence, the discipline of compassion, and the endless search for meaning … religious traditions are highly complex and multifarious" and amply show both tendencies.

Natural science looks to origins in the past, social science tries to lay out planning for the future; the question is not simply what religion has been, but what it should be; whether we are finally waking out of this darkness, or whether religion will always be a part of human life, whether we want it or not.

+

The theory of interpretation includes hundreds of lines of argument, beginning with the problem of the *text* itself: the language it is written in, when it was written, how to read it; arguing that texts are contestable and require interpretation; and discriminating between different approaches to understanding linguistic communication, which focus on the author, the intention of the author, the audience, the time and place, the physical environment, the political world, which values it promotes in society, or many other variables – psychological or economic or bound by some other contingent cause. Traditions of interpretation and commentary are born in focusing in on sacred texts and the problem of reading them, and especially whether to emphasize the authority of tradition or to stress more the importance of critical distance, reflection and objective judgment.

There is a long tradition of scriptural commentary and interpretation in each of the three main civilizations in which philosophy appears – Europe, India and China – a form of study that many western writers call 'hermeneutics' – a Greek word derived from the name of the messenger-god Hermes. This is an approach that tries to develop an understanding of religion from *within* the sphere of belief – not from the outsider's standpoint – accepting the terms of belief but seeking further understanding.

Sacred texts call upon their readers to accept the terms of belief; this is common in nearly all traditions and has a prehistoric counterpart in shamanic practices of *beckoning* spirits but not *commanding* them; also in offering cures but requiring a ready subject to benefit from them. Something like an openness and willingness to *accept* the shaman's help is gradually transformed over the generations into open and willing *assent* to a proposition, as religiosity becomes less preoccupied with practice and more preoccupied with belief. An example of this idea in Christianity is the sermon on faith in *Hebrews* 11. "Without faith it is impossible to please him. For whoever would draw near to God must believe that he exists and that he rewards those who seek him" (5-6); wherefore "faith is the assurance of things hoped for, and the evidence of things not seen" (1). The word translated 'evidence' (alternatively: proving, assurance, conviction, certainty) is *elenchus* in Greek – Socrates' word – which in the *New Testament* does not mean cross-examination, testing, giving an account for purposes of disproof or refutation, or closely examining evidence by which someone might be convicted; instead it means conviction, persuasion, proof, even revelation. The passage says that faith (*pistis*) (normally meaning 'trust, loyalty, engagement, commitment') is a kind of assurance about what we hope for, and a kind of evidence without seeing the proof. We go forward, without anything supporting us, just as if we knew, even though we do not. The secret of faith is some such presumptive belief.

We are talking about trying to understand religion by *accepting* religious belief. St. Thomas offers perhaps the most illustrious example of this strategy – or Maimonides, or Al Farabi, or Shankara – or Confucius, another teacher who interprets the sayings of the ancients. St. Thomas calls this *fides quaerens intellectum*, "faith seeking understanding." A modern exponent of the 'hermeneutical' position is the German thinker Hans-Georg Gadamer. Gadamer writes: "It is impossible to understand tradition without accepting its claim" (*Wahrheit und Methode*, 1960, p. 473). Gadamer argues that religions rest on unproven assumptions taken as facts and are therefore rightly described as *prejudices*. His approach is to develop a concept of "legitimate prejudice" in order to work around the negative judgment that prejudices always lead to error, and thus tease truth out from error. Prejudices are not merely limitations on knowledge. They are conditions of knowledge.*

Gadamer tries to unpack these ideas by introducing the comparison that *having faith* in order to know, or *accepting* in order to understand, or *prejudging* as a route to seeing, are part of a game. He tries to uncover the deep import of *play* in human experience and the widely differing *roles* that make up social life. The player – or participant, if the word 'player' sounds too trivial – in a game – a drama, a contest, a debate, a dance, a contract, a relationship – is always involved in *more* than that of which he or she is conscious. While consciously contributing to the play, the player is also being played. The player is being played by countless moves, reversals, ploys, constraints, surprises and nuances

– connections and meanings of meaning that animate the play and give the game its emerging character as an *interplay*.

This interplay presumes a prior context or contexts of assumptions, attributions and capabilities, that lend participants' actions their intelligibility and significance. The game already exists and we are new players playing it. The game exists before we do. Instead of it belonging to us, we belong to it. Tradition precedes the individual, history precedes the individual, culture precedes the individual. Gadamer argues that in trying to understand purposeful human engagements, we can aim for critical alertness and participation, but we cannot aim at wholesale critical detachment, pure observation or objective analysis. He argues that the idea of the detached observer is an *illusion*. He still wants to talk about getting things right, and erring by being too uncritical, and making the mistake of lacking any sense of history, but he thinks of these things as mistakes that players make while they are playing the game.

Gadamer argues that the attempt to think critically about virtually any subject (e.g. religion) belongs within the larger social interplay and historical flow of that which is being criticized. This is what he calls the "principle of the consciousness of the effects of human historicity" – "principle of historically effected consciousness" (*wirkungsgeschichtliche Bewusstsein*). He claims that there is no chance that we will grasp what critical thinkers are trying to accomplish if we do not become conscious of the effects of *history* on critical thinkers themselves. Critical thinking struggles to get behind the contexts of human understanding, so that it can expose the shortcomings of such contexts and succeed in overcoming them. Gadamer argues that that this effort is completely pointless – contradicting Raymond Guess' ideas about the possibility of external ideology-critique – we do not have the power to step outside our own culture and look at it from 'outside,' except in the case where we leave our culture and join another.

Gadamer reaches these conclusions mainly by thinking about language. For example, he claims that to learn a language is to become a *participant* in a linguistic apprenticeship, and that it takes some time to become fluent in expressions and turns of phrase – at the same time, when you learn a language, you also take in and internalize definite perspectives, beliefs and intentions – language learning is a kind of theater and works mainly via role-play. Language is not a set of tools to be mastered and then employed at will, but is itself active in shaping thinking, willing and judging, as well as speaking. The effects of history, it turns out, pervade language and its usage just as thoroughly as they influence the consciousness, or rationality, of individuals.

Gadamer describes language-play, culture-play, tradition-play as a seesaw interplay – there are "tendencies of meaning" that dominate the player – the thing we are trying to understand must assert itself against these tendencies – the thing makes a claim on us, which is why we have to assert ourselves against it – yet we cannot even begin to play without accepting this claim.

One way of expressing this result is to say that learning a language involves absorbing some typical prejudices. From the perspective of the Enlightenment, prejudice blunts the understanding. Gadamer treats prejudice instead as enabling understanding. He argues that, without standing in a tradition, an historic limitation or "prejudice," the inquirer *has no perspective at all.* You learn to understand what is before you in the terms your culture has given you; these become the *only* terms in which you understand at all.

Gadamer argues that tradition is wrongly understood as that which "already" possesses truth for its adherents (so that they are spared the effort of thinking about what they believe). He argues that the real significance of tradition lies in the *challenge* it addresses to the learner or newcomer. Tradition is not primarily about transmission and submission. It is an interplay, with possibilities of new understandings, confrontations, misunderstandings, and transformations – he talks about "productive misuse" and "barren propriety" as opposite kinds of problems in the interplay. Tradition is always changing. A real encounter with the tradition we are learning involves a "fusion of horizons." The horizon of understanding that the learner brings to the encounter *intersects* the horizon of some element within tradition that addresses the learner. The resulting "fusion of horizons" is not merely a merging or melting together (in which tensions are laid to rest), but a dynamic back-and-forth exchange (in which forces continue to act on one another) – an interplay in which stresses are uncovered and brought forward rather than glossed or passed over. In the interplay between learner and tradition, the learner sometimes stumbles, and sometimes makes progress towards a more inclusive and self-critical understanding, but never reaches a *perfect* or *completed* understanding. Thus the encounter with tradition is inexhaustible.

Gadamer argues: when we encounter tradition, we sometimes stumble and sometimes make progress; but the tradition we meet is never static; it changes by our interaction with it; so do we; we should not encase it in an unapproachable holiness; tradition has to live and breathe.

Perhaps Gadamer is saying something straightforward and obvious: that we can only understanding something by becoming part of it – rather than by standing outside – understanding always requires us to join in.

Gadamer's critics dismiss this idea and accuse him of three related kinds of mistakes. His attitude towards tradition seems too acquiescent; he is too ready to cede meaning making to existing authorities, which also comes out in his failure to challenge the National Socialist regime under which he lived. His concept of tradition seems to ignore the obvious fact that every tradition is a construction out of remnants of previous traditions; thus his own native German culture includes elements reaching back to the beginning of Indo-European language. His conception of tradition also seems naïve. Fanatical believers do not welcome new ideas or debate. They think they already know everything. Gadamer had this stark reality before him but did not see it.

Another approach to religion emerges from the study of everyday language. Pioneers in the analysis of language in use emphasized the *naming* relation as the model semantic connection. Thinking about names offers the paradigm that reality consists in objects. But further thinking opens up new ways of conceiving what is real.

The name 'Clark Kent' has significance because it picks out *one* individual from among the set of all possible objects. It took some time to recognize that this model is much too narrow. The Austrian thinker Ludwig Wittgenstein played an important role in advancing from this idea. Wittgenstein showed that words are less like objects and more like tools that have many different purposes, just as hammers and screwdrivers and levels and saws have distinct purposes. "Look at the sentence as an instrument and at its sense as its use." He noted that the use of language is incredibly varied (*Philosophical Investigations*, 1953):

"How many kinds of sentences are there? You might say: assertion, question, and command. – But there are countless kinds: countless different kinds of uses of what we call 'symbols,' 'words,' 'sentences.' And this multiplicity is not something fixed, given once and for all; but new types of language, new language-games, as we may say, come into existence, and others become obsolete and forgotten. Here the term 'language-game' is meant to bring into prominence the fact that the speaking of a language is part of an activity, or a form of life. Review the multiplicity of language-games in the following examples, and in others: Giving orders, and obeying them – Describing the appearance of an object, or giving its measurements – Constructing an object from a description (a drawing) – Reporting an event – Forming and testing a hypothesis – Presenting the results of an experiment in tables and diagrams – Making up a story; and reading it – Play-acting – Singing songs – Guessing riddles – Making up a joke; and telling it – Solving a problem in practical arithmetic – Translating from one language into another – Asking, thanking, cursing, greeting, praying."

This long passage from Wittgenstein's work *Philosophical Investigations* is the source for the term "language-game." Wittgenstein thought of a language-game as a whole complex consisting of thinking, speaking, listening and many different kinds of activities, all woven together. In one example he imagines a group of workers cooperating together in building a house. They point to things and blurt out single words like 'block,' 'pillar,' 'slab,' or 'beam' – they take a block and move it into place and move on to the next problem. In another example he offers the metaphor of going to the store holding several cards in one's hands – of an apple and another card with a picture of three dots – then showing these cards to the grocer, who places three apples in a sack.

112

These and many other examples point to the ways in which pieces of the game – ideas, words, actions – weave together into a story. The term "language-game" indicates that the uses to which expressions are put *have significance in a context* and are interlaced with significant actions.

Wittgenstein argues that a language-game, a context of meaning, a semantic environment or sphere of discourse, must have clear boundaries. One language-game must end where another begins. To understand a language-game, the inquirer has to map out its logical frontiers. This requires a good description of the game and all the allowable plays within it. Failure to distinguish language-games from one another results in interestingly different confusions: use mistaken for mention; fallacies of ambiguity (e.g., quotation out of context), fallacies of insufficient evidence (e.g., weak analogy), and fallacies of insufficient relevance (e.g., false analogy). What links all these mistakes together is that they all involve something like a 'category mistake.' Expressions that have significance in root contexts result in erroneous reasoning or plain nonsense when they are offered up in strange contexts. Wittgenstein says that in cases like these, "language goes on a holiday."

Consider the example of religious belief – for example, consider the language-game of Hebrew scholars discussing the finer points of *Genesis*. Perhaps one believer, in order to explain his or her point, draws a parallel between the account of Creation in the *Torah* and the account provided in modern cosmology. This kind of parallel can be fruitful yet may also be misleading. The kind of questions we want to raise in interpreting scripture are not typically the same questions we want to ask in pursuing science. To pursue the parallel very far quickly invites confusion.

The logical mapwork required for proper interpretation also includes determination of where one language-game *unites* with another. Linguistic territories have to be marked off from each other, yet not so far as to cut off one part of language from another. Language needs to retain some of the significance it has in *ordinary* contexts in order to be meaningful in special contexts (for this reason Wittgenstein's position in the *Investigations* is sometimes called 'ordinary language philosophy'). The result of qualifying *all* the senses of an expression to a special sphere of discourse is that the expression becomes meaningless.

Wittgenstein notes that the word 'God' is among the earliest learnt. We learn that God sees, punishes, rewards, and so on. Wittgenstein notes that if we use the phrase 'the eye of God' in a religious context, the term 'eye' must retain some of the significance it has normally, or in contexts that have no religious meaning. The 'eye of God' has to see like other eyes. If the 'eye of God' is not an 'eye' in any normal sense, then the sense of the term vanishes in this special context. But contexts can also merge too closely. Wittgenstein notes the danger that talking about the 'eye of God' will set us going about the eyebrow of God (*Lectures on Religious Belief*, II, III).

Wittgenstein remarks that "what we do in our language-games always rests on a tacit presupposition." Each language-game has distinct logical frontiers or boundaries that mark it out from other games, that link it to certain contexts and exclude it from others, and whose description determines the rules of the game. These rules make sense on the strength of a few key concepts. These are the "constitutive concepts" of the game. In a sense, they are what the game is about. The constitutive concept in the language-game of physical science is the notion of a physical object. This is what science is about. The constitutive concept of the language-game of religious belief is the concept of God. This is what religious belief is about.

Interpretation (as Wittgenstein conceives it), i.e. the attempt at understanding believing and reasoning in special contexts, i.e. the attempt to understand a language-game, requires a special effort and is marked by much confusion. In trying to figure out the game we are forced to ask: What is the constitutive concept of the game? What does this concept mean? Can it mean logically what it purports to mean? Is it *about* anything? Is there anything like this in the universe? Are we talking about something that actually exists? And regarding the game itself: Is this game current, or out-of-date, or entirely new? Is it ordinary language? Or is it language on a holiday? Did it ever make sense to play this game? Does it now? Will it ever make any sense to play it?

Wittgenstein notes that much of religious language has to do with absent figures and – on a line of thought very like that of Deborah Kelemen's ideas about "intuitive theism" – he compares religious language with gossip about a brother in America, a missing Aunt and a fellow at Cambridge who he bumped into even though he thought he would never see him again. He notes: we play a game in which some of our partners are ghosts.

He also notes that members of a religious community may be faithful to their creed but still have questions and difficulties and areas of doubt. In such a case, the language-game of religious belief is carried on 'internal' to the doctrine. Discussion works through the basic agreement of profession of the faith, as in the hermeneutic tradition, and seeks to clarify points by appeal to scripture, tradition, discussion and experience, e.g. Muslim scholars sometimes disagree about the meaning of the term *jihad*, 'holy war' or 'holy struggle.'

A different problem arises when religious belief is examined 'from outside' and without the framework of shared loyalty. E.g., a biologist might ask what precursors to religious behavior can be discovered among other animals, such as wolves howling at the moon; an anthropologist may seek to probe the significance of ancient cave paintings and the light thrown by ancestral forms of worship on modern religiousness; a psychologist may describe the working of the religious mind and identify some of its root causes in fears or hopes; a sociologist may examine religion as a tool for social unity, division or control;

an historian may describe the emergence of a faith, how it won adherents, and record its influence on culture for good and ill.

The point in this variety is the shifting relation between context examined to context employed. The description and assessment of the game under investigation varies with the observing perspective. Every game provides a view of itself; rival games provide distinct results when applied to the same material; external perspectives (such as Raymond Guess' ideas about external ideology-critique) tend to mix questions of meaning with political jockeying and contests over power; and it is always possible that new games may uncover levels of meaning of which current players are wholly unaware.

Different language-games are (in a sense) logically cut off from each other; their constitutive terms are mainly self-referential; this is another reason why religious language-games are so resistant to criticism from an external point of view. The proviso is that the words we use in a religious context must retain *some* of the significance they have normally, or in contexts that have no religious meaning – thus the connection to daily life saves religious talk from collapsing into nonsense – at the same time, the connection to daily life represents a (still relatively weak) reality check in religion.

Wittgenstein tries to develop a perspective from which language-play looks like a *routine practice*. The game is conceived to persist through time with more or less fixed rules, despite shifts in other contexts. He argues: words have meanings and contexts have forces. To adopt a certain idiom, and address matters by routine practice, to *apply* a practice and depend on its results, entails some persistence in that idiom. You cannot both upset the norm and still assert its results.

As a result of all these researches, Wittgenstein ridiculed approaches to religion that emphasized doctrine, and argued for the import of ritual instead. He compared religious ritual to more primitive gestures, as when a savage sticks a knife through a picture of his enemy (*Remarks on Fraser's Golden Bough*, 4). Wittgenstein argued that it is wrong to think that the savage is making a mistake. More generally, religious people are not making mistakes when they say and do various odd things. What the person is doing has a kind of magic about it. It is symbolic. It is not based on the false belief that the person depicted in the image will be harmed by stabbing it. Religious ritual is not a substitute for any other kind of action – the way magic might be confused with science – and there may be no substitute for it. It is *not* literal speech. So soon as it is taken as such, it is diminished, not just to a mistake, but to complete nonsense.

Wittgenstein's critics (e.g. David Pole, Maurice Cornforth) accuse him of regarding ordinary language as 'sacrosanct,' that he speaks for the 'status quo,' that he takes no account of change – that he argues for leaving everything as it is. Thus "philosophy may in no way interfere with the actual use of language; in the end it can only describe it" (*Philosophical Investigations*, §124).

Gadamer and Wittgenstein are hinting at something that takes root in magic, ritual and symbolism, which can flourish as tradition or degenerate into ideology. It is rooted in the life process, and is an adaptation, an emergent construction or structure, fundamental to human life. For lack of better terms, let us call it 'orienting value.'

Orienting value is shared in village life; proclaimed in imperial society; and apportioned in feudal society. Beginning in the 14th century, with the collapse of the manorial system – the organizing principle of feudalism – something completely new happens to orienting value. It becomes an item for sale.

The Greek root *oeconomia* translates as 'household.' Thus the economic problem as first formulated has to do with managing the affairs of a family. It is important to note that the Greek household was a center of production *and* consumption: the family made things for their own use, generating revenue with sales, and supplementing production with purchases – making and trading in agricultural and handmade goods. Thus the management of an economic unit – a family or clan or village or nation – has to do with production, consumption and trade.

Hunting and gathering societies, and societies based on tradition or command (so-called 'tribute' societies) do not manage these kinds of activity as we do, by the three principles of capitalism. These principles are: encouraging and celebrating the profit motive (greed, the desire to amass goods) for all members of the society; providing the stuff of life by competitive buying and selling (channeling the acquisitive drive through the demands of markets); and, lastly, leaving the problems of production and distribution to private enterprise (dividing social power between public and private, government and business). Instead, in village life, in the empire, and in feudal times, authorities kept profit to themselves; they directed production and distribution; and they enslaved or coerced labor power.

Karl Marx (1818-1883) summarized the logic of capitalism in his formula M–C–M'. M stands for capital as money, which gets transformed into C, capital as commodities, which is transformed into M', capital as more money. Thus money buys/produces commodities; commodities are sold/consumed; and sales are invested and increase by a surplus called 'profit.' The driving engine within this dynamic is the production of commodities – something economists call 'commodification' – as preliminary to the sale. Marx noted that *absolutely anything* can become a commodity. E.g., rap music expresses the outrage of a dispossessed people against the injustices of ghetto life; yet rap music becomes a commodity in the same economic system that created this dispossession; and rap music even becomes a tool in marketing strategies for sales of new goods.

Some thinkers argue that when something becomes a commodity, it can no longer serve as a vehicle for meaning – e.g. for protest – or indeed have any other significance than that of being an *item for sale* in the open market. Not everyone shares this view. For example, Theodore Adorno (1903-1969), the German sociologist and critic of Marx, reasoned that "vestiges of the aesthetic claim to be something autonomous, a 'world unto itself,' remain even within the most trivial commercial productions" (*The Culture Industry*, 1991). Whether one can *say* anything and, at the same time, also *sell* something, or whether the act of selling something changes the character of that thing and diminishes it, it seems clear that in a market economy, everything actually *produced* enters the market; thus it becomes a new element in the universe of capitalism. This universe destabilizes every kind of regime that precedes it, whether of tribute or feudal power or kingship. Capitalist economics takes into itself everything in its reach through processes of commodification, and quickly transforms threats to capitalism into new avenues for sales. Thus also capitalism promotes free exchange of all kinds and ultimately breaks down every kind of social and geographic barrier.

Figures of the Scottish Enlightenment such as David Hume (1711-1776) were the first to grasp that the changes taking place in the societies of their time arose from intermingled political, social, intellectual and especially economic forces, and that the overall effect of these intertwined forces was to weaken entrenched privilege. Hume studied the market economy of his time and gradually reached the conclusion that the psychological underpinning of this system lay in hedonism. He hypothesized that excesses of private self-seeking tend to cancel each other out in the wider context of society at large. This principle is sometimes expressed in the formula "private vices make public virtues." Hume's fellow Scot Adam Smith (1723-1790), the father of modern economics, argues in his classic work *The Wealth of Nations* (1776) that "the private interests and passions of men" are led in the direction "which is most agreeable to the interests of the whole society" by the force of the "market mechanism" – what Smith also calls "the invisible hand." The mechanism of greed, hedonism or self-seeking, when it works in the context of similarly motivated other selves, results in competition; and competition results in the distribution of goods that society wants. Smith studies capital distributions and investigates prices, wages, surpluses, shortages, and the varying relation between markets and public confidence (the "spirit of the times"). Smith sees *enterprise* at the center of commercial life, growing towards monopoly and threatened by bankruptcy. The proper function of government is to wield and retain authority for education, health, the public welfare, public works, national defense, orderly transition in bankruptcies, and the prevention of monopolies – a view that is today called 'socialism.'

Smith also began to study religion from this same perspective – looking at religious consumers driven by hedonism and religion itself as a commodity in a free market – foreseeing the kind of commerce that makes possible a Mormon in China or a Buddhist in Kansas. Smith noted the advantages that new religions have over established systems (who must struggle to "keep up the fervor and devotion of the great body of the people"). He observed that clergymen in established churches share the entrepreneur's general disdain for public power, but with the same exceptions. When orthodoxy is challenged by newcomers, ecclesiastical authorities appeal to government power to make a legal establishment of religion (Book Five).

Marx hypothesized that human history passes through successive stages of social formation, such as tribalism and feudalism and capitalism, where each new stage solves a problem created by its predecessor, but (unlike Smith) he also theorized that history progresses towards a definite goal. Marx held that revolutions are the engine of history, because the contradictions inherent in society develop of themselves and eventually explode, thus heralding new epochs. Beneath social contradictions lie economic inequities – eventually these contradictions take form as class struggles, which are contests between ruling and oppressed classes, and which have reached such a pitch in the modern world that the oppressed class cannot attain its liberation without at the same time liberating all human society from exploitation – including the exploiters themselves. Marx made the startling claim that *history itself* has the goal of producing a classless society – i.e. when this happens, history ends – alternatively he says that everything preceding this event is human "prehistory." The classless society will replace what Smith defined as "competition" with a new era Marx calls "cooperation." Thus Marx rejects perhaps the most basic characteristic of capitalism – its dependence on greed – and envisions a future state of society in which cooperation, central planning, and the abolition of social divisions will supersede acquisitiveness, market competition, and the division of social power – a system he called "communism."

Marx's attitude towards religion is complex and thought provoking. On the surface, religion is a kind of narcotic that distracts oppressed people from developing a "revolutionary consciousness." But more fundamentally, the recourse to narcotization is necessary because human beings cannot yet face themselves as the authors of their own destiny. Marx argues: God is the "alienated essence" of human reality. At a later stage in economic history, *wealth* becomes this "alienated essence." At a final stage of history not yet accomplished, humanity will take back this alienation, and human reality will assert its *own* essence. It will cease to worship an external image and placeholder for its own creative power. Marx argues that (at that point) religion will wither away – when people stop reducing themselves down to a "debased, enslaved, abandoned and despicable essence." Thus religion represents an illusory solution to the problem of human life. Religion thus far has failed to grasp what 'orienting value' really is. Genuine progress will make religion unnecessary and usher in real happiness (*Theses on Feuerbach*; *Contribution to the Critique of Hegel's Philosophy of Right*).

Joseph Schumpeter (1883-1950), the last of the great "worldly philosophers" (as Robert L. Heilbroner calls the great economists in his classic work *The Worldly Philosophers*, 1953), foresaw the rise of multinational corporations and, more generally, the advance of capitalism into global commerce, challenging the authority of the nation-state and threatening many established structures of society. Schumpeter made a particular study of the corporation, tracing its history from Roman times and the desire to preserve property relations through generations, through feudal times and the effort to avoid conveyances for the purpose of transmitting property from hand to hand, to its modern establishment as an artificial being "existing only in the contemplation of the law." Schumpeter looks at some special cases such as the history of sailing charters and the close maritime relation between merchantmen, men-of-war and pirates, noting that the "risks of wind and wave" provided a kind of training and model for "captains of industry" – also historic instances when small business corporations became colonies and thereafter nation-states (the United States and India being the most important examples of corporate nation-building). Schumpeter tries to understand the growth of corporations and their bursting of national boundaries – corporations growing outwards into the unincorporated frontier – by weaving many different kinds of facts together into general laws. Thus the same forces that explain the breakdown of villages and drive towards great cities also explain corporate conflict and mergers – the same forces that explain the advance and integration of technologies.

Schumpeter argued that religion is the model of the *corporation-without-superior* and thus the source for all other chartered authority. He notes that *corporations-without-superior* give birth to lesser corporations and serve as their superiors; also that children sometimes rage against their parents and usurp their authority; noting that religious and economic history appear to run parallel along these lines. Beneath these transformations lies the critical energy of capitalism itself. "Capitalism creates a critical frame of mind which, after having destroyed the moral authority of so many other institutions, in the end turns against its own." Free markets attack the credentials of kings and popes, yet ultimately also attack the sacrosanct value at their very center, i.e. private property itself. Unlimited growth in the context of finite resources is unsustainable – this becomes visible as the unincorporated frontier recedes – so that if capitalism is to survive it must transform itself in still new ways.

the economics of religion, 2

Two works by economists have a singular import for religious studies – Max Weber's *The Protestant Ethic and the Spirit of Capitalism* (1904) and the 1973

119

work *Small is Beautiful* by E.F. Schumacher. Weber tries to explain the economic past and Schumacher offers a vision of the economic future. Both wrestle with Smith's, Marx's and Schumpeter's pronouncements about religion. And both try to rethink 'orienting value.'

Weber begins by asking the straightforward question, *why did capitalism originate in a particular place (northern Europe) at a particular time (the seventeenth century), even though human greed is "as old as the history of man?"* As a way of getting at this problem, Weber studies cycles of agricultural production – particularly in feudal times – and he notes the following odd fact: landowners are anxious to get the harvest in and, in an effort to make greater efficiencies, they often try to pay their workers a little more than usual rates at harvest time; but this strategy has precisely the opposite effect than the one intended, i.e. raising the wage has the result that not *more* but *less* work is accomplished in the same amount of time. Weber reasoned that this is the case because the worker reacts to the increase in pay not by increasing his work but by decreasing it. More generally he concludes that "a man does not by nature wish to earn more and more money, but simply to live as he is accustomed to live and to earn as much as is necessary for that purpose." His large conclusion is that human beings had to *learn to desire* to earn more and more money in order for the new economic model of capitalism to succeed. Weber claims that men learned this new desire from Protestantism.

Weber's argument is difficult to follow but appears to contain at least these seven claims: that Calvin and Zwingli introduced the notion of *predestination* – i.e. that there is no way that a human being can affect his or her eternal fate; also, the Puritans held that, even though we cannot know what awaits us, we should conduct our lives as if we were among the elect; that the best way to banish doubt is to live a life of constant and uncomplaining labor; thus the Puritans, on the basis of earnest religious convictions, claimed that *work* has a deep ethical dimension, and that we are all called upon to take up a trade and work; but these same Puritans were extremely frugal people who did not spend the capital they accumulated; instead, they invested it; this investment provided the initial capital that set the capitalist system in motion.

"The Puritan wanted to work in a calling; but we are forced to do so. … Thus when asceticism was carried out of monastic cells into everyday life, and began to dominate worldly morality, it did its part in building the tremendous cosmos of the modern economic order. … This order is now bound to the technical and economic conditions of machine production which today determine the lives of all the individuals who are born into this mechanism. … Perhaps it will continue to determine them until the last ton of fossilized coal is burnt."

Weber offers a theory of the *religious* origins of the Western world (he also poses himself the question why capitalism did *not* develop in China and offers the response that the Chinese tradition religion denounces the pursuit of gain as unbecoming of a proper Confucian). Religion plays this directing role for economic development because it authorizes, or bans, the various ways in which 'orienting value' can express itself. Religiosity sets a tone that determines what kind of markets there will be. Religiosity puts a frame around 'orienting value' – essentially a way of talking about human motivation – and thus inaugurates a kind of experiential logic in which premises (human driving energies) lead to conclusions (advanced states of society). Hume and Smith characterize human energy as greed (hedonism, pleasure-seeking, self-seeking) and foresee greed checking greed and society advancing towards prosperity. Marx portrays human energy as alienating itself, fighting for itself, and then advancing towards self-realization. Schumpeter thinks of agency as criticism – unafraid of any foe – which must inevitably attack itself. Weber thinks of agency as effort adapted to religious conventions; the advent of capitalism transforms piety into greed, spiritual ambition replaced by the desire for economic gain; he foresees a quickening process of rationalization, secularization, and eventual "disenchantment" of society. For all these thinkers, then, the experiential logic which begins with human energies is a recursive function, probably best captured in Marx's phrase "creative destruction." The system reaches an apogee and falls back to the beginning.

Schumacher is another important voice in this discussion because he challenges a view held by all his predecessors – the view that the "standard of living" is a function of consumption. Schumacher rejects the assumption that a man who consumes more is "better off" that a man who consumes less. Schumacher notes that a *Buddhist economist* would consider this approach irrational. He argues:

"Since consumption is merely a means to human well-being, the aim should be to obtain the maximum of well-being with the minimum of consumption. . . . The less toil there is, the more time and strength is left for artistic creativity. Modern economics, on the other hand, considers consumption to be the sole end and purpose of all economic activity. It is clear, therefore, that Buddhist economics must be very different from that of modern materialism, since the Buddhist sees the essence of civilization not in a multiplication of wants but in the purification of human character. Character, at the same time, is formed primarily by a man's work. And work, properly conducted in conditions of human dignity and freedom, blesses those who do it and equally their products. . . . The most striking fact about modern industry is that it requires so much and accomplishes so little. Its inefficiency therefore remains unnoticed.

"Ever bigger machines, entailing ever bigger concentrations of economic power and exerting ever greater violence against the environment, do not represent progress: *they are a denial of wisdom.* Wisdom demands a new orientation of science and technology towards the organic, the gentle, the non-violent, the elegant and beautiful.

"No system or machinery or economic doctrine or theory stands on its own feet: it is invariably built on a metaphysical foundation, that is to say, upon man's basic outlook on life, its meaning and its purpose. I have talked about the *religion of economics*, i.e. the idol worship of material possessions, of consumption and the so-called standard of living, and the fateful propensity that rejoices in the fact that 'what were luxuries to our fathers have become necessities for us.'

"Systems are never more nor less than incarnations of man's most basic attitudes . . . General evidence of material progress would suggest that the modern private enterprise system is – or has been – the most perfect instrument for the pursuit of personal enrichment. The modern private enterprise system ingeniously employs the human urges of greed and envy as its motive power, but manages to overcome the most blatant deficiencies of *laissez-faire* policies by means of Keynesian economic management, a bit of redistributive taxation, and the 'countervailing power' of trade unions. ... Can such a system conceivably deal with the problems we are now having to face? The answer is self-evident: greed and envy demand continuous and limitless economic growth of a material kind, without proper regard for conservation, but *this type of growth cannot possibly fit into a finite environment.* We must therefore study the essential nature of the private enterprise system and the possibilities of evolving an alternative system which might fit the new situation."

Weber and Schumacher held that religious ideas underlie economic life. Weber held that capitalism creates a "disenchanted" frame of mind, reducing even the most important things in life to "income statements and balance sheets." Schumacher held that economics without Buddhism, "i.e., without spiritual, human and ecological values, is like sex without love." Unlike his predecessors, however, Schumacher is doing more than describing economic processes; he recommends that we think wisely about our motives, and the logic that follows from them; he recommends replacing idolatry with wisdom; he even recommends a new religion – one that has learned humility.

the economics of religion, 3

Capitalism, democracy, the nation-state, and the Enlightenment arose together in Western history. Historians have long debated why this is the case – why Western society came to dominate the rest of the world – and many rival hypotheses have been offered to explain this fact, including:

early adoption of agriculture, favorable climate and soils, favorable plant and animal species for domestication, plentiful food, population growth resulting in division of labor, technical specialization, advances in metallurgy, weaponry, and democratic pressure on archaic privilege a geography that favors balkanization into national states with defensible borders

relative freedom from natural disasters, offering a relief from superstition and a chance for intellectual progress

an extensive east-west axis supporting exchange of innovations and diseases; trade and commerce building cosmopolitanism, technological progress and immunity

the institution of private property, economic competition, the work ethic, consumerism

rapid increase of urbanization in medieval times, resulting in pressure on vestigial tribalism and advances in political participation

the medieval Church's hostility to endogamy (marriage within the tribe or clan) and support of consensual marriage, which reduced the power of the patriarchy (and forever altered the status of women in the Western family system)

Thus overall: the religious spirit gradually loses its footing under the impact of the skeptical, inquisitive, scientifically curious, and humanist perspective of the Italian Renaissance, ushering in the first real epoch of intellectual and political freedom, the 'Age of Reason.'

There is an appreciable link between capitalism and democracy. Capitalism supports democracy in that it upsets any and all pretenders to final importance. Something new comes along, a new consensus has to be reached by information-sharing, advocacy, compromises, purchases, votes. Weber and Schumpeter characterize democracy as a kind of market mechanism for competition between political leaders. But democracy also supports capitalism, in that the values of free speech and social mobility shape the 'marketplace of ideas' – a market whose shapes cannot be determined in advance – and democracy stokes innovation, the engine of economic growth.

Perhaps the best argument in favor of a strong link between capitalism and democracy is that *political freedom has only appeared in capitalist states*. We may not comprehend why democracy sometimes succeeds and sometimes fails in capitalist states – yet we do know that democracy has never succeeded in any state that is not capitalist.

All these developments – capitalism, democracy, the nation-state, and the Enlightenment – are disintegrative, i.e., they all result from breaking up larger wholes. If there is a trajectory of history, it is towards distribution, rather than concentration; decentralization, rather than monopoly; in psychological terms, from an external to an internal locus of control; from oppression to self-determination; in a word, towards *freedom*, precisely as Hegel taught: "the history of the world is none other than the progress of the consciousness of freedom" (*Philosophy of History*, Introduction); "in the end, freedom puts itself on the throne of the world, without any power being able to resist it" (*Phenomenology of Mind*, VI, B, III, Absolute Freedom and Terror).

If there is a force of history, it moves economic life towards capitalism, government towards democracy, and civilization towards secularism. A tentative conclusion is that no single vision of 'the big thing' in life (or the 'big other' over above us) can withstand the criticism it receives in the marketplace of ideas, and the messy democratic conversation, where everyone gets a voice.

With the advent of capitalism, orienting value becomes *an item for sale*. It is marketed, and takes new shapes as the market advances. Thinkers such as Rodney Stark, Roger Finke, Henry Ruf, Carl Bankston and Robert Wortham study the growth and decline of religious denominations. The main assumption of this work is "rational choice theory" – the idea that human beings, accessing only imperfect information, still behave in a way that is generally rational. This is true of prospective consumers acting in a market economy; it is also true of prospective believers in a *religious* economy; and studying this market gets us still closer to understanding the thought complex *religion/culture/history*. Human beings have religion because they are rational, from their sense of order and desire for meaning. Orienting value, or human motivation, or the 'religious sense' as Max Müller calls it, is reason-seeking. Because it is an emergence in the life process, because its essence is historical, the 'religious sense' is ineradicable, but it is subject to the same changes we see at work in economic and political history and in the history of ideas. Religion offers itself as the 'big truth,' the context we need to make sense of important experiences, the answer to the puzzle of life on earth. Therefore religion changes as concepts of 'big truth' evolve. The supernatural begins to disappear and naturalism advances. Newton's "divine architect," Spinoza's "*Deus sive Natura*" (God or Nature), and Einstein's talk about a "God who does not play dice" are increasingly secular. As the German theologian Dietrich Bonhoeffer said: "man comes of age."

The evidence for the trend towards secularization is real but misread if we see it narrowly as disenchantment (as Weber held). Progress towards secularization runs parallel with the spread of self-reported 'spirituality' – and even more by wild diversification in religious markets. Religious pluralism (the offer of many choices) will create a religious economy (as Stark and Finke say "There are always winners and losers in a religious economy"). A corollary here is that religious pluralism (an increase in competition) tends to increase religious participation, whereas the establishment of an official religion (a monopoly in the religious market) tends to decrease it. Rational-choice theory shows how dominant religiosity in the United States depends on open religious markets and how dominant agnosticism in Europe depends on established (closed) religious markets. This theory throws some light on how religious believers act and why religions succeed or fail in varying market conditions. Religions mediate exchanges between mortals and their gods. Some religions successfully market this service. Others fail to reach their customers or are outfoxed by competitors; they fail to foresee change or adapt to it; they misread market trends and see their products die on the shelf. Rational-choice theory of the religious economy tends to predict that, the *stricter* a church (more restrictive regarding conduct and more unforgiving regarding transgression), the *better* it tends to do in the market. Laissez-faire, humanistic and tolerant churches tend to disappear (contrary to expectations emerging in the educational process) because barriers to entry tend to raise the stock of available goods: supply decreases, demand increases, and prices rise. Thus at the same time that man comes of age and concepts of 'big truth' evolve, the defensive reaction grows alongside – the conservative instinct – secularity increases and so do spirituality, conservatism, and proliferating markets.

Rational-choice theory defines rationality as "wanting more rather than less of a good." The good in this case is a sense of order and desire for meaning – of which we are seeking more rather than less – which may take shape as an explanation, or as a sense of connection to a larger purpose – as doctrine or community. Secularism advances, and fundamentalism with it – more people count themselves 'spiritual', yet at the same time we see strict congregations growing rapidly – doctrines proliferate, 'megachurches' appear, religious markets grow and diversify and at the same time four-fifths of the population in postindustrial societies agree that religion is not very important. Hegel speaks for *freedom*, in which the struggle for the good society is about liberation, and where hierarchy and tradition are chains that must be broken – the counternarrative is a heroism of *defense* – reacting to danger, to contamination, to death – putting up barriers and defending a territory.

Schumacher studied both trends and focused on bringing intelligence to the problem of unlimited growth in a finite environment. He saw the disintegration inherent in capitalism, democracy, and political life and in the pursuit of knowledge, as well as disintegration in the religious spirit running parallel with the development of technology. His recommendation is *further* disintegration – more local control, less central order – less talk, more wonder. He argues: small is beautiful, even in religion.

Criticism of a merely *economic* understanding of religion arrives from many quarters – from those who are offended by this strategy or from those who resist the idea that everything we care about can be seen in an economic light. Just like natural science, social science tries to reduce the phenomena down to simplest principles, whereas in religion the focus is typically towards larger perspectives. Nevertheless all social scientific investigation of religion seems to converge on a few findings: we have to catch ourselves in the act of belonging, which means that we have to get free of it; religion unfolds as a kind of game; and players define a territory and ready themselves to defend it.

game theory

Game theory offers itself as the unified field theory of social science. It models the social universe. The fundamental construct in this theory is the *game*. In game theory, the game is not conceived as behavior (as in ordinary language philosophy), nor as engagement (as in hermeneutics), nor narrowly as a transaction (as in economics), but as a situation (a predicament, a decision space, a set of options). There is at least one player. Players have options – possible courses of action – which fact sets up the problem of selecting an option (choosing a course of action; settling on a strategy; devising a plan; creating a decision algorithm). The game runs through independent plays (scenes, episodes, trials, tosses, tests, tries). Players have preferences (motives, desires, values, principles). It is assumed that players are self-interested (self-regarding, self-seeking, self-centered, selfish, egoistic). It is also assumed that players are rational (minimally logical, sane, capable of appreciating reality). Since there are multiple situations (options), playing to different interests (values), play engages fights (conflicts of interest). The game takes place in a 'setting,' including the idea of a 'social situation' (a set of constraints on action) and the idea of 'local conditions' (a different set) and the idea of risk (uncertainty, luck, chance events – or, in religious language, 'acts of God'). Thus in each play there are several possible outcomes and some uncertainty about how things will turn out. The object of the game is to win. The winner gets the 'payoff' – sometimes called 'utility' – the loser gets the 'setback' – failing the goal.

The situation is human activity trying to make a go of intelligent action in life through the exercise of judgment, acting on experience, common sense and available information. The situation faced by modern man, acting rationally, on the basis of knowledge, out of self-interest and in the quest to maximize utility – is likewise the situation faced by primitive man, including the idea of freedom ('native optimism'), the idea of risk or fortune ('the aleatory factor'), the idea of interest (affect, instinct, motive), and the strategic factor – the plan to go from wish to reality – e.g. through magic or via work.

John von Neumann, Oskar Morgenstern, John Nash and others developed game theory in the 1940s. On the above assumptions and constructing mathematical models – probability theory to measure uncertainty in the outcome, decision theory to define optimal strategies, and Bayes' theorem to estimate the impact of new discoveries on decision-making (Bayes showed that evidence has a stronger confirming effect if it was more unlikely before being observed) – they worked out some basic results. They began by defining two fundamental kinds of games – competitive games and co-operative games, or 'zero-sum interactions' (strict competition) and 'non-zero-sum interactions' (strict co-operation). The theory focuses on competitive games, on the principle that players are self-interested.

Game theorists cite the English philosopher Thomas Hobbes (1588-1679) as an important predecessor, because Hobbes observed that a policy of self-interest is best served by reaping the benefits of cooperation, but not returning them – essentially, reneging on the promise to assist someone else who has assisted me. Hobbes thought that *rational* agents will perpetuate a "war of all against all" and that government must become a tyranny to threaten and exact punishment on anyone who breaks a promise. He held there are only two possible outcomes for social life: tyranny and anarchy. Reason chooses tyranny as the lesser of two evils.

The theory results in definitions of social norms as versions of Nash equilibria (no player has anything to gain by changing his strategy) that result from transforming a mixed-motive game into a coordination game. In effect, following Hobbes' reasoning, the theory derives morality from self-interest. Likewise morality is equated *conservatively* as existing norms.

Game theorists also cite Smith's background concept of the "invisible hand," or self-regulating nature of the market, and Hume's idea that "private vices make public virtues," i.e. the discovery that when each person pursues his or her own advantage in a market, the net results include distributions and prices that are beneficial to everyone in the community. The free market (competition) leads to public welfare (cooperation) – which is cooperation without coercion or, in Hobbes's terms, cooperation without tyranny.

"It is not from the benevolence of the brewer, the butcher and the baker, that we expect our dinner, but from their regard to their own self-interest. We address ourselves, not to their humanity but to their self-love, and never talk to them of our necessities, but of their advantages" (Adam Smith, *Wealth of Nations*, 1,2,2).

Smith wants to draw our attention to a free market in which trade occurs and continues over time because trading parties – competitors – both benefit from the exchange – otherwise they would not engage in it – thus the net circumstance is "win-win" and the dynamics of non-zero-sum exchange (in which competitors share in the 'payoff') supplant zero-sum scenarios (which are 'winner take all'). In mathematical terms, in any game there is a pure strategy for player 1 (a 'maximin' strategy) that guarantees player 1 a payoff not less than V, and a pure strategy for player 2 (a 'minimax' strategy) that guarantees that player 1 gets at most payoff V. These pure strategies are in equilibrium and, in general, strategic optimization through repeated trials in a decision-space converges on stable equilibria.

Game theory has been applied to religious questions since its infancy (e.g. by Thomas Bayes, 1702-1761, who discovered the key link between probability and evidence). Bayes and his colleague Richard Price thought that the theorem proved the existence of an unseen order behind supposedly random events – i.e. a proof of the existence of God. A more recent application of game theory to religious ideas is the 2009 work *The Evolution of*

God by the American journalist Robert Wright. Wright applies game-theoretic ideas to the world history of religion and draws a number of sweeping conclusions. His approach is similar to Stark and Finke's application of rational-choice economics to the growth and decline of religious denominations in different "religious markets." Wright is also looking at winners and losers in religious competition. However, his main idea is to apply *non*-zero-sum dynamics to religious competition. He thinks that the evolutionary process has outfitted the human preference system – it makes us highly self-interested; also that repeated trials in the game of religious competition impact religious institutions in powerful ways; these trials also change human actors. The net result is what he calls "the evolution of God."

Wright begins by depicting primitive religion – shamanistic religion – especially focused on the idea that tribal religion is preoccupied with placating gods, forces of nature and fate-making powers. At a deeper level religion is also about jockeying for power in the tribal hierarchy and prosecuting war against other tribes. As long as the tribe is dominant in an area, there is no reason for it to cooperate – thus "the war of all against all" – religion under these conditions remains preoccupied with magic, ritual, power symbols and apocalyptic prophesy in a believer-take-all scenario – the moral circle shrinks to the tribe or even to "true believers" in the tribe. *Our truth is the only truth*; we are the chosen people; we will not make peace with infidels. But monopoly is unstable, religious groups proliferate, populations increase and territory becomes scarce. Tribal competition increases over time and tribes are forced into compromises. Trade relations expand and tribal self-interest recommends benefits from commerce. Religion in this new circumstance evolves beyond magic, ritual, symbolism and doom-saying; it becomes more intellectual, more abstract, more moral, more tolerant, more hopeful. The moral circle expands. The roster of gods begins to include deities worshiped by other tribes. The dynamics of non-zero-sum interactions kick in; the net result over history is evolution in a positive direction: religious cooperation without coercion, religious toleration from self-interest, and evolutionary pressure on religious ideas in the direction of an expanding moral consciousness. Wright's way of saying this is that "god grows" – "god evolves."

Wright's conclusion is quite hopeful. He acknowledges that things do not seem to be going that well right now – religious controversy seems to be on the rise and toleration is becoming scarcer – he acknowledges that recent events seem to disprove his theory. Wright explains this discrepancy in the following way: evolution and non-zero-sum dynamics have stalled; the moral imagination is stuck or is even backfiring; "our mental equipment for dealing with game-theoretic dynamics was designed for a hunter-gather environment, not for the modern world."

Wright's last thought is that the moral imagination needs some "coaxing." It needs to go to some places that "it doesn't go to unabetted." As it were: the moral sense has to step in to save religion – it has to step in and prevent religion from backsliding to its magical and ritualistic origins. Game theory helps us grasp "pragmatic truths about human interaction." But these truths are not enough – we need more than pragmatism. The project of deriving morality exclusively from self-interest fails. We need "moral truth" – we must bring moral truth to our spirituality – so that god can evolve further.

the dynamics of faith, 1

The accounts from evolutionary biology, neurotheology, anthropology, and structuralism try to bring light to religion from physical science. Hermeneutics, linguistics, economics and game theory offer light from the social sciences. Paul Tillich's 1957 work *The Dynamics of Faith* tries to let religion speak for itself.

Tillich was a Protestant theologian and he comes to the problem of religion from that tradition. But he does not offer a defense of Protestantism. Instead he confronts the conflict of religious traditions with one another, describing in great detail the process by which one religion arrogates to itself the claim to exclusive truth, while casting its rivals into the background as mere superstitions. After a lifetime of studying religious controversy, he concluded that religion produces more disease than health. He held that faith confuses, misleads, and creates alternatively skepticism and fanaticism, intellectual resistance and emotional surrender. He held that a fair and critical review will always conclude with the rejection of merely *religious* assertions. Yet he also remarked that this hardly seems possible. Powerful traditions inculcate the same notions throughout the generations. Thus the immediate challenge revolves around making religion useful – not on eradicating religion – instead on making religion serve health rather than disease. More than this, Tillich held that religious language captures an elemental longing in the human spirit. Thus he committed himself to carrying on the project of religion – seeking the place of religion in the modern world – despite all his doubts about the subject. He expressed this determination in the form of a paradox: "Faith comprises both itself and doubt of itself."

There is an old saying that a paradox is merely a truth standing on its head – normally invisible because it is too close up to see – expressly made visible because it is presented in a new and striking way. Tillich thought that it was important to talk about the spirit. He hoped to reinterpret religious experience and remove its confusing and distorting connotations. He thought this was necessary – otherwise one loses the significance inherent in it. He tried to stand religious life on its head in order to draw its poison and capture its truth.

Tillich's father was a Lutheran pastor and Tillich himself from an early age felt a spiritual calling. He was ordained as a Lutheran minister in 1912. He served as an army chaplain in the trenches during the First World War. The war years shook his faith and led to many crises. He discovered the works of Søren Kierkegaard, who argued that the universe is fundamentally paradoxical, and who maintained that the individual is solely responsible for giving his own life meaning. Tillich immersed himself in existentialist thinking and found much in it to express his spiritual quest.

For Tillich, "existentialism gives an analysis of what it means to exist." "Existentialism," he holds, is a kind of protest against another view – "essentialism" – a view he attributes Hegel. Tillich says that Hegel's book *The Phenomenology of Mind* (1807) teaches "essentialism" because it claims explicitly "man has an essential nature." Existentialism is a kind of protest against this idea. Hegel describes man's estrangement from himself in the early part of his book; then he claims that man has reconnected with himself and healed himself; man is perfected, "the rational is the real, the real is the rational" – philosophy can give up being the love of wisdom and become wisdom itself. Tillich rejects the idea that man is healed and that the search for wisdom has found its goal. Instead of this, Tillich sees himself as living in a time of unprecedented horror. Over one hundred million people died in war during the twentieth century – thus we cannot believe that what is *real* is rational. The real, actual, practical, concrete, or "existential" predicament of human being is not rational – it is unrelieved suffering and war. The world as we experience it is full of pain, not harmony, as Hegel claims; not peace. The real – existence itself – is absurd.

Existentialism is one stage among many in the history of Western philosophy. The existentialist account of the project of radical doubt is neither the last stage of philosophy nor the most current. It is however the relevant stage for Tillich – the stage at which philosophy discovers the absurd. Tillich accepts the existentialist account of the human predicament – the idea that existence is *estrangement*, not reconciliation; the idea that at this juncture in history, man becomes a *thing* and ceases to be a person; the idea that history itself is *suffering* – the harsh truth of the human condition. Truth is very far from what we might wish it to be. But we must also wish to see clearly and look honestly at things, if we are to get anywhere in our thinking – at least to try – which is the existential predicament of every single human being. The truth is that "existence itself is a kind of anxiety threatened by meaninglessness" (*Systematic Theology*, 1951).

Tillich thinks of existentialism as a way of facing this anxiety – following Kierkegaard, he wants to hang on to this feeling rather than letting it go – anxiety is what comes from confronting the basic "existential givens" – it is the "dizziness of freedom" and is the only real solution left to us. "Whoever has learned to be anxious in the right way has learned the ultimate."

Tillich's starting place from existentialism is the finding that existence *has no character.* It is blank and faceless and undetermined. Thus it is not simply that human beings have no predetermined character at birth; existentialism is a radical voluntarism, and implies that a person may *choose* his or her identity at any juncture in life. A human being has no essential nature but is largely made of choices.

The idea that human beings have no predetermined character at birth is familiar from empiricism. The empiricists compared human reality to a blank slate (*tabula rasa*) and held that experience gradually inscribes this slate with substantive character. Thus Locke held that it takes some time for an individual to grow and become a person and to inhabit his own being. In stark contrast, Sartre held that an individual who "inhabits his own being" is effectively dead.

Heidegger and Sartre seize on the concept of nothingness, of being literally nothing, in order to draw attention to the contrast between being a thinking being, a conscious being, and being any other kind of being. They associate the contrast between objects and subjects with the emptiness and readiness of *consciousness* – that it is nothing in itself but is instead a receptacle, a view outwards into the sensorium – as against the fullness and finality of dead *matter.* A stone is what it is – it has this character. A human being sometimes sinks into passivity in order to evade the core problem of living; but the person who attempts to evade responsibility is responsible for undertaking this course. A stone does not make any decisions, yet a stonelike person has decided to be a stone. Heidegger states this result as a formula: "the essence of human reality lies in its existence." Sartre's more famous phrase is that "existence precedes essence." Ortega y Gasset stated the principle in concrete terms: "to live is to decide what we are going to be."

Heidegger says that the burden of having to act and form a character for oneself is not "chosen" but is "thrown" onto the individual human being – onto existence – the subject is thrown into this circumstance and cannot get out of it. Man has "fallen" into this state. That he cannot get out of this circumstance means that he must continually face this circumstance. Most accounts of human nature stress the import of the past (the human constitution or the vicissitudes of personal history) in the determination of human character; existentialism stresses the future (the problem of formulating plans for oneself and carrying them out). Heidegger emphasizes that human beings define themselves in the projects they undertake. Human reality is *projective* reality. Thus one among his definitions of *Dasein* or human reality or human being is "thrown projection." Sartre expresses this idea in the form of a paradox: human reality must carry "the burden of freedom" and human reality is "condemned to be free."

Since existence lacks all predetermined meaning, it emerges in a condition of meaninglessness.

The jump out of nowhere and into nothing – into an imagined but still unrealized future – is a development in the sense of meaning, i.e., a determination of this instinct. The determination of meaning transpires in and as *consciousness*, as conscious experience and conscious processing, i.e., as thought. Existentialism conceives human reality as reflective consciousness, as a problem for itself, a question to itself, as consciousness *of* consciousness. Heidegger states this principle in the formula: "existence is that kind of being which is an issue for itself." Thus existence is a problem for itself and is always in search of its own meaning.

A person may *create* a meaning for his or her own life by means of belief and action; a person may *disown* this creation, claiming to *discover* that life has such-and-such a meaning, and calling it 'truth' or 'religion' or 'science' or 'wisdom'; but no one can *forego* meaning and still live a human life.

Existence is also individual or particular; existence is "my existence" or "your existence" or "his existence" or "her existence." Heidegger says that "existence is *in each case mine.*" Existence is subjective, incommunicable, personal. It cannot be shared or given away. There is no bridge to cover the gap between separate existences. Consequently, there is a fundamental and insurmountable aloneness or separateness or isolation in human reality.

Existentialism stresses that existence is finite; it emerges in a distinct moment and vanishes in a distinct moment; the 'that it is' of existence is distinguished by the fact that, at one moment, it 'was not' and, at another moment, it 'is no longer.' Thus existence lacks a precedent and is not the result of any gradual development – it is comparable to turning on a light – likewise also existence does not gradually fade or wither but is gone in an instant – somewhat like turning off a light. Yet existence is *conscious* experience and grasps beforehand and continually its own approaching demise. Thus it cannot banish the thought of death from its horizon; or rather it cannot do so without descending into unconsciousness.

Just as a human being sometimes sinks into passivity in order to evade the core problem of living, a human being sometimes buries the harsh reality of impending death and finds escape in the fantasy of immortality. He imagines things and loses his grip. But there are different cases: he turns into a stone; he stands on his own two feet; perhaps he even figures out how to die. Heidegger says that in some cases *Dasein* or existence (human reality) finally comes into its own "in an impassioned freedom towards death." Death is the "possibility of the impossibility of any further existence" – death is the summation of all the conditions of the appearance of existence.

Human beings create a meaning for themselves and enact their freedom, awakening in the solitary reflection that life must be seized before it comes to an end.

Thus it is possible to live a human life in human terms. But people can also disown their creations and pretend that they are the work of ancestors or great powers or gods; or they can make the different mistake of imagining that they are gods themselves; they can even fail to live at all and instead put an end to themselves. Existentialism holds that *at this juncture of history,* existence has fallen into a condition of estrangement. It is filled with anxiety and threatened by meaninglessness. This is why the existentialist reflection on death oftentimes takes the form of contemplating suicide. Albert Camus put this idea in the formula "[T]here is only one truly serious philosophical problem, and that is suicide." Norman Brown recast the idea by talking about "the struggle of life against death." Gabriel Marcel called it "the war of being against non-being."

Facing one's death is not something a person can do once and be done with – but instead life itself becomes practice of death (the existentialists have even claimed Socrates in their ranks, since Socrates says that philosophy is a "practice of death" – William James, who talks about "using your death," is recruited too). Thus freedom is conceived as a struggle rather than a victory or completion. We can't actually attain freedom, but we can always keep fighting. The existentialist claim is that "the struggle itself toward the heights is enough to fill a man's heart" (Camus).

the dynamics of faith, 3

Tillich attempts to develop a conception of faith and of the interrelations between faiths on the strength of the existentialist account of freedom, meaningless, isolation and death. In particular, Tillich holds that faith has to do with *death* – overcoming fear of death; overcoming the temptation to escape death by wishing it away – faith as an honest confrontation with death.

His first step is to define faith as the *ultimate concern* – the most important concern in a person's life – the driving problem, the central issue in a person's life – the last thing a person would wish to lose – the innermost core – the thing that matters and makes the difference between life and death.

In a sense Tillich returns to the beginning of the reflection we are pursuing here and tries to get at the meaning of the word 'religion' in its broadest contexts – focusing especially on the idea that the word 'religion' is often used in secular contexts to indicate passionate conviction – religion as a cause, principle, or activity pursued with zeal or conscientious devotion. He is trying to capture the basic element that something *matters* to a person – he looks for this and tries to see how it works.

Tillich reasons that in every case something matters to a person – every human being takes part in the world to further a *specific* good that he seeks – thus he takes up a party cause – he selects *one* thing out of many – he devotes himself to one thing particularly and this becomes the driving issue.

Religion is rooted in the desire for meaning, but the world we actually live in is absurd. Desire collides with reality and freezes the will. We have to find a way to overcome death and live with meaning. Nothing in the world, nothing we experience, quiets this longing. The drama takes place in us, in what drives us, in our ultimate concern – what we have been calling 'orienting value.' The fact that devotion has to *limit* itself – that the search for meaning seizes on something and defends a territory – is the touchstone. To worship everything is to worship nothing. Oppositely, in worshipping *one* thing particularly, it is easy to wind up in a dead end. Human beings are limited beings and not omniscient; they make choices with *limited* knowledge; but to uphold a party cause is to surrender to a concern that is merely provisional.

Faith is a "centered act of the personality" and *not* merely an act of will, knowledge or emotion. The problem of faith thus defined is to make out the difference between a provisional concern and an ultimate concern and not to mistake the former for the latter. A provisional concern that is taken as ultimate becomes destructive – all of a person's energies become focused on an object that is unworthy of this attention – it does not belong in the center but is put there – very quickly we lose our way – we begin to make all the typical mistakes. Tillich argues that every provisional concern entails this danger – a kind of side-project looms overlarge and tends to insinuate itself as a permanent object of desire. Yet he also argues that there is no easy way to avoid this. Some important steps in the argument are as follows:

(1) Faith, the ultimate concern, is inexpressible, and cannot be captured in a rule.
(2) But in each case faith takes form – it takes shape in a symbol and in actions.
(3) Thus the ultimate concern is expressed provisionally – the whole via the part.
(4) To reduce the whole to the part is dangerous – it makes it easy to confuse them.
(5) There is no way to avoid this danger – faith has to take shape and become real.

Tillich concludes that there does not appear to be any harmless way to domesticate the driving concern of one's life. If a concern remains merely provisional, or if faith is not passionate faith, then faith remains a hesitant faith, and thus is not a real faith; because (he says) a hesitant faith leaves a person unmoved. Orienting value is always on the verge of overreaching. Real faith always involves the danger of idolatry. This is what Tillich argues in the *Dynamics of Faith* and elsewhere:

"If faith is the state of being ultimately concerned, and if every ultimate concern must express itself concretely, the special symbol of the ultimate concern participates in its ultimacy. It participates in its unconditional character, although it is not unconditional itself. The situation which is the source of idolatry is also the source of intolerance. The one expression of the ultimate denies all other expressions. It becomes – almost inevitably – idolatrous and demonic" (*Dynamics of Faith*, 1957, pp.122-123; *The New Being*, 1955, pp. 152-160).

Tillich claims that the transformation of the contingent symbol of the ultimate concern into its demonic opposite "has happened to all religions which take the concrete expression of their ultimate concern seriously." The religion of ancient Greece has a kind of advantage over rival traditions in that it *never* takes the concrete expression of its ultimate concern seriously and, therefore, can trespass any set of concrete symbols. Tillich observes that this advantage comes at great cost:

"Such an indifference to the concrete expression of the ultimate is tolerant, but it lacks the power to transform the existential distortions of reality," and "any view fully indifferent to the concrete symbols of its expression would *eo ipso* also be inert." Thus the same circumstance that makes symbols powerful and able to carry the spirit – and which drives us to act in the world on behalf of our faith – also makes them dangers that tempt us into fanaticism.

The project of faith straddles the middle ground between the false infinite and the vacuous infinite – between the transitory, mistaken for the eternal (a mere thing or symbol takes on absolute significance) and the ineffable, mistaken for the substantive (a mystery or suggestive idea is transformed into a dogma). Faith lives between overbelief and underbelief, between mere bias and blank sensing, prejudice and indifference. The circumstance is that of the believer who must balance the 'ultimacy' and 'unconditional' character he tries to express with the 'relativity' and 'contingent' character of what he actually says.

Tillich tries to wrestle with this problem by a close analysis of *symbols* and the ways in which human beings attempt to express themselves by means of symbols. At first he considers a strategy offered by his contemporary Rudolf Bultmann – a fellow existentialist and religious searcher – Bultmann reached conclusions very like those of Tillich and proposed to do away with all religious symbolism – thus e.g. he proposed rethinking Christianity without rituals and symbols – Christianity without the cross, without the resurrection, without magic – instead revising Christianity into the form of a rational and moral creed.

Tillich, reflecting on this proposal – which Bultmann called "demytholigization" – tried to square it with his intuitions about the ultimate concern. He argued: whatever we grasp as the ultimate concern, we call "god." Tillich uses the lowercase "g" to stress the necessity of having to express our faith in concrete terms. Yet the whole notion of the ultimate concern is that it transcends everyday concerns – it is the *ultimate* concern and not merely a provisional one. Thus he uses the uppercase "G" to stress the transcendence that we try to intimate using symbols. In effect, Bultmann wants to retain "god" but reject "God." Tillich objects that this strategy threatens to flatten religious language – removing it from the sphere of imagery and myth and transferring it to the world of logic and observation – conflating the holy and the profane. He proposes the strategy of "deliteralization" in place of "demytholigization." Thus the point is to make use of symbols *explicitly as symbols* and resist the temptation to read them as literal truths.

Tillich argues that people have forgotten how to interpret the old symbolism. Symbols become opaque and lose their power to carry the spirit. They lose their power because they are taken as facts. Quickly they become statements. Thus we speak about God and at once people ask us if God exists. This means that the symbol is no longer working. Instead of pointing beyond itself to allow Being to shine through, the mere symbol we call "God" has become the end of the story and the touchstone of surrendering faith. God is reduced to a hypothesis, an explanation, a purported fact. Tillich responds to the situation in which religious symbols become purported facts and loyalty tests – in which we signal our loyalty by agreeing with a proposition that we know to be false – by asserting with Nietzsche that *God does not exist*. What we are up to in speaking about God has nothing to do with facts. If we argue that God exists, then in effect we are already denying God. The very asking of the question "Does God exist?" or arguing with people for "The Existence of God" signifies that the symbols we are using have become meaningless. God has simply become another object in space and time that may or may not exist. Thus we have completely lost the track. Tillich thinks that the right thing to do now, in a world in which this mistake is made over and over again, is to *confront the dead symbol* – the Death of God – and pursue a course of thought given over to complete doubt. Then the point becomes to "discover the God who appears when God has disappeared in the anxiety of doubt" (*The Courage to Be*, 1952).

To live a while in this doubt teaches the lesson (he argues) that what we have mistaken for a mere thing and what has become blunted in a language of facts and which we now see degraded in dead symbols *is fundamental to our being*. It is "the ground of our being." It is our ultimate concern. It reappears again as soon as we care about anything in life and show who we are and what values we hold and what we trying to do in the world. God is what shows itself in our commitments. Thus Tillich holds that it is meaningless to say "I am now having a 'spiritual' experience." He wants us to get away from talking about an exotic state of mind and return to the idea of something that pervades every aspect of our lives and shines through in all our actions.

Tillich argues that the test of faith is not surrendering one's will or assent to a "faith statement" or by accepting any kind of doctrine, but instead the true test of faith is *the encounter of faith with faith*: e.g. as when the Christian encounters the Muslim, or the Buddhist encounters the Jew, but also when one person of faith (for which he or she may not have a name) encounters another person who looks out into the world in a different way. The encounter brings out the provisional character of religious symbols and raises the issue, whether to treat these symbols as symbols, or whether they will be confused with literal speech. The test can degenerate into either of two extremes: to a *tolerance without criteria* or to an *intolerance without self-criticism*.

He tries to find a way past this dilemma by thinking about what he calls the *legitimacy* of faith and by thinking about faith's ability to look at itself.

His first proposal argues for a criterion of the legitimacy of faith in the "ultimacy of the ultimate concerns it tries to express." Thus he wants to ask the question: Is this proposed object of worship actually *worthy* of worship? – Is this object really ultimate or is it merely instrumental? Thus any faith that is merely a cover for the desire to amass goods, or prestige, or power or pleasure and so on, is an illegitimate faith, because it is fails the test of ultimacy. This represents a strategy for tolerance that applies a rational criterion – but it seems a difficult one to sort out. What distinguishes ultimacy from instrumentality? What is really *ultimate* in life?

His second proposal is that the criterion for the self-criticism of faith is its self-consciousness of the contingency of its symbols. Faith must (as it were) get free of itself and then return to itself – it must upend itself and become a humble confidence. Faith that must be expressed in *this* particular way, or with *these* particular words, or with *this* particular symbol, risks falling into the false consciousness of an absolutist claim. *If I actually have faith in what I believe, I should not fear having to find new ways to express it.* This represents a rational criterion for religious self-criticism – but again also represents a very daunting challenge for believers. Tillich argues that in most cases the symbol overwhelms the reality it was meant to express.

Tillich is defending the claim – completely at odds with familiar ideas about faith – that religious conviction *must be questioned.* The problem of the encounter of faith with faith cannot be reduced to *respecting* other peoples' beliefs, precisely because these beliefs claim so much – because they aim at the 'ultimate concern' – because they profess to be fundamental. In some cases conscience seems to demand actively *opposing* other peoples' beliefs. In some cases – e.g. because of the pompous way in which it is expressed – even *ridiculing* belief makes more sense than respecting it. Respecting peoples' beliefs often amounts to patronizing them – taking them to be children – to avoid hurting them or spoiling their illusions. It is equally misguided to 'respect' beliefs by adopting a relativist standpoint, because doing so ends up equating belief with blind partiality.

Tillich argues: we do not respect people's beliefs by treating people like helpless children or by regarding what people care about as nonsense. We respect belief by subjecting it to ruthless critical analysis. We respect the believer by treating him as an adult – responsible for his belief, and answerable for it.

Thus the ultimate concern shows itself in what kind of person I am, what kind of life I am leading, what I do when I am challenged to account for myself and to be counted in society as a real person furthering real aims.

Tillich offers a vision of religion as a program for action in which my inwardness and engagement with the thing that matters most to me effects an important change in me, so that my focus turns outwards in order to act – to live creatively within my mortality and to advance the driving value in my life.

+

What are we left with when we *explain* religion? Working through a broad sample of findings from religious traditions, and collecting arguments from natural and social science – from theology as well – the inquirer cannot help but sense a vast array of opinion – belief, doubt, speculation, hard evidence – as if one had entered a crowded room where everyone was speaking at once.

Does this image explain anything? I think it does. It illustrates the idea that this is something we do – religion is something we do. It shows that this 'something' takes myriad forms and excites great passions. This thing wells up or insinuates itself and stamps a person's character. It gets under one's skin. It brings people together and sets people against each other; it takes form as communities of different kinds. The religious sense shows itself as this noisy, unruly, contentious crowd.

It also shows itself as opposites; a search for meaning, a way of fitting in; taking a stand or leaving things alone; calming anxieties or checking pride; it disintegrates and assembles. The sense for the sacred appears to open up a horizon between extreme other-worldliness and extreme this-worldliness – basic ways of looking at the world that reveal something about human beings – part of being a human being is sensing this continuum and finding a place in it. There are basic opposite strategies of caring about something, focused either on holding on or letting go. Thus we see in opposites, by opposites – we see by seeing problems – the human way of seeing is an interpretative kind of seeing in which the thing we are looking at is also our sensibility – it is what it is but also what we bring to it.

Religious lore and explanations of religion both seem to show us that the underlying human drive – what I have been calling 'orienting value' – something that *wants* very powerfully – sometimes holding on and sometimes releasing – that awakens to some truth or frees itself from some error – this thing that sees by seeing problems, also makes *choices*.

Xenophanes imagined that horses might make gods for themselves in the shape of horses. If this were the case, it would be enough simply to be a horse in order to be counted among the faithful. Every people in the ancient world had a god to worship, and many people still do. But it is not enough simply to be human in order to have what one believes be respected. We bring human problem-making sensibility to experience – we make each other pass tests – we see that the other person can get it wrong – worship becomes a fight, instead of a kind of horse-sense that we all have, just by being human.

(9) true worship / false worship

Let us examine religious choice and try to make out the difference between true worship and its counterfeit.

The root of the word 'idolatry' is Greek: *eidolon* (idol) + *latreia* (service). *Eidolon* derives from *eidos* (form), a term whose ultimate Indo-European root is *weid-* (to see). Some important derivatives of this root include the words guide, wisdom, unwitting, envy, idea and history.

Some meanings of the word 'idolatry' are: worship of idols, of statues, of merely physical things; blind or excessive devotion; veneration of images, of mere nature, of heroes; fetishism; covetousness.

We say that false worship is 'idolatry', the worship of idols; idolatry is also an overreaching admiration for something. This thing in us that *sees* by seeing problems – that sees, and has ideas, and searches – can fail by touching the wrong things, aiming at the wrong things, but also has degrees and can be too much or too little. The implication is that false worship has mistaken its object or is false by a misplaced intensity.

There are important prohibitions against idolatry in many ancient traditions, notably in the *Torah* and the *Tao Te Ching* and the *Upanishads*, that get at these ideas in different ways.

The first three laws of Moses have to do with God, gods, names, images and service – in particular, the second commandment bans the making of images and worship of them – "you shall not bow down to them and serve them" (*Deuteronomy* 5,8). The Psalms remind us that idols are merely "silver and gold, the work of men's hands" – "like scarecrows in a cucumber field," meant to frighten us – "like who made them," unable to speak, unable to hear, with no life in them (135).

In the Chinese tradition, the first chapter of Master Lao's book begins with the statement that "the Tao that can be named is not the eternal Tao; the name that can be named is not the abiding name; but the Tao is eternal and nameless and uncarved" – with many further passages warning the searcher not to confuse the sign of a thing with the thing itself (*Tao Te Ching*, ch. 1).

The sacred *Vedas* from ancient India are unique among ancient religious texts in that the earliest statement of its creation myth is immediately followed by a passage that throws the myth into doubt (*Rig Veda* X 129). The *Chandogya Upanishad* pursues a long reflection on this theme that rejects names, images and physical things as guides in the discovery of reality, on the model that the spirit likewise cannot be found in the body wherever we look yet nonetheless this unseen thing breathes life into us (VIII, 7-12).

Clearly *idolatry* is a central issue in religious life. The Roman Catholic and Greek Orthodox churches split over this issue; Islam forbids all depiction of Allah; Ch'an Buddhism is often called "the philosophy of silence." In some traditions there is a taboo even against *thinking* about God.

139

Just as the term 'religion' is used in secular contexts to indicate passionate conviction, the term 'idolatry' is used in secular contexts to indicate misplaced valuation. This is a basic opposite: getting it right or failing, both in myriad examples.

Philosophers have often used the term 'idolatry' importantly in their thinking. Bacon used the term 'idolatry' to describe the conservative instinct and the unwillingness to open oneself up to new data and ideas; Marx used the term to describe the underpinnings of greed; Adorno used it to describe the disease of nationalism and the exaltation of leaders. The Israeli intellectual Yeshayahu Leibowitz (1903-1994) used it to describe the Zionist's worship of a certain plot of land. He held that divinity *transcends* nature, with no remainder; neither nature, nor history, nor any people within it, can carry divine significance; holiness is confined to God and cannot be predicated of anything existing in the world.

A cluster of problems gather around the word 'idolatry' originating in the root idea of impulse, desire, love or aspiration; including the idea that this root form of care, devotion, valuation, worship or piety is a fundamental category of human being; also the idea that worship may be misdirected, censurable, diverted from its real aim, and thus idolatrous; questioning love that can be too weak or strong, and thus under- or over-reaching, insensible or idolatrous; or arguing for a democracy among impulses, or against impulse having any measure at all; or arguing the claim that devotion, honor, worship or veneration imply an objective content or, arguing the contrary, that questions of value are like questions of taste, which by the principle *de gustibus non est disputandum* are unaccountable; thus by steps raising the general question about the nature of orienting value. Religion puts a frame around value – around human motivation, human care, human intention – orienting value is reason-seeking and religion offers itself as reason-giving.

From Tillich we learn that orienting value is always on the verge of overreaching – faith verges on idolatry – the spark of interest that makes us love also tempts us towards fanaticism. Without the spark and without love, we are powerless to accomplish anything, so that indifference lies on the other side of fanaticism. We have to be tempted, and thus not indifferent; we have to resist temptation, and thus practice dispassion. Tillich studied these currents and tides and called them The Dynamics of Faith. Tillich's argument highlights the close relation between true faith and false faith, worship and idolatry, love that is blessed and love that becomes cursed. He observes that it is easy to mistake the *symbol* for the *reality* it is meant to portray and thus fall into the position of the idolater. He argues that the demonic is right there, right next to the sacred, and comes from wrongly loving. He explores the relation between worship as such and the risk of idolatry, beginning the inquiry from two premises: that *care* is a fundamental human capacity like seeing or breathing; and that this fundamental root of *care* deserves thought.

The idea that human beings routinely value the wrong things is familiar from the Eden story. Easton's 1897 *Dictionary of Bible Studies* lists 18 Hebrew words translated as "idol" in different contexts – also translated "god," "image," and "statue." Gnostic writings from a century or more before the advent of Christ call the Earth a prison-house and disparage all human accounting of good and evil.

The idea that human beings mistake illusion for reality has its classic account in the Myth of the Cave. Plato conceives that human life transpires in darkness; that people spend their lives gazing at shadows; that they are oblivious to their bondage and ignorant of who they really are.

Tillich argues that idolatry is the elevation of something preliminary to status of something final – "something essentially conditional is taken as unconditional, something essentially partial is boosted to universality, something essentially finite is given infinite significance." This view assumes that is possible to discern which among human cares are merely provisional and which are final. Thus it appears that the charge of 'idolatry' is made from the standpoint of (presumed) knowledge, since to describe a form of worship as *false* worship implies a standard of correctness. One way to work around this requirement is to adopt a wholesale *skepticism* concerning all human cares, as we find e.g. in Stoicism.

Stoicism offers the ideal of *ataraxia* (indifference) as a response to the problem of mistaken valuation – we can be certain to avoid worshiping false gods, if we no longer worship anything at all. The Stoic proposal is sometimes expressed in the motto *nil admirari* – to admire nothing – not to wonder any more or stand in awe, not to kneel before anything, not to sacrifice one's intelligence, not to fear. Bertrand Russell, and Richard Rorty, in later times, argued for ridding ourselves of *worshipping* anything, calling out worship as a craven thing, beneath self-respecting creatures.

The Stoic proposal is noble – admirable – but it also seems wildly blind. Everyone sees that *a life without passionately caring about something* is no kind of life. Human being is much more likely to achieve its fulfillment in passion than in indifference. This may even be an explanation for religion itself – to be tied to something, to care about something and sense that it matters – zeal, devotion, passion, faith, belief. Religiosity is almost a synonym for humanity.

But zeal is also wildly blind – the spirit of reason seems to advise us that worship is virtually *always* misdirected – that human beings mistake illusion for reality and value the wrong things. The animist, the Christian and the Fascist have in common a concentration of personal energies towards the superpersonal goal. They may even share some common ways of thinking and a kind of jargon of devotion. How do we make out the different forms of zeal and set them in some order? How can we even tell them apart?

In their recent study *Idolatry* (1998), Moshe Halbertal and Avishai Margalit argue that there are three fundamentally different kinds of idolatry, which they call "replacement," "extension," and "inversion."

The first category, "replacement," assumes the definition of idolatry "worship of an alien god in place of the true god," and then replaces the (presumed) true god with a new and false ideal. In a sense this comes of the biblical idea that what we do, following the Lord, is religion, and what other people do, in foreign lands, is worshipping idols. The authors refer to the charge against so-called "secular humanism" in this light as replacing true worship with scientific naturalism, i.e. the pursuit of scientific reason, without regard to concepts of the sacred or of god. From the standpoint the true worship, they argue, the "divine" standard is *replaced* here by falsehood. Thus idolatry means: turning away from the true god and worshipping another.

Their second category, "extension," assumes that the charge of 'idolatry' may be directed everywhere in experience, since any kind of human *desire* may be accounted a form of worship. There are as many forms of idolatry as there are false gods. Idolatry means: censurable desire, i.e. wanting the wrong thing, seeking the wrong thing, loving the wrong thing. But human beings *always* want the wrong things. William James reaches a similar conclusion in *The Varieties of Religious Experience* and notes that a root of all religiosity is "an uneasiness ... a sense that there is *something wrong with us* as we naturally stand" out of which religions make ideas of sin and moral wrong. "The individual, so far as he suffers from his wrongness and criticizes it, is to that extent consciously beyond it" and has a chance to learn in this new position (XX, Conclusions). Thus the true faith and opposite of idolatry is *iconoclasm*, idol-smashing. When we talk about idolatry in this sense we are trying to model true worship, worship without sin, perfect worship – imageless worship – worship without names or limits or failings of any kind, so that all that is left for us to do is turn away from everything before us. The sense that something is wrong becomes the act of turning away. Wittgenstein also reflected on this problem and reached the conclusion: "All that we can do is to destroy idols – and that means also, not making any new ones – not even out of the 'absence of idols.'" We have to turn away even from the idea that turning away is important. What is left is the process of thinking, clearing away mistakes, idol-smashing, and silence. Thus idolatry means: breaking this silence – not being able to stand it – falling back to the weakness of wanting the wrong things. Idolatry in this case is not about replacing the true god with a false ideal, but about not having the strength for real worship.

Their third category, "inversion," represents a form of argument in which the traditional opposition between believers and unbelievers is maintained, but in which the valuation of the opposition is inverted. The division of the world is between "the community of faith" – the *cult* – and the secular world, i.e. the *infidels*. Inverting this hierarchy means praising doubt and condemning believers. Halbertal and Margalit cite Feuerbach, Nietzsche and Russell as examples of thinkers who pursued this strategy – these thinkers all argued that the *believer* is the true idolater, because he stops *looking* for truth and *enshrines* it instead.

Halbertal and Margalit eventually conclude that the modern development of the term *idolatry* has proceeded so far that it is no longer possible to maintain a concept of the absolute (God, god, divinity, deity, the holy, the sacred). Thus in our time worship and idolatry have merged. Thus to take up a stand against idolatry is to abolish the absolute, i.e. a rejection of every *ultimate* concern. The stand against idolatry is a stand against desire itself.

Sartre takes a position like this and argues for the conclusion that desire *per se* is the desire to be God. For Sartre desire is not always on the verge of overreaching, but instead desire always overreaches; it has to, because it is trying to lay hold of the entire world, of Being itself. Man possesses a comprehension of the being of God, not from wonders of nature or the moral law, but from his experience of reaching towards God – which Sartre defines as "the permanent limit in terms of which man makes known to himself what he is." "Man is fundamentally the desire to be God." "Man is the being whose project is to be God." Desire is never mere desire but is towering desire. Desire always gets out of hand and becomes demonic; in this world of extremes, we can no longer pull evil apart from good or tell them apart (*Being and Nothingness*, 1943)

Tillich would reject this interpretation and trace the error at its source in its presumption that idolatry comes from the standpoint of presumed knowledge and is "turning away from the true god and worshipping another." The error here is the idea that there could be a true god – God – because God is not a god or a being or anything that exists. "God cannot become one of the innumerable objects in space and time that may or may not exist. This is not the idea of God at all."

Karen Armstrong puts this point as follows: "Idolatry has always been one of the pitfalls of monotheism. Because its chief symbol of the divine is a personalized deity, there is an inherent danger that people would imagine "him" as a larger, more powerful version of themselves, which they could use to endorse their own lives – ideas, practices, loves and hatreds – sometimes to lethal effect. There can only be *one* absolute…" Armstrong sees idolatry as a mirror of narcissism and notes that when one thing is made supreme, it becomes a kind of need to destroy everything that opposes it. "We have seen a good deal of this kind of idolatry in recent years" (*The Case for God*, 2009, p. 322). Armstrong is arguing against holding one thing supreme, as idolatry, as arrogance, as presumption, as putting ourselves in the place of the absolute, as narcissism: if we hold one thing supreme, it will be ourselves.

Tillich warns us that a man-made idea of God could never be an adequate representation of transcendence – to think so is idolatrous – which is where he makes his transition from describing to preaching – this is where he finds his message. He wants us all to grow out of idolatrous worship and leave it behind. "The concept of "Personal God," interfering with natural events, or being an independent cause of natural events, makes God a natural object besides others, an object among others, a being among others, maybe the highest, but nevertheless, *a* being. This indeed is not only the destruction of the physical system, but even more the destruction of any meaningful idea of God. ... Even the Supreme Being is a *being*, the final item in the series. It is therefore an "idol," a human construction that has become absolute" (*Theology and Culture*, 1964, p. 129).

Tillich holds that worship of beings with names such as Jehovah, Jesus or Allah, is fundamentally idolatrous, and is not radically different from the worship of tyrants, which has not been rare in history; this is a kind of worship that led to more than one hundred million deaths in the last century. Tillich also denies that the charge of idolatry presumes a state of perfect worship. It is not because we have found a better symbol for what "God" means that we can smash mere idols as false images of the highest truth. We have no such knowledge and there is no perfect symbol. We can, however, tell when a symbol has died and when it is being used in a literal manner; we can tell that it has lost its power; we can see without claiming to know.

loyalty to loyalty

Tillich would argue that it is possible to distinguish between authentic faith and false faith even if we do not possess a *final* form of worship or a *perfect* worship or *the one and only* right formula for the absolute.

Applying Tillich's two principles to the problem of idolatry, we might argue the following:

(1) The charge of false worship implies that the (censured) object of worship is unworthy because it is preliminary, provisional, contingent, accidental – not unconditional but radically conditioned. The proof of the charge has to come out in an investigation of *what* the religion worships – what the person worships in secular contexts – the object of desire – but here the inquiry faces an obstacle in that for the most part the object of worship cannot be laid hold of or specified very far or called to account or cross-examined.

Tillich accepts believers' claims that we can only understand what it is like to worship after their fashion from the inside. But he rejects its relevance. This is why we judge a faith by its works. What kind of actions does it sponsor? What does it prohibit? How does it impact the lot of its believers? What role does it play in society? What good does this bring to the world?

(2) The charge of false worship may represent an attempt to dictate *true* worship – claiming sole prerogative, privilege, exclusivity – with the result that the (presumed) true form of worship now proclaims that the true faith has to be expressed in *this* particular way, or with *these* particular words, or with *this* particular symbol – so that it quickly falls into the false consciousness of an absolutist claim. Thus the critic of idolatry must subject his own faith to the same measure or be accounted a hypocrite.

Tillich once remarked "the idea that the human mind is a perpetual manufacturer of idols is one of the deepest things that can be said about our thinking of God" (*A History of Christian Thought*, 1969, p. 264). Because this drive is so deep in us and goes to our ultimate concern, we must study ourselves; we must judge faith by works; we must subject our own faith to an intolerant criticism.

The American thinker Josiah Royce wrestled with the problem of false worship in his 1908 work *The Philosophy of Loyalty*. Royce framed the problem of worship, devotion, care or value in terms of the basic concept of "loyalty" – offering a critique of false worship in terms very like those which Tillich offered. Royce observed how often tyrants demand unwavering loyalty, and how often religion degrades into a loyalty test; religious freedom has to be won in a contest of political loyalties, and politics seems to instruct us to look for solutions from broader loyalties. Royce wanted to speak to loyalty as a *virtue* rather than an invading demand on the personality. He reasoned: first there is a cause, then the demand for loyalty to the cause; then competing loyalties conflict, which puts the question to the believer, *loyal to what?*; but most importantly, exchanging one loyalty for another, or conquering others for the sake of any single loyalty, is vain; it is vain because it does nothing for the increase of loyalty in the world. Royce thinks that loyalty inspires noble virtues such as unselfishness, courage and compassion, but also fierce honesty and integrity; loyalty is a kind of signal of the noble character, which is then the "broader loyalty." This insight moves him to examine how loyalty to a party cause alters the quality of mind of the loyalist. He offers a test of party cause, whatever cause it may be: which is, whether my loyalty and worship of this cause works for the increase of these virtues in others. Thus it is better to increase these virtues in loyalists to other causes than to convert them to my cause. Royce calls this "the loyalty to loyalty" – "choose your cause and serve it, so that there will be more loyalty in the world rather than less" – "serve the cause to which you are loyal, but above that, be loyal to loyalty."

+

At a certain point in history, all these ideas fade into insignificance, and the role of choice in religion is reduced down to *one* choice, *one* dilemma, *one* value, i.e., the choice between theism or atheism.

(10) theism /atheism

The English word 'God' (Dutch *God*, Danish *Gud*, German *Gott*, Sanskrit *ghuta*) derives from the Indo-European root *gheu(ə)-*, 'to call, invoke.' The English word 'giddy' derives from the same root; originally the term meant 'possessed.' It gradually took on senses like 'insane' and 'happy.'

The Greek term *theos*, 'god,' which is the basis of English words like 'theism' and 'atheism,' also 'enthusiasm,' derives from the IE root *dhēs-*. This root is the basis for words like feast, festival, festive (Spanish *fiesta*, French *fête*, Latin *festus*), all having the sense 'holy day' i.e. holiday, as well as words like fanatic, profane, fantastic (French *fanatique*, Greek *fanatikos*, Latin *fanum*), having to do with the *fanum*, the temple. *Theos* links the idea of the holy (god) to a second signifier, e.g. to time or place. The time that is set apart is God's time (the holy day, holiday). Profane things are *pro-* (in front of, outside of) the *fanus* (the temple), i.e. irreligious, irreverant, unconsecrated, unholy, secular. The fanatic is someone who is in the temple and (in a sense) cannot get out of it (thus the idea of excessive devotion).

A third important IE root for religious terms is *dyeu-*, 'to shine.' This is the basis of the Sanskrit term *deva*, 'god,' 'divine,' the Avestan terms *dava*, *daeva*, 'spirit' or 'divine,' the Latin terms *Deus, Ios, Iove, Jupiter* (*Io Pater*, father-god), all with the sense 'divine,' 'god' – also the Latin terms *Diana, dies, diurnus*, day, daytime, brightness – the Greek terms *Zeus, Dios, delos*, 'bright sky,' 'clear,' also French *Dieu, adieu* (compare to English 'goodbye,' i.e., 'God be with you'). The English terms Tuesday, divine, jovial, Jupiter, journal, adjourn, and journey have the same derivation. This term links the idea of god to the sky.

Indo-European roots tend to lead us back to Zeus, the sky-god atop Mt. Olympus. Semitic roots draw us to Jahve, the sky-god atop Mt. Sinai. Both are weather-gods and volcano-gods. Both are sky-fathers.

The Semitic root *hyy, hwy, hyh*, is hypothesized to mean life or water. This appears to be the basis of the most ancient Sumerian god name *Ea*. In Hebrew, it is the verb 'to be.' This root is the basis for the sacred name, also called the tetragrammaton or simply 'the name' (*Ha Shem*) – YHWH – also *Yahweh, Jahve, halleluyah* (also note the expression *Baal Shem*, 'master of the name,' which incorporates the Assyrian expression *Ba'al*, meaning 'master,' 'lord,' or 'god'). This root is also the basis of names such as Jah, Jehovah, Joshua, Jeshua, Yeshua (Jesus); also names ending in *–yah* (Matthew, Isiah, Jeremiah, Nehemiah). The root survives in the English term 'abyss.'

The Semitic root *ˀl, *ˀil-, ˀilāh-* is the basis of the Sumerian term *Enlil* (god of gods), the Akkadian term *Babylon* (gate of God), the Hebrew forms *El* (God), *El oha* (mighty God), *El ohai* (my God), *El ohaynu* (our God), *El ohim* (the gods), *El elyu* (God most high), *El shaddai* (God of the mountains), also *Peniel* (face of God), *Israel* (fight with God), *Azazel* (desert God), *Bethel* (house of God), *Gabriel* (strength of God), *Nathaniel* (gift of God), and generally names ending in *–el*; also in prefix forms such as *Elizabeth* and *Elijah* and the like. The same root (*ili*) underlies the Aramaic term *Elaha*, and the Arabic forms *Al, Allah, ayatollah*. Because of the long Muslim occupation of Spain (711-1492), many Arabic words were taken into Spanish; thus the ancient root *ili* survives in the modern term *olé*.

The ultimate root meaning of the term *El* and its later forms is disputed. Some scholars relate it to the Semitic root *alih*, which indicates fear; another explanation is the Semitic root *uhl*, meaning strength.

Inside the sanctuary in the city of Mecca which the Arabs refer to as the *Ka'ba* (the basis for the English word 'cube') there are said to be three hundred and sixty five idols, representing gods from many earlier periods in Middle Eastern history, including all the gods mentioned above as well as Hubal, Syrian god of the moon; al-Uzza ('the mighty'), also known as Ishtar, Astarte, Inanna, Anunit, Atarsamain, Isis, Esther and (to the Greeks) Aphrodite; also Allat, Manat, and al-Kutba; also many Egyptian gods and Sumerian gods and Akkadian gods; also Jesus and his holy mother, Mary.

By tradition the *Ka'ba* was erected by Adam, the first man. It is said that the flood destroyed the edifice and that Noah rebuilt it. The shrine was forgotten for centuries until Abraham rediscovered it. It was here that he offered his son Isaac for a sacrifice and where Isaac was spared (Arabic *Ismail*).

The only god not represented in the *Ka'ba* is the 'Creator God,' 'King of Gods,' 'Lord of the House,' also known as *El, Allah, Jehovah, Jahve,* and *Jah*. This is considered a sign of respect. In Arabic, the period preceding monotheism is called the *Jahiliyyah* – 'the time of ignorance.'

A similar inquiry into Chinese linguistics, mythology and history points to what scholars call 'heaven worship,' a religious system predating Confucianism, Taoism and Buddhism in China. Polytheistic and localized cults overlapped in worship of the 'Supreme,' whose name literally is 'sky-god.' The Chinese root *–ti* is the basis for many important religious terms including *ti* (lord), *ti an* (sky lord), *shang ti* (high lord), *huang ti* (yellow lord), *ti en* (heaven), *ti en ming* (mandate of heaven), *shang ti taiyishen* (supreme ultimate high lord), *yuanshi ti an zum* (lordly celestial primordial beginning).

It is said that there are twelve major language families – Indo-European, Afro-Asiatic (including all Semitic languages) and Sino-Tibetan – we have looked at roots from these three systems – the nine remaining families are: the Niger-Congo, Austronesian, Dravidian, Altaic, Tai-Kadai, Austro-Asiatic, Uralic, Papuan, and American. Taken all together, these account for nearly all world languages. A glimpse into any of these language systems, with a focus on religious language, soon discovers god-terms, mythologies and genuine histories – creation myths, sacred places, stories of First Man and First Woman – all intertwined, in complex intersections with rival traditions, and in general leading back to a few basic linguistic roots – among the first we learn.

For example, in the Siouan language base (which includes Lakota, Dakota, Nakota, Mandan, Crow and many others) the common root for religious terms is –*kan*, as in *wakan, wakanda, wakan tanka, tunkanshila*. These terms refer to leaders, to the chief, but also to the Great Spirit conceived as an inherent life force or principle; also to rites and supernatural ideas.

In the Athabaskan language base (which includes Native American languages spoken in Alaska, the Yukon, Northwestern Canada, Washington, Oregon, California, and Northern Mexico, also including Arizona, New Mexico, Utah, Oklahoma and Texas) the root is –*aan* as in *aankaa wu, aan yadi, dik aan, aan sati, aan kaaxu*, with exactly the same references: chief, spirit, life, rites.

The overriding conclusion of these inquiries is to support the claim that god-speech is ubiquitous – an anthropological invariant – thus occurring everywhere and at all times – so widespread as to include every culture on this planet and every period of history.

In god-speech there are two important but separate elements: (1) a referent in evidence, and (2) a referent not in evidence.

The worldly referent

(the sky, the sun, the moon, the stars, weather phenomena, smoke, mist, an oath or a promise, a great howl or yell or scream, the action of calling out, the action of setting apart, the action of dividing or fixing a boundary, a totem plant, a totem animal, breath, a life, a father or mother or ancestor, a ruler or chief or person of social standing, an elder, even the tribe itself…)

is presented in some connection to an unworldly referent, a referent that is not in evidence which, despite this condition, is taken to be

(the crucial thing, the real thing, the important thing, the main thing, the thing behind everything else, the thing above all other things, the fundamental thing, the first thing or last thing, the inner nature or metanature or supernature or counternature, the transcendent, the level below or outside, deeper or higher than everything else…).

This is the origin-point of religion – returning to the root sense of *religare*, to tie or bind – at the juncture of the thing we can see and its unseen, difference-making, unworldly counterpart.

The reference to the unseen counterpart implies a kind of sympathetic magic – a magical connection to the 'Big Other' (however defined) – part of whose magic is brought back home.

Call this 'the God hypothesis' – asserting the existence of the unseen, intangible counterpart – the unseen basis of the seen and our magical connection to it.

The God hypothesis in cultural and historical perspective is a near invariant, but also shows amazing, even confusing variety, and has important exceptions.

A good example of an exceptional position is Buddhism, which in the Theraveda tradition – the "Way of the Elders" – makes no mention of God or any other supernatural idea. Theraveda Buddhism is not unbelieving but (it claims) undistracted (that is, it does not ask such questions). The Buddha said that questions about God and otherworldly things "tend not to edification" or are of no use, since whether God exists or not, whether there are any gods at all, or even whether there are 'religious experiences' or not, makes no matter; whatever the case in all these examples, there is *suffering*; answers to questions like these have no bearing on suffering; and so they are nothing.

The tradition of Theraveda Buddhism has often been advanced as evidence that it is possible to live without asserting the God hypothesis.

There is also a famous story about Napoleon and the great mathematician and astronomer Pierre-Simon Laplace. Napoleon tried to challenge the scientist by asking him why there was no mention of God in his book on astronomy. Laplace said in response: "I have no need of that hypothesis."

Some thinkers have rejected philosophical, ethical and scientific theories as exceptions to ubiquitous god-speech, arguing that even in these cases (which may even be expressly atheistic) there is an assertion of an *unseen counterpart* – an underlying truth, not in direct evidence, which is taken to be the crucial thing, the foundation or 'point' of the phenomena – which we may as well call 'God.'

The variety of God concepts is confusing because it is so vast – including philosophical, ethical and scientific ideas vastly compounds the problem – since every story is different – every one calls out some special name – every one has a different truth to champion and a different point to make.

Granting this – accepting a broad idea of what is going on with this concept – granting a basket of stories and many collections of theories – consider the idea of a still larger context.

Suppose that God is a supercontext, a kind of big X to which various examples, small x, are referred – a unworldly referent in terms of which worldly things are given a new significance. This implies that (1) there is another, still bigger X that has the same relation to big X that big X has to x, or (2) the supercontext has this relation to itself.

In the former case, the 'still bigger X' is the God-figure, and big X has a lower status.

In the latter case, there is no new context, no new big context or new supercontext. On this assumption, the 'Big Other' has a different character – it gets to be a 'Big Other' and it doesn't need any help – it can be what it is on its own – it does not require any further explanation. God on this model is a kind of ultimate self-sufficiency – the one thing that is a context for itself – the one thing that is its own explanation – i.e. the totality of everything that exists; the universe.

atheism

Atheism has a long history in China, India, the Middle East and Europe, as ancient as belief itself. The same transition from prehistory into history that turns primitive ritualism into positive doctrine also creates negative critique – belief as much as doubt – theism as much as atheism.

Pragmatism reminds us that belief is not one thing but many. It is the 'Big Other' in the form of the local culture. Institutional religions are cultural artifacts – things created by humans which give us information about a people. The mind is also a kind of archaeological site, where we dig up attitudes and beliefs that speak to us from a single locale. Looking at language worldwide shows many ways of naming 'Big Other,' such as the Greek *theos*, Sanskrit *ghuta*, and Sumerian *Ea*. Looking at culture we can also see what atheism has been in many different times and places.

Atheism has been naturalism, as in ancient China, some of whose books date back five thousand years. Much later, the 'Hundred Schools' period in Chinese history (dating from the eighth century BCE) includes several atheistic positions, including the speculations of the school of Names and the Legalist school. China today, with its roughly 1.3 billion inhabitants, is officially atheist, the only such nation in the world.

The *Rig Veda*, dating from an ancient period in Indian prehistory – perhaps as early as 2000 BCE – allows itself to state and examine several atheistic arguments. The Lokayata (or 'Critical') school, also called Carvaka, dating from the fifth century BCE, expresses a vision of strict materialism. Important later figures in Indian thinking, including many writers in the Mimamsa (or 'Exegesis') school, state atheistic positions (Shabara, ~200 CE, Kumarila Bhatta, ~700 CE).

From the cross, Jesus cries out "My God, my God, why have you forsaken me?" (*Mark* 15. 34). He is quoting from the opening verse of *Psalm* 22. The verses continue:

Far from my rescue are words that I roar.
My God, I call out by day and You do not answer.
I call by night, but I find no rest.

Jewish tradition holds that the *Psalms* are the work of King David, who is thought to have lived around the year 1000 BCE. Thus Jesus is quoting a text that for him is nearly 1000 years old. The text is ancient, but it is also highly sophisticated, and continually switches back and forth between conviction and doubt. *Psalm* 13 wonders where God is hidden, *Psalm* 14 wonders if He exists at all, *Psalm* 19 announces that the heavens declare the glory of God, Psalm 22 laments the emptiness of the world without Him. *Psalm* 53 condemns a cynical and unrighteous age but also explicitly raises the atheist argument: "The fool says in his heart, 'There is no God.'" Likewise God looks down from heaven on the sons of men, but the wise are all fallen away and no one does good works. Every atheist in Jewish tradition thereafter tries to speak up for "the fool" – a tradition continued by Christian authors in the Middle Ages; an example is Gaunilon's piece "On Behalf of the Fool," a product of the Benedictine community in Alsace, dating from around 1100 CE – the contemporary philosopher Ibn Warraq continues this tradition in Islamic scholarship.

Ecclesiastes is perhaps the most unbelieving book in the Bible – "vanity of vanity, all is vanity" – God may be in heaven, but we are here on earth – the meaning of existence is hidden, and none of us achieves wisdom – you may fear God, but you cannot understand Him – you cannot even be certain that He exists. By tradition (doubted by scholars) *Ecclesiastes* is the work of David's son, Solomon the Wise, an important figure also in Christian writings and in the *Qur'an*. The *Qur'an* says that Sulayman, son of Dawud, had wisdom to control the wind and could understand the language of birds (27,16; 34,12).

It is striking that a man thought to be wise beyond all other men among Jews, Christians and Muslims – a storyteller (*Proverbs*), philosopher (*Ecclesiastes*), and love-poet (*Song of Songs*) – is unafraid to doubt the existence of God, to voice these doubts, to dismiss his own and everyone else's wisdom – Solomon builds a temple for Yahweh and a resting-place for the Ark, but also shrines to Ashtoreth, Milcom, Chemosh, and Molech – Love-Goddess, Bull-God, Destroyer-God, Fish-God.

Greek writers beginning with Diagoras, Prodicas, Kritias, Theodorus, and Euhemerus – figures of the fifth century BCE – express a deep skepticism on religious questions. Diagoras stated flatly that there are no gods and that he will not be scared into any fairy-tales or pretended magic or other foolishness. Critias is perhaps the sharpest critic. The following passage (fragment 25) has to represent a milestone:

"Then when the laws prevented men from open deeds of violence, but they continued to commit them in secret, some man of shrewd and subtle mind invented for men the fear of gods, so there might be something to frighten the wicked when they acted, spoke or even thought in secret. There is, he said, a tremendous spirit that never dies, that hears and sees everything, exceedingly wise, which is the *divine nature*. This is the seductive story he told with lying words. He gave the gods a dwelling place to strike fear in the hearts of men, in the heavenly vault, whence come lightnings and roars of thunder, and the starry face and form of heaven, wrought beautiful by the cunning craftsmanship of time; where the meteor falls from the sky, and liquid rain that descends to earth. He surrounded men with these fears and wonders and gave the Deity a fitting home in a fitting place, to extinguish wrongdoing by means of fear...this is how men came to believe in the existence of gods."

The orator Lysias tells stories of the "hell-fire club" in ancient Athens – a band of unbelievers who deliberately chose unlucky or forbidden days on which to dine together and mock the gods. Disbelief, rationalism, natural philosophy and the Sophistic movement all began together in the lifetime of Socrates – an important aspect of the atmosphere in which Plato and Aristotle both grew up. Plato was moved to construct a philosophical theology because the popular worship of his time was crumbling away. He tried to save belief – but it is more significant that he was free to criticize it.

François-Marie Arouet, better known by his pen name *Voltaire* (1694-1778), David Hume (1711 –76), Denis Diderot (1713-84), Claude Helvétius (1715-71), Jean d'Alembert (1717– 83), Paul-Henri Thiry, baron d'Holbach (1723-89), Adam Smith, the father of modern economics (1723–90), and Edward Gibbon, perhaps the greatest historian of all time (1737–1794), among many other luminaries of the European Enlightenment, all ventured atheist arguments, defending both freedom of inquiry and, especially, religious freedom, including the freedom *not* to worship.

Hume, for example, argued that the conception of God, creator and preserver of the world, who must be omnipotent and omniscient and supremely good, is logically incompatible with the existence of suffering.

The solution of his epoch was to remove the acceptance of the idea of God from rational or logical control – as an item of faith it could not be questioned – thus we worship God without understanding. Hume argues that reason leads us into doubts we cannot or should not sustain.

The crystal clarity of the atheist thinker Arthur Schopenhauer (1788-1860) makes the point that religion must surely have a bad conscience (and fear to be looked at too closely) since we are so often forbidden, under pain of severe punishment, to mock it (*Parerga and Paralipomena*, "On Religion," 8). Schopenhauer was the most popular writer of the succeeding age and was a favorite of such freethinking authors as Ludwig Feuerbach (1804-72), Karl Marx (1818-83), Friedrich Nietzsche (1844-1900), Sigmund Freud (1856-1939) and H.L. Mencken (1880-1956).

All these writers question what it is that we are really worshipping in overt acts of religious devotion. Feuerbach, for example, held that religion is a mask for a kind of narcissism:

"Religion is consciousness of the infinite. Religion therefore is nothing else than the consciousness of the infinite in our own consciousness; or, in the consciousness of the infinite, the conscious subject has for his object the infinity of his own nature. Therefore God is nothing else than man: God is, so to speak, the outward projection of man's inward nature" (*The Essence of Christianity*, 1841).

Nietzsche perhaps should be singled out at the summit of atheist thinking, having declared that "God is dead" (*The Gay Science*, 1887). Nietzsche declares that we have killed God, we have killed religious belief, whatever this belief may have been in the past. Thus he declares that in present-day society we have cleared the way ahead of us, we have finally stood up on our own two feet to take responsibility for ourselves, now we are ready to have the courage of our own convictions. We can stop cowering before idols of power or authority or respectability – feelings that have almost nothing to do with the original motives of worship – which (he claims) may simply be the desire to serve some worthy purpose.

Bertrand Russell (1872-1970) was a fierce advocate for atheism, arguing that religion is fear:

"The whole conception of God is a conception derived from ancient Oriental despotisms. It is a conception unworthy of free men. When you hear people in church debasing themselves and saying that they are miserable sinners, and all the rest of it, it seems contemptible and not worthy of self-respecting human beings. We ought to stand up and look the world frankly in the face. We do not need…words uttered long ago by ignorant men. We need knowledge, kindness and courage. We need a fearless outlook and a free intelligence."

Atheism has been many things: naturalism, materialism, skepticism, doubt, sobriety, political consciousness come of age – cynicism, scorn, bravado, satire – moral outrage, freedom of inquiry, humility, self-deprecation, a rejection of every conceit and vanity – a self-assertion of reason, science, a kind of self-confidence, courage rather than fear, freedom from superstition, and reflective calm (*ataraxia*). Atheism has been loneliness in a world without God, despair in a moment of pain – atheism has been calling for help, and has been the fool who says in his heart, 'There is no God.'

The variety of ideas about atheism is dizzying and again every version champions a different truth. Granting this – granting a broad idea of what is going on with this concept – granting a bundle of arguments and many collections of theories – consider the idea of the *belittling rejoinder*.

Suppose then that X is the starting point but by means of the belittling rejoinder X reduces to x. Then x is either the least of all or there is something even less important than x. If there is something even less important than x, as in 'it's just x,' then by steps we will arrive at the least important thing of all. And that is nothingness.

Atheism is a polemical concept; it exists to oppose a prior hypothesis. The Romans, for example, considered the new sect called 'Christians' to be atheists, because they disbelieved in the Roman gods. A polemical concept is one that enters into and takes a side in a controversy – *polemos*, the Greek term for struggle, conflict, war. Therefore atheism has meaning in a prior context of theism.*

If theism is assertion, then atheism is denial
If theism is God, then atheism is man
If theism is belief, then atheism is doubt
If theism is fear, then atheism is courage
If theism is other-worldly, then atheism is this-worldly
If theism is superstition, then atheism is realism
If theism is mysticism, then atheism is naturalism
If theism is credulous, then atheism is skeptical
If theism is heaven, then atheism is earth

The anthropologist Paul Radin's work in the 1930s discovered a correlation between the economic level of society and nature of its supernatural beings. Civilizations with a food-gathering or fishing-hunting economy worship or fear inconsistently defined spirits. When the method of food production evolves into agriculture, caste and class systems emerge and a priestly class who find it necessary or profitable to elaborate the nature of a supernatural being. The historian of technology Lewis Mumford shows how agricultural record keeping systems gradually evolve into writing systems (late fourth millennium BCE), quickly exploited for reverence and skepticism. Huge beings who lord over the universe have an earthly correlate in mighty grain-kings presiding over Nile, Euphrates and Indus river valley civilizations – theologies follow empires – where religious skepticism is born in the same moment, in some examples within the priestly class itself. Ssu-Ma Ch'ien (145-86 BCE), the ancient Chinese historian, records that the 'Hundred Schools' in Chinese thinking – some of which assert a God and some of which deny this – resulted from the breakup of the ruling clan in the latter centuries of the Chou dynasty, when government officers lost their positions and scattered throughout the countryside. Without an imperial patron, they turned to teaching in a private capacity. The Mohist school, theist, came together among the former guardians of the Chou temples. The Legalists, atheist, had served in the ministry of justice. Thus in a given case there may be a difference in office, and economic, class and caste differences may also play a part in the conflict between theism and atheism. Theism develops the logic of the still bigger context, atheism the logic of the belittling rejoinder.

The polemic of belief and doubt takes form in ever-expanding shapes, such as the conflict between Mo Tzu and Han Fei Tzu – the Mohist school, which stood on the principle of love (*jian ai*) vs. the Legalists, who elaborated the principle of power (*shi*) – or the Athenian debate about *physis* (nature) and *nomos* (law) – or the current debate about how life began on earth.

What is it that we are denying if we take up an atheistic position? There is no general answer to this question, outside reference to a cultural context. The Carvakas attacked Brahman, Diagoras of Melos attacked the Olympians. From the standpoint of polytheism, all monotheists are atheists, since they disbelieve in gods, excepting only one. Jainism, which may be the world's oldest religion, describes divinity as *man's* highest attainment – Buddhism is also ancient and dismisses talk about gods as completely irrelevant to insight. If God is the universe, or a stand-in for a self-explaining context, then atheism appears to be self-contradictory, since the universe exists, including atheists. Yet on atheistic logic, even the universe is something about which we can say, 'it's just x,' which may not need any amendment. Probably this is not the kind of thing that is at stake in religious arguments. For the most part, the God hypothesis is *not* about the universe, not about logic, mathematics, physical law or science – Einstein often talked about God but also stated very clearly that he was an atheist. At a certain point in history, the God hypothesis gets reduced down to monotheism – the assertion of the Supreme Being – which makes atheism a claim about a very specific and controversial 'Big Other.' Atheism today is about monotheism and also about the advance of science since the Enlightenment. Atheism is the claim that a being who is all-powerful, all-knowing, compassionate, who created the universe, who hears our prayers and can intervene in human affairs, does not exist.

Plato held that "all mankind, Greeks and non-Greeks alike, believe in the existence of gods" (*Laws* 886a). His lectures, however, concerned the break between the *theologi* and the *physiologi* – the introduction of explanation in terms of physical necessity, which he says was begun by Thales of Miletus (Aristotle, *Metaphysics* A 983). This conflict continues through history and even divides a person from himself: "I believe as a Christian what I cannot believe as a philosopher" (a note from the Renaissance Averroist Petrus of Mantua, 1462-1525). Marx writes that "the abolition of religion as the illusory happiness of people is required for their real happiness – the demand to give up illusions about its condition is the demand to give up a condition which needs illusions" (Marx and Engels, *On Religion*). But against this consider the words of the German thinker Jürgen Habermas, often considered the greatest living philosopher, whose work is usually seen as broadly Marxist in nature. In an interview in 1999, Habermas said: "For the normative self-understanding of modernity, Christianity has functioned as more than just a precursor or catalyst. Universal egalitarianism, from which spring the ideals of freedom and a collective life in solidarity, the autonomous conduct of life and emancipation, the individual morality of conscience, human rights and democracy, is the direct legacy of the Judaic ethic of justice and the Christian ethic of love. This legacy, substantially unchanged, has been the object of a continual critical re-appropriation and reinterpretation. *But up to this very day there is no alternative to it.* And in light of the current challenges of a post-national constellation, we must draw sustenance now, as in the past, from this substance. Everything else is idle postmodern talk."

Charles Darwin (1809-1882), who plays a central role in this debate, wrote that "I feel deeply that the whole subject is too profound for the human intellect … Let each man hope and believe what he can" (Letter to Asa Gray, May 22, 1860).

Thus the polemic of belief and doubt appears inexhaustible; as soon as belief is introduced, so is doubt; thus thoughtfulness converses on with itself. Nonetheless we see more if we return the focus to a period preceding belief. Primitive religiosity is the background for theism and atheism; religion was initially about magic and practical action, about what people *did* and not what they *thought*; beliefs and likely even ideas played no part in the earliest stages of religious life; there were no doctrines or explanations; and no doubt could have been raised. In religion we celebrate the sacred through dance, art, ritual and sacrifice. With the change from prehistory into history, all religions developed an intellectual tradition and a preoccupation with doctrinal correctness; and in reaction skeptics create matching traditions of scorn and doubt. Theism and atheism are opposite reactions to the loss of the previous world of rites, and when we return the focus to the epoch of human prehistory, we see an enormous expanse of time. The archeological record suggests that the first modern humans appeared somewhere between 250 to 150 thousand years ago, whereas agriculture and everything that follows from it cannot have begun more than 10,000 years ago. The reign of magic covers a period of unimaginable stability – followed by a period of unceasing social change. Wittgenstein is correct when he says in *Remarks on Fraser's Golden Bough* (1930) "simple though it may sound, we can express the difference between science and magic if we say that in science there is progress, but not in magic – there is nothing in magic to show the direction of any development."

Primitive society is stable, but makes no progress. There is no polemic in it to drive a conflict between belief and doubt. Thus the same circumstance that introduces belief, and ultimately leads to monotheism, also introduces rapid social and technological progress. The aspect of religion that is age-old excludes problems of fanaticism; the aspect of religion that emerges with farming, and which leads to innovation, critical thinking and social justice, rises up with fanaticism. Occam's razor – the principle of simplicity – works on religion as much as science, and makes us insist on *one* thing and one only.

Schopenhauer and Feuerbach and Nietzsche and Russell tend to equate religious belief with fanaticism. These thinkers make little room for an open kind of worship, *not* fanatical, the worship of a person who can enter a temple and also leave it behind. They make little room for a poetic frame of mind that finds a way to worship, but also stays clear of religious inquisition. They all note exceptions to the rule – discovering examples of an open kind of worship – but they also argue that these are rare – very rare – returning to the reality that the history of religion is dominated by fanaticism and (as Gibbon notes) is largely a register of crime, folly and misfortune.

Members of the "hell-fire club" and strident atheists today may look like mirror images of their opponents. Fanatical belief is the root cause of atheism and tends to produce its matching negative. Thus atheism turns from debunking fairy tales and becomes a crusader against all belief of type X (however defined). It becomes a new form of intolerance. Marx, for example, developed a critical and skeptical position regarding religious belief, emphasizing its uses in statecraft, following Enlightenment thinkers such as Voltaire and Gibbon. He exposed the ways in which religious devotion distracts people from taking positive action in this world. But he also saw the depth of religion as an outlet for the sense of injustice and longing for a better world:

"Religious suffering is, at one and the same time, the *expression* of real suffering and a *protest* against real suffering. Religion is the sigh of the oppressed creature, the heart of a heartless world, and the soul of soulless conditions. It is the *opium* of the people" (*Contribution to the Critique of Hegel's Philosophy of Right*).

Yet this same thinker, who saw so clearly into the workings of religious oppression, and who understood the political import of religion as an impetus for change, must have forgotten these lessons; for he devised the groundplan for a totalitarian régime bent on controlling what people think – not to convince, but to terrify them – to dictate 'revolutionary' thought and ban 'counter-revolutionary' thought – to define thought-crime and eradicate thought-criminals.

The fanatic cannot abide us worshipping any other god but *his* god, which he declares to be *the* god.

The American thinker Henry David Thoreau notes that the fanatic adopts his own scheme as the framework of the universe. The fanatic cannot be satisfied until every other scheme is laid waste. The fanatic thinks that he has learned the "alphabet of heaven" and insists that we learn it too. He has no patience with people who are still unsure, who have doubts, who still want to think. Thoreau notes that this same mistake in forcing a conclusion is easy to find on either side of a question – for and against any given claim – fanatical advocate vs. fanatical opponent – yet it grows up especially around the Prime Assertion – the God hypothesis – and also the Prime Denial – atheism. Thus it appears that the polemic of belief and doubt unfolds a dynamic of fanaticism and progress. Passionate conviction and defense of a cause stand on one side of human psychology; throwing off superstition and refuting foolishness stand on the other side; vehement advocacy and ruthless criticism grow up together, test one another, and ignite new developments.

fanaticism

We can admit fanaticism and progress provisionally as data for our study. We can also remind ourselves that religious studies are political studies; the philosophy of religion enters a contested space of ideas; at the end of the day there will be something to disagree about. Politics ensures our freedom, without which we have the monotony of one truth lifting or oppressing us all. A quick conclusion is that an end to religious controversy would probably render society sterile. The seesaw antagonism of belief and doubt is a liberating instability; but the order of things with which we are familiar is itself deeply unstable; and the process of change, for which progress is an optimistic name, brings tragedy as well as comedy. There is a sense in human beings that looks for order and a different sense that welcomes liberation. Studying religion, we want to make out the various forms of zeal, but we also have to study the idea of progress and make clear how it applies to religious life.

Beginning with fanaticism: belief in God is fanatical in some cases and poetic in others; atheism is fanatical in some cases and liberating in others; there is something like a humble theology and also a humble atheism.

Does the theist want to make us the gift of a life-altering truth? Or is he simply spreading an infection? Does the atheist want us to think for ourselves? Or does he just want to win another argument?

A tradition called "weak theology" began in the 1960s – some thinkers associated with this school include Harvey Cox, J.J. Altizer, Paul Van Buren, William Hamilton, Mark C. Taylor, Jean-Luc Nancy, Philippe Lacoue-Labarthe, Bernard Stiegler and John D. Caputo – meant to bring humility to religious thinking. Some important ideas in this school include: getting away from proselytizing; getting away from overpowering people with a religious message; to learn how to sense mystery, live with it, and develop a mindfulness and life practice that includes it; to cultivate silence and "unknowing" as an orienting force and joyful support to everything one does; to get away from dogma, the need for certainty, and conformity in opinion, and to move towards building community via humaneness rather than common beliefs; and to practice and encourage thoughtful dialogue.

John D. Caputo in particular writes about "the weakness of God" and argues for an understanding of God as "an unconditional claim without force." God, like desire, exists in the space between what exists and what does not; God is hope in the sense of dynamic potential; God is not a force that intervenes in nature but a claim that a human being feels the pull of and incorporates by practicing mindfulness, humour and charity (*The Weakness of God*, 2006).

The British philosopher Julian Baggini defines atheism as "open-hearted commitment to truth and rational enquiry." Atheism on this conception stands as a complete opposite to militancy, hostility and strident rejection of other peoples' beliefs. It has nothing to do with dogged conviction or belligerent belief (*Atheism*, 2003). On Baggini's reasoning, Christopher Hitchens's recent work *God is Not Great: How Religion Poisons Everything* (2007), despite its avowed atheistic theme, is closer to religion than irreligion. Einstein, Carl Sagan and Steven Weinberg all express something like a *reverent* atheism, wonder-struck at the majesty of nature.

Advocacy is a given, but not fanaticism. Zeal need not be fanatical, nor skepticism either – that is, the *ultimate* concern, which calls to us in even moment of our lives, and the love of truth, which is an *absolute* demand, are both *human* occupations – they are ours to do with as we choose. The study of the irrational and immature elements in our nature should help us counteract them. Psychological insight looks at the *way* a person is devoted to his values – like a fanatic, without coming to terms with infantile longings we are all born with; or with some humor, which has learned to smile at some of our childish fears, and has come some way towards accepting the brief span of a human life.

There appears to be a connection between fanaticism and the basic human division into in-groups and out-groups. The generations continue to socialize children into the in-group of the parents – to take on their prejudices and become the victim of prejudices against them. The basic psychology of conformity has tremendous survival value: the helpless child's pattern for survival becomes the parents', and learning happens via identification and sensitivity to parental cues. Thus the imposition of an aggressive identity on trusting children foments intellectual violence – unshakable belief, blind faith, absolute certainty, mindless conformism – as well as violence in the world – since an identity that resists change also tries to subjugate every other kind. Philosophers remind us that the child learns by believing the adult and that doubt is something we learn very gradually. Some of us grow into adulthood without modifying the second-hand ethnocentrism we received from our parents; but even a young child can become skeptical about parents' attitudes and ideas, simply by pursuing an argument a few steps further. Prejudice feeds on abstraction, but also dies with details. The family is primary, but the individual emerges.

The mind becomes a battleground between childishness and insight, slogans and experiences, emotionally powerful simplifications versus the ability to think for oneself.

Fanaticism is a disease and spreads without any effort. Humility is a cure yet must be explicitly practiced. Bringing humility to thinking – religious thinking and irreligious thinking – is a recent common theme across this boundary. The idea is to bring more to the discussion from Socrates – taking the position of a thinker who is more focused on ignorance than knowledge; more focused on searching than converting. Socrates brings people together in order to seek for knowledge. He is not trying to persuade anyone, he is not selling anything, he is not campaigning against anything. The contemporary Italian philosopher Gianteresio Vattimo tries to capture the essence of the problem, common to theism and atheism, in terms of what he calls the "triumphalist metaphysics of aggressive certainty." "When someone wants to tell me the absolute truth, it is because he wants to put me under his control" (*After the Death of God*, 2007).

Thus the first result of the present study of the thought-complex *religion/culture/history* is that whatever a person believes, the trick is to believe it with some humility. The trick is to acknowledge how little we know, and not arrogantly claim that we alone see the truth. Not *what* we believe, but *how*.

progress

Schumacher's famous essay "Buddhist Economics" (1966) portrays the conflict between the stagnation of traditional societies and the heedless growth of modern materialism as a false choice. He rejects the equation of progress with advances in technology or with rising standards of living. He tries to define progress in terms of self-consciousness, wariness about one's own footprint, enlightenment and community. The Nobel laureate Amartya Sen's 1999 work *Development as Freedom* offers a similar argument, defining poverty as "a deprivation of basic capabilities, rather than merely as low income." Real progress allows people to realize their capabilities – human freedoms are the means of development as well as their ends – the overarching concern has to be the process of enhancing human freedom and working towards social arrangements that bring this about. As with the discussion of Robert Wight's work above (pp. 62-4), the point is to bring an *ethical* dimension into thinking about history, human life today and future planning.

Belief and doubt, theism and atheism, the seesaw antagonism of advocacy and skepticism – this is the panorama we are regarding – and at first the main issue that jumps out from this history is fanaticism and the problem of tempering religious zeal. Yet this history also shows a very clear line of development. It begins with magic and ends with ideology. It becomes less a sense of grandeur and becomes more a normative form of thought. Less a set of practices, more a set of rules. Still: these comments ignore the most important event transpiring in this history, i.e. its very evident *progress*.

What begins with invoking the spirits, animal sacrifice, ecstatic visions, branding rituals and fearsome tribal deities becomes a call to welcome the stranger, to love mercy, to do justice, to learn humility, to feel compassion, to offer service at every opportunity, even a commandment to love our enemies. Religious history raises the problem of fanaticism but also confronts us with increasingly sophisticated moral ideas that gradually get extended to everyone in the community, and to all communities, ultimately to life itself and even to inanimate matter.

We can get a hold of some of the significance of this change by thinking about the idea of progress itself and whether it makes sense to talk about progress in philosophy, or in ethics, or in religion.

French philosophers of the eighteenth century hoped to improve the state of society by the gradual triumph of reason over prejudice and knowledge over ignorance. They sought to replace age-old superstition with the new spirit of scientific curiosity. They thought they were working for democracy and the improvement of society. Their work led, unexpectedly, to violent revolution. They failed to allow for the strength of human passions. They failed to recognize how much liberty depends on differences and dis-agreement, rather than sameness and central planning. They failed to see politics as a support, rather than the enemy, of enlightened society. They made the very mistake that most offended them in their rebellion from the church – they created an orthodoxy that tyrannized over unbelievers. Perhaps the world can become increasingly better in terms of some value people can agree about, but this change cannot be *imposed* on society, or it will not take. The lesson appears to be that progress follows an internal logic. It depends on bringing everything in on the same footing, bringing everyone to the table and creating a context for exchange.

If we look at philosophy, ethics, religion, this is precisely what we *don't* see – we don't see everything brought in on the same footing, we don't see bringing everyone to the table, we don't see a common basis for exchange – instead we see separate tables, we see insular discussions, we see separate communities steeped in their own histories and principles of interpretation. The contrast with science is striking. There are no contemporary defenders of Ptolemy, Copernicus or Newton, all claiming to have the best theory of the physics of celestial motion. "Nor are there contemporary mercantilists or physiocrats, as there were in the eighteenth century, all claiming to have the best theory of economics" (James Sterba, *The Triumph of Practice Over Theory in Ethics*, 2005). There are no contemporary defenders of the phlogiston theory of heat, or of Lamarckism, or of phrenology, or of the flat earth. We do not have contemporary defenders of these theories because the scientific community adopts *common* foundations of evidence and argument. But this is not the case in philosophy, or ethics, or in religion, where competing schools constantly challenge the foundations of all their rivals.

Thus there are contemporary defenders of Socrates and Spinoza and Heidegger in philosophy; there are contemporary defenders of Epictetus and J.S. Mill and Nietzsche in ethics; and there are contemporary defenders of Judaism and Christianity and Islam in religion. There is absolutely no doubt that there is progress *within* these traditions – for example, within Judaism, which begins with fear of the sky-father Jahve and gradually becomes the ethic of social justice. But there is little progress between them. Aristotelians talk to Aristotelians, utilitarians to utilitarians, and Hindus to other Hindus.

The problem we are left with in religion, as in philosophy and in ethics, is the problem that we began with in this study – the problem of irreducible plurality – what Hannah Arendt feared would become a "permanent theatre of war." She looked forward to a time in which every such insular group would renounce its claim to binding authority and universal validity – instead to bring its insights, and look for others' insights, in a new world-conversation – not challenging the other group's very foundations, but seeking to learn.

Habermas has written that "the world's religions resist becoming happy participants in a companionable pluralism" and that cosmopolitanism, committed to pluralism, "cannot affirm the absolute rightness of anything" except its commitment to talking, and listening, and going on. Thus the impasse from centuries past is still with us – we can look forward to a world conversation, but it does yet exist – it remains for us to create it.

Thus the second result of the present study of the thought-complex *religion/culture/history*: recognizing that whatever we believe, other people believe something else; thus the trick is to believe and to make room for others to believe, as they determine. Someone who disagrees with me is nonetheless my opposite in a political struggle that serves us both. Our conversation, and especially our disagreement, is liberating. Not *what* we believe, but *with whom*.

Philosophy looks for the grounding form, the transcendental form, and the distorted form – the origin of a thing, its essence, and its characteristic dysfunction. In the case of *religion/culture/history*, the groundform is ancient religiosity: the religious instinct in its humblest form. The essence is the 'big truth': the truth that human beings need a context to make sense of their lives. And the characteristic dysfunction is the devolution from wonder to dogma: the decay of religiosity from the sense of astonishment to the demand of submission.

Unearthing the groundform of religion makes it possible to see the coherence of theism and atheism as opposite reactions to the loss of a common world of rites. Belief and doubt are identical twins, latecomers in religious history, and completely irrelevant to the root forms of religious feeling, which are closer to celebration and thankfulness for the brief chance we have at life.

Laying hold of the essence of religion reveals that religion is an outcome of human reason, even if it is misplaced in given cases. Religion springs from the sense of order and the desire for meaning, which means that it is susceptible to reason and to offers of meaning. The order of things that it looks for is exactly the order of things that it discovers. Reason that we find inside ourselves is reason that we discover in the cosmos. The unworldly referent is intimate. Religiosity throws up intelligence and kinship at once.

When we see the dysfunction in a thing we see its weakness, and where its strength can be tested. The weakness in religion is human weakness – the weakness in 'orienting value' – something that takes root in magic, ritual and symbolism, which can flourish as tradition or degenerate into ideology. It is rooted in the life process, and is an adaptation, an emergent construction or structure, fundamental to human life. It is shared, proclaimed, apportioned – sold, traded, produced, consumed – hoodwinked, robbed, coerced, enslaved – it must be limited and kept under control, it is just on the verge of overreaching – this well of energy or motivation – which finally disintegrates – which is returned, renewed, redeemed – promised, betrayed, inflated, weakened – a claim without force, which somehow we make felt.

Religion that was hard work, holding the problem in one's character, reading the old symbolism, empowering symbols and resisting symbols, honoring and keeping one's honor, religion as quietism, unknowing, humble practice and human seeking … This becomes religion as the situation you are in, as the game – as what you carry on from the *inside*, as a *part* of, as player, played, involved, comingled; which becomes religion as arrogance, as assertion, as agreement, as subjugation; as who one is, as signaling loyalty, as the test; which becomes religion as submission, as thoughtlessness, as mindlessness, unconsciousness, oblivion.

The difference between strength of character and weak self-hatred; serving the cause become blank servitude; championing the good become imposing the good; good become evil.

Following the argument through these discoveries, an initial thesis begins to form itself – a new conception to be tested by the *elenchus* – whose precursor forms were first articulated by Socrates, St. Paul, Voltaire and Hegel.

Lego is to speak, *elego* is to answer back, to cross-examine, to test, to try the case. Socrates describes thought itself as exactly this speaking and answering back that tries a case. Socrates feels his own ignorance and thinks that it is his duty to expose it and work on remedying it. He thinks that everyone else is in this same position and that everyone has this same duty. Socrates' conception of the *elenchus* encapsulates an ideal of society in which people rid themselves of presumption and practice dialectic as a way of caring for their souls.

"So too now I say this is what I am doing, investigating the argument on my own behalf, but equally well on behalf of my other companions; or do you not think that it is a common good among virtually all human beings, for each thing to be completely evident, as to what it is in reality?" (*Charmides* 166d4).

Aristotle, reflecting on Socrates' project, argues that Socrates thought he was helping himself, and helping other people, as was his religious duty, because "the purpose of life is the knowledge of virtue" and because he thought that as soon as one knew justice as it really is, then one would be just (*Eudemian Ethics* 1261 b3 ff). Aristotle questions whether it makes sense to think that knowing the definition of good makes you good – but he also argues that Socrates makes a beginning for philosophy in his very clear concept of thinking as the refutation of presumption.

The term *elenchus* undergoes a revolutionary change in the language of the *New Testament*, as for example in Paul's letters, and notably in the discussion of faith in the Epistle to the Hebrews, chapter 11. "Faith is the assurance of things hoped for, and the evidence (*elenchus*) of things not seen" (*Hebrews* 11:1). Socrates' word has been transformed here and no longer indicates a test of any kind or the result of testing, but instead a state of perfect assurance that has no precedent or basis of any kind. The anonymous author of *Hebrews* is trying to make a case for the pre-eminence of Christianity over Judaism. The essence of the argument is the strange idea that, unlike Socrates and all those who have seen the fruition of their work, the heroes of faith do not see this fruition, but instead "they see and greet it from afar" but still remain strangers and exiles on earth; "they are seeking a homeland" but have not arrived there yet; "they desire a better country and a heavenly one" and even though they do not discover heaven on earth they "die in their faith" (11:13-16). It is as if, in place of reasoning from premises to a conclusion, and then feeling a sense of assurance that comes from working through the steps, another path opened up, not through reasoning, but through desire.*

Voltaire satirizes the logic of desire in works like *Candide* and *Zadig* as innocent, even brave hopefulness, fatal to reason, common sense, practical reality and ultimately even to justice. "Superstition sets the world in flames, and philosophy quenches them." Philosophy develops itself as scientific thinking, and we owe to science, rather than wishing, all the progress of history. History is the sequence of stages through which humanity must pass before it can arrive at knowledge and consciousness of itself.

Hegel thinks that this culmination occurs in his own lifetime, in his own thinking, in himself. Hegel awakens to a comprehension that assembles the understanding *of all times past* as it arrives at knowledge and consciousness of itself.

With these steps as precedents, we have a chance to look back on the history of ideas and look ahead some way forward. Socrates argues against presumption; Paul argues for it; Voltaire argues against it; Hegel again for it. Meanwhile these thinkers have all successively much greater audiences and at the end of the series the entirety of world culture appears on the same stage. Thus it becomes possible for all of us to argue about all of history, about every culture, about every belief and every doubt that human beings have raised.

Today, perhaps for the first time, it is possible to look at the whole of human thoughtfulness, to have Europe and India and China before us simultaneously.

I am looking at the future as a single moment in which myriad accounts are contemporaries for a present, living mind, seeking knowledge and consciousness of itself. Religion, philosophy and ethics have to date made no progress that is general, but only relatively to traditions and national histories. I am looking at a future in which religion, philosophy and ethics have arrived together at a moment of renunciation of all binding authority and universal validity; they are become symbols, wisdoms, failures, thought-paths and thought-lessons open to each other; they are become offerings from which thinking can take what it will.

I am asserting that Aristotle, Daniel Dennett, Lao Tzu and Vatsayana are contemporaries – I am imagining philosophy as enlightened humanity in conversation with itself – I am looking for an enlarged perspective and for a truth-content that survives this larger course of scrutiny.

This is my thesis and my conception of the *elenchus*. The *elenchus* was initially a method of refutation, aimed at exposing pretensions to knowledge; it became a hope and a flight to the hoped-for end; it became a vision of human progress through scientific research; it became an awakening in a fullness of world-historical understanding; finally it disintegrated into examined lives.

Thus the trick is to acknowledge diversity and the insularity that goes with it. Truth cannot be universally valid and identical for everyone, but is that by which the believer lives and realizes himself. It has a meaning in a context and is not universally valid for everyone – but from this step, by small steps, truth becomes what each of us can wrest from personal histories and choice – which again is perhaps only a way of recognizing that human being is personal.

Beginning with the personal does not mean ending with the personal; I am concluding that a person has to earn an understanding of truth for himself, but I am not asserting that truth is private; I am asserting that what I love is public and will show itself in what I do. I am saying: I have to begin with myself. If I do not take things personally, then I will not care about anything; but the inquiry shows, that *a life without passionately caring about something* is no kind of life, and that human being is much more likely to achieve fulfillment in passion than without it; but again passion is blind and must be led through the *elenchus*.

Reason-seeking finds reasons, wanting to be tied to something becomes being tied to something, wanting something to matter becomes having something matter; but we want to live examined lives, and so in every case it is not enough that we care about something and that something matters; we have to examine our reasons and take a close look at the thing we love.

We look for a foothold outside our narrowness – we watch over ourselves to warn for narrowness – we accept manyness but demand criticism – we reject stupidity but acknowledge ignorance – we discover strength by what we test – we see without claiming to know – we see that the *way* we love is everything, since without paying much attention or taking things for granted and settled, without any need to look again, the thing we love becomes evil – we also see that we are not doing this by ourselves – philosophy takes place in every person – every person can also refuse philosophy.

The point of view taken here is *comparative religion*. By definition, this point of view is for comparison. I am not for any one thing, but for many. I am for taking experience in rather than pushing it away. I do not see the earth beneath my feet as the enemy of heaven. I do not set reason against emotion. Both guide and both fail; both can become a prison. I have a home ground and I am part of a very large whole. I have two eyes, but they are not at war.

I can make out the rough outlines of a point of view – what I am for and against – the brief outcome of my experience studying comparative religion. I am *against* the psychology of fanaticism – arrogance, idolatry, intolerance, and ignorance. I am *for* a humane psychology – humility, curiosity, welcoming, and intelligence. What counts is, whether there is humility; whether there is some search going on; whether there is some comparison; whether there is philosophy.

Religion is far older than philosophy. The sense for the sacred is far older than the power of reason. But at a certain juncture in human history reason emerges and spirituality alters by being examined. The history of ideas as I conceive it marks a significant break at the birth of agriculture, cities, patriarchy, writing – including records of the first stirrings of philosophy as we think of it today, working with ideas and arguments – also the beginning of war; and the first theologies and doubts. Man comes of age, as Bonhoeffer says, which means that he can farm, build cities, make war, write his history, think, believe and doubt. Philosophy is another product of the Bronze Age and sun worship rather than devotion to the Great Mother.

Let us say that philosophy – *radical critical inquiry* – breaks down into differentiable types or trends – such as, going after the whole; staying on the side of ignorance; speaking from experience; a focus on structure; a focus on moral ideas; assembling what is known. I see examples of all these trends in my mind's eye from Western, Chinese and Indian thinkers – also from African, American and Oceanic thinkers – I see ancient examples and modern practitioners. I see in my mind's eye these irreducibly different kinds of human expressiveness. Human beings have set out at least on these several paths, in lands far apart and wildly different epochs on the timeline, to conduct philosophy.

These are conversational strategies, or actor's parts, or different sorts of people and sensibilities, and might be rehearsed in one's own mind, or in a family, a neighborhood, a state or empire. These are ways to talk – perspectives, languages, vocabularies – different practices of philosophy – these are basic philosophical orientations – these are questions from different questioners. Socrates is telling us that we conduct this work in our own minds, by ourselves, in a silent conversation of the soul with itself; in which we take the part of saying and also answering back; expanding or reducing, taking a next step or returning back to the beginning. The dialogues appear to rehearse these same basic strategies: a focus on the whole, on ignorance, on experience, on structure, on moral ideas, on knowledge.

Let us say that philosophy breaks down into differentiable types or trends – then we are likely to discover schools of theology that follow all these same lines of thinking – philosophy and theology may even be indistinguishable if we reach back far enough. Arguably, Heraclitus is a philosopher (a metaphysician or cosmologist) but also a theologian. Plato is a moralist, yet again a moral theologian. Spinoza, Shankara and Vivekananda are philosophical holists, but they also make theological claims. Sextus Empircus is a skeptic; so is Nagarjuna; and both talk about God. Plato offers the idea that philosophy begins in wonder, and theologians such as Schleiermacher, Barth and Tillich argue that worship begins from wonder, too.

If philosophical orientations are basic irreducibles, then we should expect to find a *rationalist* atheism (as with the Carvakas or Daniel Dennett), and also a *rationalist* form of theology (Parmenides, Zeno, Anselm, Spinoza). Rationalists of all stripes share a common orientation to the world. God-speech is not therefore a defining orientation for these thinkers. Regardless of the prime denial, or prime assertion, these thinkers think about the world in fundamentally similar ways. Rationalism is just one case. Presumably the principle is general. Thus there are *empiricist* theologies and *empiricist* atheisms – e.g. Aquinas argues from his observations of nature, and so does Richard Dawkins. Dawkins and Aquinas may therefore be kindred thinkers. Their antagonism is an artifact of current politics, current trends in popular culture – in the thirteenth century and presently. Likewise there are perceptualists among believers (Berkeley) and atheists (Russell).

The *primacy of philosophical orientation*, deeper than theology or atheism, argues for normalizing variety. We cannot get holism, skepticism, empiricism and rationalism down to one position, except to the Socratic position of examining. We cannot reduce ethics, epistemology and cosmology down to one theme – we have to accept this variety and go on with argument – or else cut away from Socrates and examining life. Thus the primacy of philosophical orientation means normalizing the variety of ways of looking at the world – since the philosophical orientation to the world is irreducibly plural – where also normalizing variety means normalizing incompleteness. There is no unified field theory of philosophy. We cannot reduce down all the phenomena to one equation. There is no final resolution of philosophical wonder. There is no rational exclusive claim to truth – in Tillich's language philosophy works with provisional claims; it reaches but falls short of the absolute.

Tillich held that "no church has the right to put itself in place of the ultimate." He held that it was impossible for any one tradition to contain the "infallible truth of faith." The fundamentalist appears to say: 'if I do not count my faith as absolute, it is merely one faith among others, and so it means nothing.' It appears to be nothing, because it is not everything. It is as if the tribe required itself to rule the globe – that if the tribe merely rules itself, it is nothing – if the self merely rules itself, that is nothing – it must grow outwards and crush all others. Tillich responds: "The same criterion is valid with respect to the whole history of religion and culture. The criterion contains a Yes – it does not reject any truth of faith in whatever form it may appear in the history of faith – and it contains a No – it does not accept any truth of faith as ultimate, save the one that no man possesses it."

Philosophy also reaches to the idea that we cannot make an ideal out of not reaching an ideal. There is no point in persevering in philosophical inquiry if we cede from the outset that we cannot answer our questions. We always have to challenge the idea that there is no point in thinking anymore.

We have to put up new challenges. Philosophy is just as much assertion as it is critique. We always need a current pretender, an orthodoxy, a reigning truth. We are lucky if we have something to fight. The touchstone is the creation of a tradition of critical discussion. Anaximander arrived at his theory by criticizing Thales' theory – Thales founded this new tradition of freedom of thought – "he seems to have created the tradition that one ought to tolerate criticism" – the pupil is encouraged not to revere his master but to criticize him – this is a new kind of framework, not for heresies and schisms and banishing dissenters, on the theory that the most important thing is to keep the doctrine pure, but for challenge, innovation, new questions and ideas, on the theory that the most important thing is to know – "thus knowledge proceeds by way of conjectures and refutations" (Karl Popper, *Back to the Presocratics*, 1958).

Heidegger's classic *What is Called Thinking?* from 1954 reaches back to an idea that he was working with in 1919 in his confrontation with Jaspers and their discussions about philosophy – an idea about going on with philosophy even after we realize that we cannot resolve our questions – as a young man he called it "incessant actualizing," "continual renewal," "constant renewal," "constantly standing at the starting point" and "an infinite process of radical questioning that always includes itself in its questions and preserves itself in them." He talks about *staying in the process of questioning* expectations and *preserving oneself in problematizing* experience. After all his life experiences, he talked about Socrates instead. He argues that we all feel the storm and blowing winds of thinking so strongly that we run to seek refuge. Socrates, however, the "purest thinker" of all, stands out. "All through his life and right into his death, Socrates did nothing else than place himself in this draft, this current, and maintain himself in it" (*What is Called Thinking?*, Part 1, Lecture 1, Summary and Transition).

Thus the solution to problem of the philosophy of religion is to make a religion of philosophy.

+

Hsun Tzu argues that the sage does not seek to understand heaven. The Buddha rejects religious questions as of no help for suffering. Suffering, he claims, supersedes all our scruples.

Socrates would argue that theism and atheism and cosmology and like studies are all pretty far from the immediate problems of human ignorance facing moral demands. Philosophy in Socrates' version is simply the obligation to think. But as we have noted in our discussions, if this stripped-down Socratic quest to become and remain thoughtful evolves into any sort of definite *philosophy*, such as rationalism or skepticism or empiricism, then this new creation is on a par with atheisms, theisms, and other isms …

Philosophy descending into 'philosophies' and 'isms' is unproblematic as long as the new creation (whatever it may be) then becomes a new object of scrutiny and is made to answer the Socratic *elenchus* and cross-examination. This activity seems to me the core concern of philosophy, though we often let our curiosity wander off into distant corners of the intellectual universe. We just have to learn how to get back to the core concern of thinking.

There is a legend according to which, of the ten parts of wisdom in the world, nine are in Jerusalem. I am lucky to have had a chance to travel to Jerusalem and see for myself. I don't know about all nine parts of wisdom, but I did find a few. I thought I would talk a bit about my experience in Jerusalem, and what I am able to make of it, as a way of bringing this study to a close.

Jerusalem draws pilgrims from around the globe, including believers of many stripes, but also philosophers and spiritual seekers and scholars – I got interested in philosophy as a young person and I confess that I have an enormous respect and curiosity about religious lore – also I've been teaching philosophy and comparative religion for several decades – so, my journey was a life chance for me, I dug in very deep and tried to take advantage of being there to learn what I could. When I arrived at the airport I had kind of a funny experience, which is that people kept asking me for directions, even though I had never been there before. And when I got into the city itself, the same thing kept happening to me. I also ended up translating for different people who were staying at my hotel and also at a bar where I stopped in to get a drink. I found a tour guide but I ended up giving him a good deal of background about the city and I even gave him several books I had brought along on the trip. I was talking to him about Jerusalem in the period around 60,000 BCE and the different archeological finds regarding early man and stone tools and weapons, and about the Natufian culture and some finds in the Shuqba cave in the Judean mountains, which date from about 15,000 BCE. I thought to myself, since I was giving directions and translating and doing all this talking and teaching, that instead of finding wisdom in Jerusalem, I seemed to be bringing it. And I wondered if that might be the point.

So I was feeling pretty good about myself and I got hungry and decided to find a place to eat and I made out, in my OK Hebrew, that the name of a restaurant right in front of me was my own name and, I thought, well, maybe I should go in there. So I went in but they said there was a private party and I couldn't eat there that day, so I was ejected from myself in a sense and that seemed kind of weird. Later that evening I went to a bar and got to talking with an Israeli man who was about my age and he asked me about myself and what I was doing there. And I told him a little bit about myself and we started talking about the Jewish people, who number only 14 million or so, whereas there are about 2.3 billion Christians in the world and 1.5 billion Muslims, so that this little place, this patch of ground has such a big role in history, since almost 2/3 of the world follows a religion born in this desert country. But this man said to me that American Jews like me aren't really Jews and he sort of dismissed my way of looking at the problems over there.

So I said to him that it was funny because in America I am Jew whether I want to be or not and I used to get in fights when I was a kid because people would give me a hard time about being Jewish – but now I am over here in Jerusalem and people tell me I'm not a Jew – so it looks like I can't win no matter what I do. And he said that, *all right*, with an answer like that, you must be a Jew. So I thought to myself again that I did not come to Jerusalem to find out who I am, but to bring who I am to this city and add my part – just adding my voice to the conversation.

So the next day I was walking in the old city, where there is the Jewish quarter and the Armenian quarter and the Muslim quarter, and it's kind of like a crazy mish mash of narrow alleys – the middle eastern bazaar that we have all seen in films – with many people inviting you into their shops and proudly displaying knick knacks and tchotchkes and touristy things, but also the local version of a supermarket – just broken up into little pieces – also little synagogues and mosques right next to places where you buy spices or tooth paste. And I was wandering around aimlessly and it happened that a couple of guys got into a fight right next to me and I pretty much had no choice but to push them apart and thankfully some other folks there helped out and we separated these two people and I never did figure out what the argument was about. And I thought to myself, I did not come to Jerusalem to find peace, but to make peace.

So I think that what all these little episodes were teaching me was something that I did not need to come to a faraway place like Jerusalem to find out, but was in front of me all the time, which is that it's up to me to bring enlightenment, good will and peace wherever I happen to be – really we have to bring this stuff with us wherever we go.

Now I lugged a whole lot of books with me on my trip and I also hung out in several terrific little bookstores looking for more – I had a chance to study some ideas from Judaism, Christianity and Islam that I have been puzzling about for a long time and I thought I would close here by talking about a couple of these – but the theme is the same: that you pretty much have to bring your game wherever you happen to be.

One passage in the Bible that always drove me nuts is from *Proverbs* (9:10) and also *Ecclesiastes* (12:13) which is about the fear of God – "Fear of the Lord is the beginning of wisdom" and "Now everything has been said, and here is the conclusion: Fear God and keep his commandments." Now I guess what bothers me about these passages is that there's this idea that we should live our lives in fear, as if a lightning bolt were about to shoot down at us at any moment. So as I wandered through the aisles of some wonderful very cramped bookstores smelling of people and coffee and old pages, I looked for commentaries on several passages by ancient scholars such as Rabbi Hillel and Rabbi Eliezer and Maimonides and Hasdai Cresdas, and after reading through some of them and arguing about them with friends, I finally got it.

It's sort of like this. You are invited to the royal palace – you are going to have an audience with the King. And so you take a shower, clean up, make yourself presentable – after all, you are going to see the King. And when you are presented to the King you're on your best behavior; your back is straight and you want to put your best foot forward and bring the best version of yourself, the *big* version. I think that what this is saying is that in the presence of something you honor, in front of something that you care about, that matters to you, your ideals, your values, the things you cherish, when you have these things in mind, then you're in the zone – you rise to the moment and do your best work. And this is what is meant by: 'the Fear of God.'

Now I always liked some passages in *Philippians*, in the New Testament, from St. Paul, such as where he talks about *kenosis* – which is an interesting Greek word which means something like 'emptying' – capturing the idea that religion can inspire an open, welcoming receptiveness, rather than being a stricture of doctrines and dogmas and do's and don't's. Paul says that sometimes we get down in the dumps and lose faith in ourselves. His advice always made sense to me and I still think it is powerful – he says, if you lose heart – then "whatever is true, whatever is honorable, whatever is just, whatever is pure, whatever is beautiful, if there is anything excellent, if there is anything worthy of praise – then think on these things."

So, a last word from the third tradition. It's strange that the best-selling poet in the United States is not Walt Whitman, or Alan Ginsberg, or Billy Collins or even Paulann Peterson, who is the Poet laureate of Oregon – the best-selling poet this year and pretty much every year in our country is Jalal al-din Muhammad Balkhi, known as Rumi, a Muslim, and Sufi mystic, who dates from the 13th century. One of Rumi's lines is *We are not here to take prisoners*, which is his advice to parents in raising children and also to priests who get a bit overheated in their sermonizing – in general the idea of leaving people to their own thoughts and their own path. He also says, *Stain your prayer rug with wine* – knowing that Muslims must pray five times a day and also that wine is forbidden – in effect he is saying that we are fallible creatures and we all fail, but somehow we must accept our weakness and also realize *that everyone can see it* – but you have to go on anyway.

So, putting it all together, what I came to from my pilgrimage, is that it's up to each one of us, it's up to me to bring the big version of myself to the problems of everyday life; and I have to 'Present the King' (as it were) to myself – that is, I've got to keep my values right in front of me where they can see me; and if I get down, all I have to do is look around and see something good, something true, something honorable, something beautiful, or something just – and that will help me get back to myself; and, lastly, if I fail, as I am very likely to do, and I spill wine on my prayer rug, then I shouldn't worry about that too much, but just get back to being a pilgrim, and having some values, and trying to do some good.

Notes

This work is the result of decades of study and a complete bibliography for it would run to many pages. In lieu of a lengthy list of original and secondary sources, and in the present moment when the ability to source texts is easier than it has ever been, I offer a few notes here to help the reader trace back the main lines of thought developed here to earlier thinking.

Where I am quoting from a text I try to indicate that in the text. Where I am influenced by a thinker I try to indicate that too; and below are some notes that expand on sources that have helped me to form my way of looking at this subject. The result, whatever its limitations and shortcomings, is mine.

I consider myself a student of languages and I have gotten into the habit of consulting dictionaries as beginning points for much of my thinking. From Novalis I have learned that word histories stand to philosophy as experiments do to science. Learning about the words we use to articulate important ideas, in different language families and languages, from different periods and places, is hugely important for philosophy.

I consider myself a student of history and a great many historians are consulted, questioned, defended and disputed in this work. Several notes below speak to my approach to history, historians, and how history and philosophy emerge together.

I consider myself a student of Socrates, Plato and Aristotle and I like to consult all of them on questions that come up for me in philosophy. Many other thinkers have had a large impact on the way I think about the world. I immediately think of Shakespeare – also Kant, Gibbon, Darwin, Nietzsche, William James, Freud, Jaspers, Heidegger, Wittgenstein – also Confucius, Molière, Martin Buber, Hermann Hesse, D.H. Lawrence, Plutarch – especially the Buddha. I studied with Hans-Georg Gadamer in the 1970s and his conception of hermeneutical understanding made a lasting impression on me.

Even as a child I had a passion for philosophy and a fascination with religion. Many people – searchers, doubters, scholars, believers – have taken me in over the years, given of themselves and helped me become a clearer thinker. My debt to them is inestimable. I tried to repay it forward by becoming a teacher. Most of my life I have worked in education and I have tried to model intellectual search for new generations of seekers. My hope is that this work will be of some use to people who ask themselves the sort of questions that have been my companions for a half-century or so.

(note to page i). World population figures culled from reports by the United Nations, the BBC, the US Department of State, the Central Intelligence Agency, and the Pew Research Center (also the Pew *Global Attitudes Project*).

(note to page vi). Some resources on declining religiosity among youth and generalized increase in spirituality:

http://www.pewglobal.org/question-search/?qid=408&cntIDs=&stdIDs=

http://pewresearch.org/pubs/614/religion-social-issues

http://www.pewforum.org/Age/Religion-Among-the-Millennials.aspx#beliefs

http://www.mccrindle.com.au/resources/whitepapers/Emerging-Trends-Enduring-Truth_The-Spiritual-Attitudes-of-the-New-Generations.pdf

http://www.usatoday.com/news/religion/2008-06-23-pew-religions_N.htm

http://www.pewforum.org/Other-Beliefs-and-Practices/Many-Americans-Mix-Multiple-Faiths.aspx

See also *After the Baby Boomers: How Twenty- and Thirty-Somethings Are Shaping the Future of American Religion* by Robert Wuthnow (2007) and *Souls in Transition: The Religious and Spiritual Lives of Emerging Adults* by Christian Smith and Patricia Snell (2009).

(note to page 1). Regarding the Sanskrit term *dharma* and its translation into English as 'religion,' see Rabindranath Tagore, *Sadhana: The Realization of Life*, 1913. Tagore notes that "when any wrong is done, we say that *dharma* is violated." English speakers might say that doing wrong goes against their religion. But Tagore says that *dharma* also has the sense that when wrong is done, "the lie has been given to our own nature." English speakers might talk about the thing they care about most as their *religion*, but the word 'religion' does not normally point to human nature, but instead a kind of framework for it.

(note to page 4). In this text I am arguing that the literature on religion seems to divide into two rough groups – for and against – and as my study strategy I am pursuing the idea of doing *neither* of these, but *searching*. I am calling this (1) appreciative inquiry, which is a way of saying yes to what a tradition is saying and trying to go with a charitable interpretation, and (2) critical inquiry, which is a way of saying no, not so fast, and offering an account that shows fidelity to the text, and (3) a balance of the two. An example might be table manners. In China, people use chopsticks to eat. In Europe, people use knives, forks, and spoons. We could study table manners from one side or the other, arguing against chopsticks or forks. We could study them appreciatively, not arguing against them but showing how these customs came to be dominant in these different geographic regions. And we could blend both inquiries, arguing against and for and balancing these perspectives, until we thought we had a good idea about the history and significance of table manners. The goal is not to enforce the Fork ethic or the Chopstick way of life, but to see them both as *human* phenomena, and then step back and ask questions about human experience more generally, and why people bother to be polite at the table at all.

In logic there is the duality of charity and fidelity – i.e. when you are looking at an argument, you can make it as strong as possible before you assess it; or you can make it as faithful as possible to what the text (or person) actually says, even if it offers a weak argument. In the latter case you may end up arguing against a straw man. In the former case you may end by analyzing an argument that is much better than the original.

My strategy is to try to look at religion charitably, with better arguments for it than religious people typically offer; also critically, using arguments that show religion in the cold light of reason, without worrying if anyone is offended; and then, after trying both these strategies, to step back and ask big questions about religion that move outside the question of for or against, looking for the larger human element.

I do not see religion vanishing (or being replaced by scientific thinking) in my lifetime, or in the lifetime of anyone alive in my day or even in the foreseeable future. I am arguing that it will be with us like war, disease, marriage, music, dance, controversies about education, political contention ... and so on. It is an enduring feature of human experience. This has made me want to understand it by learning about it in many different ways and working through many sorts of explanations of religious phenomena. Philosophy as I understand it sends me on this mission, in the same way that the call to an examined life drives us to learn as much as we can and try to apply this learning to further the good. Probably the thinker who has influenced me most on the question of religion is Paul Tillich, whose work *Dynamics of Faith* is quoted at various places in this text. I was led to study Tillich from reading existentialist philosophers, especially Heidegger. The point of the study of religion (as Tillich argues, for example, and as explicated further in chapter 8 of this text) is to interpret religion in ways that support a progressive agenda. We can criticize it and help it evolve. We cannot kill it (as some advocate) and (even imagining that we could) doing so might well make things worse rather than better (see the comments about this issue by Habermas on p. 147).

(note to page 13). Ibn Khaldun's dates are 1332-1406. Considered a father of cultural history, sociology and economics – as well as several other fields – he was also a theologian. It would be strange not to count him a believer (though his perspective is full of skepticism and irony; his definition of government runs as follows: "an institution that prevents injustice, other than such as it commits itself."). As a believer, Khaldun acted as lawyer, scholar and jurist in the *Shariah* tradition (Islamic religious law).

Leonardo da Vinci's dates are 1452-1519. Leonardo freed himself from all human conventions. In his notebooks he wrote: "Whoever in discussion adduces authority uses not intellect but rather memory."

Francis Bacon's dates are 1561-1626. In Bacon the transition to an empirical standpoint is complete. Bacon argued that the reasoner must free himself from his own personal standpoint; from all ideas that arise in social life; from all trade and economic life; and even from all previous artistic productions. The thinker should proceed from fact to law via induction. Everything else is prejudice.

Voltaire's dates are 1694-1778. He brings all these previous steps of free inquiry together in the *Essay on Manners* (1753), the first work of expressly 'skeptical' history.

(note to page 24). The Welsh philosopher H.H. Price (1899-1984) developed ideas about belief under its traditional description as a mental event and also under the newer hypothesis that belief is a disposition (*Belief*, 1969). The main arguments he had for this were about how we acquire beliefs. He thought they came on gradually in social learning. He didn't think most people have a Cartesian kind of process going on where they would sort out their various beliefs. He was skeptical about the credentials for all such belief but did not want to paint a picture of people who, like scientifically minded philosophers, think they are accepting and rejecting propositions on the basis of evidence. He thought this was a pleasant fiction that people concoct about themselves. He advocated something resembling an empiricist attitude and a sort of experimentalism about theism. He argued to the odd conclusion that theistic ideas are empirically testable because they imply that people have spiritual abilities of some sort; however, when it comes to *testing* all he is able to come up with is *try it and see what happens*. His version of pragmatism makes him drop the question that he begins with – whether theism makes any sense at all and deserves our attention, other than to dismiss folk delusions – replacing it with questions about happiness and engagements that make us happy. His result is a vague and idiosyncratic version of Christianity. Price is another thinker who travels a very long way only to return back to his parent's home.

Price was interested in the distinction between *believing that* and *believing in* and hoped that the latter concept would help to clarify what is going on in religious life. Propositional belief grows by precedents and degrees into confessional belief. His critics countered with ideas about programming that instills attitudes about facts (and what count as facts) and values (including religious values). On this model even an automaton can have religious beliefs.

(note to page 25). J.L. Austin (1911-1960) came along and his idea seemed much more powerful – not the idea that belief is a disposition, which is a sort of a background-thing that would show itself when the topic came up, and that lives in a kind of murky unconscious – he talked about belief as performance, as behavior, as publicly observable stuff – reasoning that when you say that you *believe* something, you are impinging on what others can and do believe, just as actors on the stage interact with and change each other's emotions. So, on this model, there is no private belief. Belief is public. If it is public, it lives in the public, it is fair game, and we can study it out in the open. Then we see that it comes in degrees – as in, *absolutely certain* belief, and middling, regular sorts of belief, and vague and even half-doubting belief ... from an extreme on one end of a continuum to an extreme on the other ... from shouting to whispering and everything between – with all the variety that it takes on in myriad shapes of language and behavior and interaction.

I accept this kind of account much more than I support Price's way of looking at things. I think the point about degrees of belief makes sense on Austin's theory. What this means for my account is that if religious belief is just another kind of belief, then we can study it and criticize it appropriately like ordinary factual kinds of belief, against a matching epistemic standard (Austin and Wittgenstein both noted that we do not look for the same standard of exactness in all things). My quotation from Locke (p. 28) is intended to reinforce the point that belief ought to be *criticized* and that as rational animals we can never simply *accept* the word of authority.

However, I also see that if we look at religious belief in context (as it functions for people in daily life) it does not appear to follow the model of factual sorts of belief, even if it claims that it is factually true (which of course is typically laughable, but that is not the point) – the point here is that religious people introduce a special category of belief that is privileged and cannot be looked at square on, despite Austin's point that belief is public and therefore fair game for analysis – religious people do this whether they see it or not. Thus they introduce a split in their minds and, in effect, compartmentalize themselves into normal people and (at the same time) weird-religiously-thinking people. This text explores a number of theories that try to account for this psychological change, e.g. in the form of confirmation bias (the attempt to exempt favored ideas from scrutiny) or as pluralistic ignorance (no one believes, but everything thinks that everyone believes, and authorities scare off dissent; private disdain mixed with public support helps to prop up a false consensus).

As Austin shows, when I declare my belief, I am proposing a kind of guarantee. I am saying: I stand for this belief. This makes it easy to confute analysis with insult (people will be wary of challenging a person's belief, offering criticism, if they are seen to be making a personal attack). There is a close connection between who I am and what I say in public. If I separate this connection, I begin to look like a hypocrite. 'What I believe' and 'who I am' get pulled apart – but they also get some breathing room – though it may also seem like I have lost faith in my belief. Perhaps it looks like I don't stand for anything and what I say is merely words. But if I give people a chance to criticize what I say, I have a better chance of learning, also of making some progress.

(note to page 26). In the interests of balancing appreciation with criticism, I ask myself the following question: let us grant this psychological split and unwarranted protection of favored thinking; is there any parallel among people who are not religious? Is this (even more generally) normal human behavior, rather than being some extraordinary psychological failure restricted to religious people? The answer I come to is yes – a very large yes. Poetry is an example. This is the example I use in the text. But love is another. Most of our thinking regarding love is magical thinking ... exactly the same illogical mish-mash that we see in religion.

The conclusion I come to is that if religious people were to look on their beliefs as poetry or as love – keeping it in this kind of frame, which is *personal* – this would be fine with all of us and many fewer problems would result (they would be the kind of problems that come up in interpreting poetry and in our love lives, that sometimes cause pain and even violence, but not war). It would be a helpful acknowledgement and a step towards humility that might empower progress in society. It is precisely because religious believers are *not* satisfied with poetry (or love either) that they get into trouble. They claim (then) that certain magical beliefs be taken, not as magic, but as fact. Supernaturalism, mixed with naturalism, becomes toxic, and explodes.

(note to page 32). Critical thinker: I mention this phrase several times in the text. What is a critical thinker? The quotation from Locke on page 28 begins to get at this idea. Critical thinking is sensitive to evidence, respectful of evidence, moved by evidence. It has to be learned and is a skill. It is sensitive to context. It welcomes learning, is open textured, welcomes challenge, is falsifiable. It gives up a favored idea in the face of a better argument. It may still *love* a dethroned ideal, but cannot uphold it in the face of persuasive reasoning. It rejects consolations and delusions that make us feel good. It lies somewhere between the principle *fiat iustitia pereat mundus* (let justice be done, though the world perish) and the idea that philosophy is *ancilla vitae* – the servant of life – philosophy tries to live in but also outside of society.

(note to page 41). Confucian ethics are focused on love – probably several other religious traditions might claim this. Taking 'love' very narrowly as physical affection shows some surprising results here. The neuropsychologist James Prescott developed a cross-cultural statistical analysis of 400 preindustrial societies and concluded that belief in gods who intervene in everyday life is correlated with societies which discourage physical affection, especially in infancy and adolescence; spirituality of a different kind, in which the divine is further away but physical affection is approved, takes a more amorphous shape and seems less menacing ("Body Pleasure and the Origins of Violence," *Bulletin of Atomic Scientists*, November 1975).

In this case physical affection appears to be the active variable, which takes the two psychological forms of punishing or friendly conscience. Prescott's work suggests that religiosity varies inversely with love.

Paul MacLean's model of the brain, popularized by Carl Sagan in his 1977 work *The Dragons of Eden*, hypothesizes three basic brain structures:

R complex (*reptilian*: brain stem, cerebellum; instinct, autonomic systems)
Limbic system (*mammalian*: amygdala, hypothalamus, hippocampus; emotions)
Neocortex (*human*: cerebral cortex; speech, reason, higher-order thinking)

In MacLean's model of the brain, three separate systems run concurrently, each with its own form of intelligence, memory, subjective feeling, and orientation in space and time ("outer sense" and "inner sense").

MacLean speculates that different parts of the brain may constellate different god concepts: a god with teeth; a loving god; a thoughtful god. *The Triune Brain in Evolution* (1990).

(note to page 77). Another side to the victory of Christianity over all its rivals is the ways in which the Latin language was transformed when it became the vehicle of a new faith. The stately Latin of classical times had already become an ever-changing pidgin for a vast multiethnic empire. The conversion of the empire also created a new standard language, which we now associate with piety. See Nicholas Ostler, *Ad Infinitum: A Biography of Latin* (2007).

(note to page 88). The list of luminaries from Arabic intellectual history is long – at the same time it seems obvious that they have been given too little respect in Muslim society. As the Pakistani thinker Mubarak Ali has written: "Societies which believe that they have found the truth do not bother to look at the changing times to realise that a new concept of truth has emerged as a result of human progress in knowledge ... The main task of philosophy is the pursuit of truth as it constantly probes and searches truth which evolves with time ... Generally in a Muslim society and particularly in Pakistan, there are poets, writers and religious scholars, but no philosophers, thinkers and scientists whose approach to knowledge is analytical, empirical and rational." Most of the thinkers mentioned in this passage of the text – Al-Kindi, al-Razi, al-Farabi, Ibn Sina and Omar Khayyam – were condemned by Al-Ghazali, considered the second most influential Muslim after the prophet. Ibn Rushd tried and failed to reverse the course of obscurantism preached by Al-Ghazali.

Mubarak Ali refers to the contemporary politician and father of Pakistan Mohammad Iqbal (1877-1938) as another victim of the same stagnant kind of thinking. Iqbal preached against the study of philosophy and exhorted people to believe in truth inherited from their ancestors and accepted as it is. Ali writes eloquently about the virtue of philosophy and vice from avoiding it:

"Western society inherited the philosophical legacy from Greece and added to it new ideas and thoughts which enriched the western civilization. In the 17th and 18th centuries, there was a scientific revolution which presented the universe from quite a different angle. The enlightened movement was based on reason, knowledge and progress which gradually transformed the society. The age of enlightenment produced great philosophers and thinkers whose ideas guided the society to abandon outdated traditions and values and create new values for the new age. It unfolded a new truth which superseded old and obsolete ideas. The process of western thinking and its search of truth did not end with the enlightened period. It continued to search for the truth. Later the Romantic Movement challenged the enlightened ideas and tried to understand nature and man differently with passion rather than reason. Positivism, nationalism, socialism and feminism movements followed, with the result that there were innovations and changes in art, literature, architecture and social, and cultural values of the western society. The new philosophical thoughts created a dynamism which discovered new versions of truth.

"The problem of Muslim society has been that it is afraid of new ideas and new truth. It is particularly fearful of philosophy as it creates doubts and questions the existing truth.

182

"In the absence of new philosophical ideas and believing in the unchanging truth, the society has become stagnant and intellectually barren. It fails to understand not only its own environment but also the global process. It relies on poetical and theological emotionalism and encourages our intellectuals to borrow western ideology without changing and understanding it. Although ideas develop as societies evolve, our intellectuals try to implant advanced ideas in a backward society which are not accepted by the majority of people.

"As our society believes in absolute truth, it is not ready to accept any new ideas which contradict or challenge it. This leaves no space for thinkers and philosophers to create new thoughts. The only use of philosophy is to support religious belief. ... Philosophy plays a vital role in a society only when it is liberated from faith and can bring about radical change. Whether this is possible in the Muslim society or not, is a question we must analyze and respond to" (http://dawn.com/2012/09/02/past-present-in-quest-of-truth).

Thus we need intellectuals such as Rhazes and Avicenna and Omar Khayyam, but we also need an environment in which thinkers like these can flourish and help improve society. This goes to the point on p. 83: We can only be human if our institutions let us ... Religion is a universal, but freedom is not.

(note to page 99). Richard Dawkins argues that religion is a by-product of primitive credulity (just as Spinoza argues, cf. p. 25 above). We survive by passing on the accumulated inheritance of previous generations:

"On this model we should expect that, in different geographical regions, different arbitrary beliefs, none of which have any factual basis, will be handed down, to be believed with the same conviction as useful pieces of traditional wisdom such as the belief that manure is good for the crops. We should also expect that superstitions and other non-factual beliefs will evolve locally – changing over generations – either by random drift or by some sort of analogue of Darwinian selection, eventually showing a pattern of significant divergence from common ancestry."

Experience needs to be passed on in order for children to survive; thus there is a selective advantage in unquestioning acceptance. This is a generally valuable rule from an evolutionary point of view, but also predisposes us to error. See *The God Delusion* (2006), chapter 5 (the quotation is from pp. 205-206).

(note to page 109). What the Roman church calls *fides quaerens intellectum*, the Arabs call *'ilm al Kalam*. Faith traditions have hermeneutical traditions, often many such, as in different schools of interpretation of sacred texts. But the point made above by Mubarak Ali is germane – "philosophy plays a vital role in a society only when it is liberated from faith and can bring about radical change" – a change that took roughly a millennium in western society. A recent work tries to heal the break between reason and faith and explore ways to integrate them: Richard Rubenstein, *Aristotle's Children: How Christians, Muslims and Jews Rediscovered Ancient Wisdom and Illumined the Dark Ages* (2003).

(note to page 154). Atheism is apparently a function of context. This may also be true of belief. We are talking about things going on inside the human mind. Human consciousness is something that occurs when you have something like 10^{11} neurons and 10^{14} synapses. What would consciousness look like if we have 10^{20} synapses or 10^{30} or even greater numbers? Carl Sagan suggests that a consciousness of this order would have roughly the same relationship to us as we have to the ant (who have perhaps 250k neurons). Religion makes sense for us, perhaps, but not for the ant, and not for an intelligence far beyond our ken. See *The Varieties of Scientific Experience: A Personal View of the Search for God* (2006), chapter 6.

(note to page 164). While I was thinking about some of the problems taken on in this work, I had the good fortune to get into dialogue with my friend the atheist philosopher Peter Boghossian. Boghossian proposes to dispense with faith, taken as a delusory knowledge claim. See *Against Faith* (2012).

Boghossian's studies bring up the huge questions that emerge out of Western philosophical history in the medieval period. For over 1000 years Western philosophy was the *ancilla theologiae*, the handmaiden of theology – philosophy the servant of faith. Much amazing work was done in philosophy during this period – Augustine, Bonaventure, Anselm, Duns Scotus, William of Ockham, Albertus Magnus, Aquinas. There is the interesting push-and-pull between followers of Plato like Augustine and followers of Aristotle like Aquinas. This same dynamic exists in Judaic, Christian and Islamic philosophy pretty much from the end of the Hellenistic period to the beginnings of the Renaissance. Aquinas refers to this whole period and his own investigations as *fides quereans intellectum* – faith seeking understanding – as if faith were the questioner and intellect/understanding was the person being interrogated.

Philosophy was the handmaiden of theology; then, freed from the yoke around its neck, it recovered the humanistic tradition from the ancients; this created the conditions in which empirical science was born. But then philosophy became *ancilla scientia* – philosophy became the handmaid, the servant, of science. The history of philosophy seems to suggest that philosophy has to take an instrumental role. Philosophy has to serve a purpose – thus the clarification of thoughts that philosophy undertakes has to serve a purpose – hopefully, a socially useful purpose. Boghossian's studies provoke us into asking the question *What purpose is philosophy intended to serve?*

Philosophy (I argue) has to be *ancilla vitae* – the servant of life. Thoughtfulness is a good in itself and a pleasure to engage in. But thoughtfulness brings us to moral conclusions and thus directs us from thought to action. Philosophy serves a purpose and has thus an instrumental role – but not, apparently, that of upholding a cause, in which it differs from advocacy such as we see in religious life. Thoughtfulness serves life by examining it. Thoughtfulness serves life by creating more thoughtfulness.

Question: If philosophy is a way of emancipating ourselves from stupidity (superstition, epistemic arrogance), then – once we are emancipated – what do we do with thoughtfulness?

Answer: We never emancipate ourselves from stupidity – there is no step beyond thoughtfulness.

A good place to see this is in the *Euthyphro* and Socrates' discussion there about piety (*to hosian*). Socrates is challenging this person who sees himself as knowledgeable about the gods, about ceremonies, about duties, sacrifices, rituals – Euthyphro is very cocksure about his 'knowledge' – so much so that he is willing to go to the law courts to sue his father who, he thinks, is guilty of impiety and should be punished. Socrates of course is also charged with impiety. Now Euthyphro is certainly someone who would agree that faith makes claims about knowledge – although his vocabulary is very different than the one we are using – he thinks he knows what piety is and he can cite many examples of piety – pious deeds, pious men. But then he has a conversation with Socrates. In order to be pious, it seems that we have to know what piety is. Things that please the gods are pious. But are they pious because they please the gods, or do they please the gods because they are pious? And in the end the conversation is (of course) *aporetic* – it leads nowhere – it goes around in circles. Euthyphro is forced to admit that he does *not* know what piety is.

Euthyphro doesn't have any problem using the **concept** of piety (though 'concept' is not Greek – Solon calls it *aphanes metron*, a non-appearing measure, Plato calls it *idea* – on this see Hannah Arendt, *The Life of the Mind*, 1971; One/Thinking, p. 170). But when he examines this thing – whatever it is – his clarity vanishes and he realizes that he does not know what he is talking about. Socrates wants to start the conversation all over again when they discover that neither of them knows what piety is. Euthyphro walks away.

Now Socrates is challenging Euthyphro's arrogance, his knowledge claim, his cocksure attitude, and he wants to bring Euthyphro to the same condition that he himself is in – which is not knowledge but instead ignorance – self-conscious ignorance, radical ignorance, a comprehensive disavowal of knowledge; also humility in place of arrogance; I would add irony in place of seriousness (the weighty earnestness that makes Euthyphro sue his father).

But here is what strikes me: Socrates is *not* trying to make Euthyphro less pious. Likewise, when he is talking about courage with Laches and Nicias, there is the same result. But he is not trying to say that these men are not courageous or that there is no bravery in Athens. Socrates considers justice, piety, temperance and courage to be virtues – even though he cannot define any of them – he cannot say anything definitive about these ideas.

What I take this to mean is that Socrates is encouraging us to become thoughtful. Becoming thoughtful is dangerous. It will spoil our illusion that we know what we are doing. But this is the right kind of life for us – the examined life – in spite of all its difficulties. The point is: Socrates is *not* arguing for any kind of result that would make further thinking unnecessary. He wants us to think, to stay in thinking, and bring this problem-seeking behavior with us to all life's experiences. But he is not trying to take anything away – except arrogance. He is not trying to make people less just, virtuous, temperate or pious. That would imply a new creed – a new result – a new account of piety or courage – but the whole point is that *he has no results*. There is, instead, the work of thinking. Boghossian argues that reason shows us that certain positions are *a priori* irrational and thus can be rejected out of hand. Thus I can reject the notion that the moon is made of cheese. And for similar reasons he argues that we can and should reject faith also. Thus the effort of thought appears to be aimed at removing whole sections of social life and perhaps offering new rituals to replace them. This strikes me as different than the project of making people more thoughtful and less arrogant – I would argue that philosophy is not about disabusing people of false beliefs and replacing them with true ones. It is more about teaching a general attitude of humility – of thoughtfulness – something applicable in all situations and in every sort of culture – whether we worship trees or gods or stones or nothing at all – whatever tradition we belong to.

My position, which I think is the Socratic position, is that I do not care if a person is religious or irreligious – I do not care what beliefs or symbols or rituals are dear to her, or whether she is devout or an atheist – this is not the essential thing; and we can find the "spirit of intolerant zeal" among believers and non-believers, and even among philosophers. A point of view is not a fanaticism; nor is a *view* progress of itself. People become zealous or fanatic;

people refuse progress or make it. The essential thing is not the idiom in which a person makes a life, but that the person is *thoughtful*. That she examine her life. This does not square with rejecting specific claims, *in favor of* different accounts. It squares with rejecting arrogance. Thoughtfulness does not make us attack people – individuals or groups – but what they *say*; we owe people respect, but not their beliefs. We investigate belief and test it; we offer belief and subject it to the same criticism; it's not about *what* the person thinks, but *how*.

Interestingly, Socrates does not say that he is refuting doctrines, but persons. Belief does not live in some abstract space, but in everyday human action. The call to an examined life is about changing the way people think, to make them *different kind of people*, angry rather at themselves than at others, and anxious to think. Socrates comes to the strange idea that the greatest good for a human being "is to have discussions every day about virtue" (*Apology*, 38 a3).

Taoism	Buddhism	Confucianism

Sources	*Sources*	*Sources*
I Ching (2900 BCE)	Siddhartha (b. 563 BCE)	I Ching (2900 BCE)
Tao Te Ching (?)	Tripitaka (5th c. BCE)	Confucius (b. 551 BCE)
LaoTzu (b. 604 (?) BCE)	Dhammapada (5th c. BCE)	Analects (circa 479 BCE)
Liezi (5th c. BCE)	Chinese Canon (1st c CE)	Six classics (5th c. BCE)
Yang Chu (c. 380 BCE)	Tibetan Canon (12th c)	Chung Yung (5th c. BCE)
Chuang Tzu (c. 280 BCE)		
Tao Tsang (4th c)	*Early forms*	*Early forms*
	Codification of the Sutras	Ju school (literati)
Early forms	Rules for the Sangha	Idealism (Mencius)
Philosophy of Escape	Ashokan proselytism	Realism (Hsun Tzu)
Philosophy of Change	Ghandara culture	
Higher Point of View	Silk Road	*Divisions*
		Ying Yang school
Divisions	*Divisions*	Metaphysics
Tao Chia/Philosophy	Theravada	Neo Confucianism
Tao Chiao/Religion	Mahayana	The Two Schools
Neo Taoism	Vajrayana/Tantra	School of Principle
Dark Learning	Ch'an	School of Mind
Feng Liu/Romanticism	Pure Land	
		Thinkers
Thinkers	*Thinkers*	Mencius
Kuo Hsiang	Asoka	Hsun Tzu
Chiang Liang	Nagarjuna	Ssu-ma T'an
Li Shao Chun	Asanga	Ssu-ma Ch'ien
Wang Pi	Vasubandu	Liu Hsin
Ku Huan	Bohdidharma	Tsou Yen
Kuo Hsiang	Buddhaghosa	Tzu-ssu
Hsiang Hsiu	Dignaga	Kung sun-Lung
Liu Yi-ch'ing	Dharmakirti	Cheng Hsuan
Liu Hsun	Santideva	Tung Chung Shu
Wang Jung	Nagasena	Yang Hsiung
Wei Hua Ts'un	Prajna	Wang Ch'ung
Chen Tuan	Linji	Li Ao
Sun Tzu	Gampopa	Han Yu
Wang Bi	Naropa	Chou Tun-yi
Wei Boyang	Milarepa	Ch'eng Yi
Kuo Tsiang	Dogen Kigen	Chu Hsi (Chu Tzu)
Lu Dongbin	Takuan Soho	Chang Tsai
Wen zi	Chogyam Trungpa	Fung Yu lang
Den Ming Dao	Rahula Walpola	Tu Wei Ming

Judaism	Christianity	Islam

Sources		
Tanakh (1000 BCE)	*Sources*	*Sources*
Mishnah (2nd C.)	Paul's letters (~54-58)	Qur'an (610-632)
Midrash (3rd)	Mark (~75)	Hadith (8th – 10th)
Talmud (5th)	Matthew (~80)	Sunnah (8th – 10th)
Zohar (12th)	Luke (~85)	Ijma (8th – 10th)
Kabbalah (16th)	John (~100)	
	Fathers (1st - 5th)	*Early forms*
Early forms		Sunni
Sadducees	*Early forms*	Shi'a
Pharisees	Ebionite	Sufi
Essenes	Gnostic	Mutazili
Zealots	Pauline	
	Arian	*Divisions*
Divisions		Khajirite
Orthodox	*Divisions*	Wahhabi
Conservative	Roman Catholicism	Ijtihadi
Reform	Eastern Orthodoxy	Druze
Karaite	Coptic Christianity	Baha'i
Ethical Culture	Protestantism	
	Unitarianism	*Thinkers*
Thinkers		Al-Basri
Hillel	*Thinkers*	Rabia
Shammai	Tertullian	Ibn Hanbal
Rashi	Athanasius	Al-Kindi
Philo of Alexandria	Augustine	Al-Hallaj
Josephus	Anselm	Al-Farabi
Saadia Gaon	Aquinas	Al-Razi
Bahya ibn Paquda	Erasmus	Ibn Sinna
Yehuda Halevi	William of Ockham	Al Ghazali
Hasdai Crescas	Martin Luther	Ibn Rushd
Maimonides	Søren Kierkegaard	Ibn Arabi
Israel ben Eliezer	Karl Barth	Rumi
Baruch Spinoza	Rudolf Bultmann	Ibn Khaldun
Franz Rosenzweig	Paul Tillich	Muhammad Iqbal
Martin Buber	C.S. Lewis	Ibn Warraq
Abraham J. Heschel	John D. Caputo	Tahir Ul Qadri
		Mubarak Ali

- Library
- Refine Result
  Peer Review.
  Clinical trial.
  - control trial.
*. Random - control | Clinical ;
      trial!   trial.

Made in the USA
Charleston, SC
20 March 2013